CIVIL LIBERTIES IN AMERICA

A Reference Handbook

Other Titles in ABC-CLIO's
CONTEMPORARY
WORLD ISSUES
Series

Books in the Contemporary World Issues series address vital issues in today's society such as genetic engineering, pollution, and biodiversity. Written by professional writers, scholars, and nonacademic experts, these books are authoritative, clearly written, up-to-date, and objective. They provide a good starting point for research by high school and college students, scholars, and general readers as well as by legislators, businesspeople, activists, and others.

Each book, carefully organized and easy to use, contains an overview of the subject, a detailed chronology, biographical sketches, facts and data and/or documents and other primary-source material, a directory of organizations and agencies, annotated lists of print and nonprint resources, and an index.

Readers of books in the Contemporary World Issues series will find the information they need in order to have a better understanding of the social, political, environmental, and economic issues facing the world today.

CIVIL LIBERTIES IN AMERICA

A Reference Handbook

Samuel Walker

CONTEMPORARY WORLD ISSUES

A B C  C L I O

Santa Barbara, California
Denver, Colorado
Oxford, England

Library of Congress Cataloging-in-Publication Data
Walker, Samuel, 1942–
    Civil liberties in America : a reference handbook / Samuel Walker.
        p.   cm. — (Contemporary world issues)
    Includes bibliographical references and index.
            ISBN 1-57607-927-9 (hardcover : acid-free paper)
            ISBN 1-57607-928-7 (e-book)
    1. Civil rights—United States.   I. Title.   II. Series.

KF4749.W35 2004
342.7308'5—dc22

                                                                2004003211

08   07   06   05   04   10 9 8 7 6 5 4 3 2 1

This book is also available on the World Wide Web as an e-book. Visit abc-clio.com for details.

ABC-CLIO, Inc.
130 Cremona Drive, P.O. Box 1911
Santa Barbara, California 93116-1911

This book is printed on acid-free paper ∞.
Manufactured in the United States of America

Contents

1

Introduction

Civil liberties are the individual rights people have over and against the power of the government. Civil liberties are a fundamental element of a free society. The purpose of this chapter is to provide a basic introduction to the subject of civil liberties in the United States. It defines civil liberties, explains the legal basis for civil liberties, outlines the scope of civil liberties issues, and explains briefly the process by which abstract civil liberties issues become law.

The first section of this chapter provides a basic definition of civil liberties. The second section clarifies the relationship between civil liberties and civil rights. The third section explains the legal basis of civil liberties in the United States: in the U.S. Constitution; the constitutions of each of the fifty states; and in federal, state, and local laws. The fourth section outlines civil liberties controversies. The fifth section describes how the courts, and the U.S. Supreme Court in particular, operate in defining civil liberties. The final section discusses the place of civil liberties issues in the larger context of U.S. society and politics.

Definition of Civil Liberties

Civil liberties are defined as *the rights enjoyed by individuals over and against government* (Handler, 1994:78). The place of individual rights has been especially prominent in the Anglo-American legal tradition, which emphasizes limited government. The dissenter—the individual who stands up for his or her beliefs or challenges the government—is a heroic icon in the Anglo-American political tradition. American culture honors such people for exhibiting courage and strength of conscience. American society especially honors those who took a lonely stand for what they believed was right and who were subsequently vindicated by history (Glasser, 1991; Hentoff, 1980).

The basic civil liberties principle was expressed very eloquently by U.S. Supreme Court Justice Robert Jackson in a famous 1943 decision affirming the right of school children who were members of the Jehovah's Witnesses to refuse to salute the American flag. Justice Jackson wrote: "If there is any fixed star in our constitutional constellation, it is that no official, high or petty, can prescribe what shall be orthodox in politics, nationalism, religion, or other matters of opinion or force citizens to confess by word or act their faith therein. If there are any circumstances which permit an exception, they do not now occur to us" (*West Virginia v. Barnette*, 1943).

The distinguishing feature of totalitarian societies is the absence of civil liberties. In the totalitarian state, the individual is entirely subservient to the state. Nazi Germany and the Soviet Union are examples of totalitarian societies in the twentieth century. There are no rights of freedom of speech, freedom of the press, or freedom of assembly. The person who openly disagrees with the government is likely to be arrested and imprisoned and perhaps even executed. Individuals in totalitarian societies also do not enjoy due process rights. Generally, they are presumed guilty from the start. Nor do totalitarian societies provide equal protection of the law. Nazi Germany not only murdered millions of Jews in the Holocaust but also imprisoned and executed homosexuals, mentally disabled persons, Gypsies, and members of other groups.

The law and cultural traditions of many societies that are not necessarily totalitarian place far less emphasis on the rights of individuals. Continental European countries, for example, give more power to government and emphasize the obligations rather than the rights of citizens. Many societies have a communal or communitarian culture that emphasizes conformity to established societal traditions rather than the rights of the individual (Etzioni, 1993; Glendon, 1991).

Religious practices dramatize the difference between civil libertarian and communal values. In many countries around the world today, there is an official state religion, and dissent from official religious beliefs is regarded as heresy and as a crime against the state. Most countries of the world have official, state-sponsored religions. Even in England, with a fairly strong civil liberties tradition, the Church of England is the official religion of the state and is financially supported by the government. The U.S. tradition, based more on civil libertarian values, emphasizes dissent, nonconformity, and the separation of church and state (Curry, 1986; Hall, 1998).

The contrast between the American civil libertarian tradition and the more communitarian values of other countries is evident in the provisions of virtually all of the international human rights statements (Brownlie and Goodwin-Gill, 2002). The 1948 Universal Declaration of Human Rights is a good example. The Universal Declaration, adopted by the United Nations after World War II as a statement of basic human rights, was designed to influence the law and practices of countries around the world. Although the Universal Declaration affirms the values of freedom of speech, religious liberty, equality, and due process of law, it also allows for certain limitations on individual rights.

Article 29 of the Universal Declaration allows for restrictions based on "the just requirements of morality, public order, and the general welfare in a democratic society." Yet the history of civil liberties in the United States indicates that some of the greatest limitations on rights have been justified in terms of morality (e.g., censorship of sexually oriented expression), public order (e.g., bans on demonstrations), and the general welfare (e.g., censorship of allegedly offensive forms of expression) (Glasser, 1991; Walker, 1999). Article 29 and other portions of the Universal Declaration of Human Rights are excerpted in Chapter 5.

Civil Liberties and Civil Rights

The relationship between civil liberties and civil rights is often misunderstood. As understood by most Americans, the civil rights movement refers to the struggle for equality on the part of African Americans (Bradley and Fishkin, 1998; Nieman, 1991). The general term *civil rights* also applies to issues of equality for other groups: ethnic minorities, women, people with disabilities, gay and lesbian people, and other groups.

Because of the special history of the civil rights movement in the United States, some people tend to regard civil liberties and civil rights as separate issues. It is more appropriate, however, to regard civil rights as *one area* of civil liberties. Equal protection of the laws is one of the four major areas of civil liberties along with First Amendment rights, due process of law, and privacy (see the next section, Civil Liberties Controversies). Equal protection encompasses the right to be free from discrimination in employment, housing, public accommodations, the administration of criminal justice, and many other areas of life. It encompasses not just African Americans, but also Latinos, other racial and ethnic minority groups, women, people with disabilities, as well as other groups (Karst, 1989).

Civil Liberties Controversies

Civil liberties involve a wide range of issues and controversies. This section lists the major categories of issues and some of the most important controversies in each one.

First Amendment Rights

1. Freedom of Speech

Do citizens have the right to criticize the government in wartime?

Does the First Amendment protect "hate speech," defined as making derogatory or inflammatory statements about religious and racial groups?

2. Freedom of the Press

Does freedom of the press include the right of newspapers to publish secret government documents? Can the government issue a "prior restraint" on the publication of secret documents?

3. Freedom of Assembly

Does the freedom of assembly include the right of a group to parade through a neighborhood whose residents' hostility to the group creates the possibility of disorder?

Can the government set limits on the nature of protest demonstrations in front of abortion clinics?

4. Religious Liberty

Does the First Amendment allow members of a religious group to engage in rituals that are generally illegal, such as using peyote or sacrificing animals?

Does the First Amendment allow the government to provide public funds to social service programs run by religious groups?

5. Freedom of Association

Does the First Amendment prevent the government from investigating peoples' membership in groups that advocate changing the form of the U.S. government?

Second Amendment Rights

1. Does the Second Amendment grant to individuals an absolute right to own guns?

2. Can the government restrict gun ownership by people with criminal records?

Equal Protection of the Law

1. Does the Fourteenth Amendment guarantee of equal protection apply to lesbian and gay people?

2. Are race-conscious affirmative action plans consistent with the Fourteenth Amendment?

3. Can the police stop and question members of certain racial, ethnic, or nationality groups because members of those groups are more likely to engage in certain criminal activity? Or is "racial profiling" a violation of the Equal Protection Clause of the Fourteenth Amendment?

Due Process of Law

1. The Fourth Amendment guarantees protection against "unreasonable searches and seizures"—but what exactly is an unreasonable search? Does the Fourth Amendment protection cover your trash cans? The drawers in the desk at your office?

2. The Fifth Amendment guarantees protection against self-incrimination. What exactly does this cover? Is it constitutional to use as evidence a confession to a crime made by a person who has not first consulted a lawyer?

3. The Sixth Amendment guarantees a fair trial, including the right to an attorney. Does someone receive a fair trial if his or her attorney fails to raise certain objections to testimony presented by the prosecution at trial? What if the lawyer falls asleep during the trial?

4. The Eighth Amendment guarantees protection against cruel and unusual punishments. Is the death penalty cruel and unusual? Is it cruel and unusual to keep a prisoner in facilities that are not sanitary?

The Right to Privacy

1. Since the Bill of Rights does not mention the word "privacy," what is the constitutional basis for a right to privacy? Is sexual activity between two adults completely private? Is the material on your computer's hard drive private?

2. Can the government maintain files on citizens' spending habits, travel, and other personal information? Is it legal for the government to keep a file on what groups you belong to or what places you have traveled to?

The War on Terrorism

The war on terrorism involves a number of civil liberties issues that cover most of the categories listed above.

1. The Patriot Act authorizes the government to conduct wiretaps without a judicial warrant. Is this constitutional under the Fourth Amendment?

2. In response to the terrorist attacks of September 11, 2001, the Federal Bureau of Investigation questioned about 5,000 men of Arab background. Is this a form of discrimination based on national origins?

3. The U.S. Department of Justice announced plans to eavesdrop on suspected terrorists in jail and their attorneys. Does this violate the Sixth Amendment right to counsel?

The Legal Basis of Civil Liberties

The Bill of Rights

Civil liberties in the Unites States are guaranteed by the first ten amendments to the U.S. Constitution, referred to as the Bill of Rights; the three Civil War amendments—the Thirteenth, Fourteenth, and Fifteenth Amendments; and the Nineteenth Amendment (see Sidebar 1.1).

The Bill of Rights, which was adopted in the form of amendments to the U.S. Constitution in 1791, evolved out of a long struggle in English and American history that began with the Magna Carta in 1215 (Brant, 1965; Schwartz, 1977, 1980). Excerpts from the Magna Carta and other documents leading up to the Bill of Rights are reproduced in Chapter 5.

The protections provided in the Bill of Rights were designed to protect individuals against government infringements on their liberty, even when government policy represents the views of the majority in society. The First Amendment, for example, protects the right to express opinions that the majority find offensive. In the era of racial segregation (roughly the 1890s through the 1960s), white majorities in southern states passed laws restricting the rights of African Americans, including the creation of separate school systems, the denial of voting rights, and other violations of individual rights. In the civil rights era (the 1950s through the 1970s), these laws were declared unconstitutional (Nieman, 1991).

The imposition of racial segregation by white majorities in the South during the era of segregation illustrates the basic tension between civil liberties and the principles of democracy. Democratic self-government is based on the idea of majority rule, but the Bill of Rights says that there are certain things the majority cannot do. The majority cannot decide to discriminate on the basis of race. The majority cannot decide that certain ideas are illegal. The majority cannot pass a law that favors one religion over others. The majority cannot pass a law that invades individuals' privacy. The role of the Bill of Rights in a democratic society was explained by the U.S. Supreme Court in a 1943 case striking down a law that compelled school children who were members of the Jehovah's Witnesses to salute the American flag in violation of their religious beliefs (Peters, 2000). The Court explained:

> The very purpose of a Bill of Rights was to withdraw certain subjects from the vicissitudes of political controversy, to place them beyond the reach of majorities and officials and to establish them as legal principles to be applied by the courts. One's right to life, liberty, and property, to free speech, a free press, freedom of worship and assembly, and other fundamental rights may

Sidebar 1.1 Text of the Bill of Rights

Amendment 1
Congress shall make no law respecting an establishment of religion, or prohibiting the free exercise thereof; or abridging the freedom of speech, or of the press, or the right of the people peaceably to assemble, and to petition the Government for a redress of grievances.

Amendment 2
A well regulated Militia, being necessary to the security of a free State, the right of the people to keep and bear Arms, shall not be infringed.

Amendment 3
No Soldier shall, in time of peace be quartered in any house, without the consent of the Owner, nor in time of war, but in a manner to be prescribed by law.

Amendment 4
The right of the people to be secure in their persons, houses, papers, and effects, against unreasonable searches and seizures, shall not be violated, and no Warrants shall issue, but upon probable cause, supported by Oath or affirmation, and particularly describing the place to be searched, and the persons or things to be seized.

Amendment 5
No person shall be held to answer for a capital or otherwise infamous crime, unless on a presentment or indictment of a Grand Jury, except in cases arising in the land or naval forces, or in the Militia, when in actual service in time of War or public danger; nor shall any person be subject for the same offence to be twice put in jeopardy of life or limb, nor shall be compelled in any criminal case to be a witness against himself, nor be deprived of life, liberty, or property, without due process of law; nor shall private property, without due process of law; nor shall private property be taken for public use without just compensation.

Amendment 6
In all criminal prosecutions, the accused shall enjoy the right to a speedy and public trial, by an impartial jury of the State and district wherein the crime shall have been committed, which district shall have been previously ascertained by law, and to be informed of the nature and cause of the accusation; to be confronted with the witnesses against him; to have compulsory process for obtaining witnesses in his favor, and to have the Assistance of Counsel for his defence.

Amendment 7

In Suits at common law, where the value in controversy shall exceed twenty dollars, the right of trial by jury shall be preserved, and no fact tried by a jury shall be otherwise reexamined in any Court of the United States, than according to the rules of the common law.

Amendment 8

Excessive bail shall not be required nor excessive fines imposed, nor cruel and unusual punishments inflicted.

Amendment 9

The enumeration in the Constitution, of certain rights, shall not be construed to deny or disparage others retained by the people.

Amendment 10

The powers not delegated to the United States by the Constitution, nor prohibited by it to the States, are reserved to the States respectively, or to the people.

The Civil War Amendments

Amendment 13

Neither slavery nor involuntary servitude, except as a punishment for crime whereof the party shall have been duly convicted, shall exist within the United States, or any place subject to their jurisdiction. . . .

Amendment 14

All persons born or naturalized in the United States, and subject to the jurisdiction thereof, are citizens of the United States and of the State wherein they reside. No State shall make or enforce any law which shall abridge the privileges or immunities of citizens of the United States; nor shall any State deprive any person of life, liberty, or property, without due process of law; nor deny to any person within its jurisdiction the equal protection of the laws. . .

Amendment 15

The right of citizens of the United States to vote shall not be denied or abridged by the United States or by any State on account of race, color, or previous condition of servitude. . . .

. . .

Amendment 19

The right of citizens of the United States to vote shall not be denied or abridged by the United States or by any State on account of sex. . . .

not be submitted to vote; they depend on the outcome of no elections (*West Virginia v. Barnette*, 1943).

A scanned image of the original Bill of Rights may be viewed on the Web at *www.law.emory.edu/erd/docs/pict/bill.jpg*.

State Bills of Rights

The constitutions of each of the fifty states also contain bills of rights (Maddex, 1998; Tarr, 1998). Sidebar 1.2 contains an excerpt from the constitution of the state of Oregon.

As the free speech clause of the Oregon constitution illustrates, many state bills of rights use language slightly different from that of the U.S. Bill of Rights. Moreover, in some cases state supreme courts have interpreted their state bills of rights to provide greater protection than that provided by the U.S. Bill of Rights as interpreted by the U.S. Supreme Court (Tarr, 1998). For example, some state supreme courts have ruled the state constitution provides a right to privacy that is much broader than any U.S. Supreme Court ruling has provided. State supreme court rulings, of course, apply only to the people in that state and have no authority in other states.

The Concept of "State Action"

Civil liberties laws protect individual rights against actions by government. Thus, some "state action" must occur for these laws to apply (Handler, 1994:521). The Bill of Rights does not protect individuals against actions by private individuals or organizations. For example, if a radio station fires a talk show host because he said things that offended certain listeners, it would not be a violation of the host's First Amendment rights. The firing would be a private action. However, if a *public* radio station, such as a

---

Sidebar 1.2   Section 8 of the Oregon Bill of Rights

Freedom of speech and press. No law shall be passed restraining the free expression of opinion, or restricting the right to speak, write, or print freely on any subject whatever; but every person shall be responsible for the abuse of this right.

state university radio station, fires a talk show host because of his views, it could be a violation of the host's First Amendment rights. A public radio station is a government agency, and thus the firing would involve state action. Similarly, a private employer can require certain hairstyles (e.g., no long hair for men; no "Mohawks"), whereas a public employer cannot (some police officers, for example, have sued and won the right to wear beards or long hair) (Hunt and Strongin, 1994; Repa, 2000).

Federal Laws Protecting Individual Rights

Individual rights are also protected by federal laws. Title VII of the 1964 Civil Rights Act, for example, outlaws employment discrimination on the basis of race, color, religion, sex, or national origin (see Sidebar 1.3). The statute is intended to enforce the principle of equal protection of the law, which is also guaranteed by the Fourteenth Amendment (Karst, 1989).

State Laws Protecting Individual Rights

Many state laws also protect civil liberties. Most are similar to their counterparts in federal law. Some state laws provide protections that are not guaranteed by the Bill of Rights or by federal law. The Illinois Human Rights Act, for example, prohibits discrimination on the basis of sexual orientation (Sidebar 1.4).

Local Laws Protecting Individual Rights

Finally, many cities and counties have laws or ordinances that protect civil liberties. The Seattle employment discrimination law bans discrimination in more areas than does federal law, in particular discrimination based on sexual orientation (see Sidebar 1.5). As with state laws, there is considerable variation among local ordinances, and many provide greater protections than federal or state laws.

Executive Orders and Individual Rights

Individual rights can also be protected through executive orders. At the federal level, the president of the United States can issue executive orders directing the activities of federal agencies. Executive orders have the full force of law.

Sidebar 1.3   Unlawful Employment Practices

SEC. 2000e-2. *[Section 703]*

(a) It shall be an unlawful employment practice for an employer:
   (1) to fail or refuse to hire or to discharge any individual, or otherwise to discriminate against any individual with respect to his compensation, terms, conditions, or privileges of employment, because of such individual's race, color, religion, sex, or national origin; or
   (2) to limit, segregate, or classify his employees or applicants for employment in any way which would deprive or tend to deprive any individual of employment opportunities or otherwise adversely affect his status as an employee, because of such individual's race, color, religion, sex, or national origin.
(b) It shall be an unlawful employment practice for an employment agency to fail or refuse to refer for employment, or otherwise to discriminate against, any individual because of his race, color, religion, sex, or national origin, or to classify or refer for employment any individual on the basis of his race, color, religion, sex, or national origin.
(c) It shall be an unlawful employment practice for a labor organization:
   (1) to exclude or to expel from its membership, or otherwise to discriminate against, any individual because of his race, color, religion, sex, or national origin;
   (2) to limit, segregate, or classify its membership or applicants for membership, or to classify or fail or refuse to refer for employment any individual, in any way which would deprive or tend to deprive any individual of employment opportunities, or would limit such employment opportunities or otherwise adversely affect his status as an employee or as an applicant for employment, because of such individual's race, color, religion, sex, or national origin; or
   (3) to cause or attempt to cause an employer to discriminate against an individual in violation of this section.
(d) It shall be an unlawful employment practice for any employer, labor organization, or joint labor-management committee controlling apprenticeship or other training or retraining, including on-the-job training programs to discriminate against any individual because of his race, color, religion, sex, or national origin in admission to, or employment in, any program established to provide apprenticeship or other training.

Sidebar 1.4   Illinois Human Rights Act

It is the public policy of this State: (A) Freedom from Unlawful Discrimination. To secure for all individuals within Illinois the freedom from discrimination against any individual because of his or her race, color, religion, sex, national origin, ancestry, age, marital status, physical or mental handicap, military status, or unfavorable discharge from military service in connection with employment, real estate transactions, access to financial credit, and the availability of public accommodations.

Source: (775 ILCS 5/1-101) (from Ch. 68, par. 1-101)

President Lyndon Johnson, for example, issued Executive Order 11246 in 1965, directing federal agencies to have affirmative action plans for employment (Urofsky, 1991). In 2000, President Bill Clinton issued Executive Order 13145, prohibiting federal agencies from discriminating on the basis of genetic information (e.g., DNA information indicating that a job applicant had a predisposition to developing a certain disease or disability). Executive Order 13145 is reprinted in Chapter 5.

Sidebar 1.5   Seattle Municipal Code

Unfair employment practices designated. It is unfair employment practice within the City for any:

A. Employer to discriminate against any person with respect to hiring, tenure, promotion, terms, conditions, wages or privileges of employment, or with respect to any matter related to employment.

. . .

C. Employer, employment agency, or labor organization to print, circulate, or cause to be printed, published or circulated, any statement, advertisement, or publication relating to employment or membership, or to use any form of application therefor, which indicates any preference, limitation, specification, or discrimination based upon race, color, sex, marital status, sexual orientation, gender identity, political ideology, age, creed, religion, ancestry, national origin, or the presence of any sensory, mental or physical handicap.

Executive orders can also be used to violate civil liberties, however. One of the greatest violations of civil liberties in U.S. history was Executive Order 9066 (see Chapter 4), issued by President Franklin D. Roosevelt, authorizing the evacuation and internment of the Japanese Americans during World War II (Irons, 1983). Executive Order 9066 is reprinted in Chapter 5.

State governors have the authority to issue state-level executive orders, and mayors have the power to issue such orders at the municipal level.

Law, Public Opinion, and Behavior

The subject of the law has several different dimensions. Political scientists make a distinction between formal legal doctrine (the law on the books), public opinion (what people think about the law), and behavior (how people act and whether their behavior conforms to the law) (Casper, 1972). These distinctions are especially important for civil liberties, because there are many instances in which people object strongly (public opinion) to a law (for example, a new Supreme Court decision) and simply ignore it in practice (behavior).

For example, the Supreme Court has ruled that prayer in public schools violates the Establishment Clause of the First Amendment. That ruling represents *constitutional law doctrine.* Many people do not like that interpretation of the Establishment Clause. Their views represent *public opinion* about the law. There is evidence, however, that some schools still permit prayer or other religious exercises in violation of the law. Those practices represent the *behavioral* aspect of civil liberties.

The extent to which people and organizations conform to the law is a major issue in the translation of the promises of the Bill of Rights into daily reality. There is evidence, for example, that police officers do not advise suspects of their rights, in violation of the U.S. Supreme Court's 1966 *Miranda* decision (Human Rights Watch, 1998). Similarly, prisons maintain certain inhumane conditions (e.g., inadequate ventilation, overcrowding) even though the courts have held these conditions to be unconstitutional (Fliter, 2001).

In short, one of the major issues regarding civil liberties is the extent to which people are able to actually enjoy the freedoms to which they are entitled according to the Bill of Rights and the courts.

The Role of the Courts

Interpreting the Constitution

The courts interpret the meaning of the Constitution and the Bill of Rights and apply them to particular cases. The exact words in the provisions of the Bill of Rights are vague and ambiguous, which leaves open a number of fundamental questions. What constitutes "due process of law"? What is "cruel and unusual punishment"? What is "speech"? Is a physical gesture a form of speech? Is a protest armband speech? Is burning the American flag a form of speech (Goldstein, 2000)? Is burning a cross a form of speech protected by the First Amendment (Cleary, 1994)? These are the type of questions that the Supreme Court answers.

The meaning of due process at any given moment, therefore, depends on how the courts have interpreted it. As a result, the meaning of each provision of the Bill of Rights is constantly changing. The scope of free speech is very different in 2001 than it was in 1970, and even more different than in 1930. On occasion, the Supreme Court reverses one of its previous decisions and, in doing so, either expands or contracts the scope of civil liberties. In 1986, for example, the Court decided in *Bowers v. Hardwick* that the Constitutional guarantee of a right to privacy did not include the right of two people of the same sex to engage in sexual relations (Walzer, 2002). But in 2003, in *Lawrence v. Texas*, the Court dramatically reversed itself and ruled that such relations do enjoy constitutional protection.

The power of the Supreme Court to interpret the meaning of the Constitution is not explicitly stated in the Constitution but was established in the famous case of *Marbury v. Madison* (1803) in a bold ruling by Chief Justice John Marshall (Simon, 2002). On the occasion of the 200th anniversary of the *Marbury v. Madison* decision, law professor Joel B. Grossman (2003) wrote an essay for the Freedom Forum explaining, as the article's subtitle indicates, "The Reasons We Should Still Care About the Decision." He points out that "virtually all constitutional law courses in U.S. colleges and law schools begin with the *Marbury* case. And there are good reasons for this." The decision raised "a host of fundamental questions relevant to any country with a constitution and courts: What should the role of constitutional courts be? What should the shape and extent of judicial review be? What are the limits of judicial activism? Why are checks and balances and the idea of limited government essential to constitutional govern-ment? How can, and why should, a country commit itself to con-stitutional rule and the rule of law?" All of these questions are directly relevant to a system of government based on a constitu-tional framework and to how individual rights are to be pro-tected under such a system.

The text of the First Amendment says that "*Congress* shall make no law" [emphasis added]. The courts, however, have inter-preted that phrase broadly, and as a result, First Amendment rights include, for example, protection against violations by the executive branch of the federal government and by state govern-ments.

Many conservatives believe that the Supreme Court has interpreted the Constitution too broadly and that justices have substituted their own values and beliefs for the original meaning of the Constitution, or the original intent of its framers (Bork, 1990). Most legal scholars, however, believe that the original intent point of view is not valid. First, they argue that the special virtue of the American system of constitutional government has been its capacity to adapt to changing circumstances—new tech-nologies and changing social mores, for example. Many new issues have arisen over time. The framers of the Constitution never discussed the issues of pornography or hate speech, and they had no way of imagining the Internet. Second, they argue that it is impossible to determine exactly what was the original intent of the framers of the Constitution. We have only an incom-plete record of what the participants at the 1787 Constitutional Convention in Philadelphia said. And when the Constitution was ratified by each of the states, we do not know that those peo-ple thought they were adopting. In short, attempting to adhere to the "original intent" of the framers is impossible, because we cannot know what they intended in all circumstances (Levy, 1988).

How the Supreme Court Operates

The U.S. Supreme Court plays the leading role in defining the scope of civil liberties. The formal process for Supreme Court cases is described in the Rules of the Supreme Court, which can be found on the Supreme Court Web site *(www.supremecourtus. gov)*. Briefly, the Supreme Court operates as follows.

1. *A case or controversy.* The Supreme Court rules only on specific cases or controversies that come before it. It does not issue advisory opinions or anticipate issues that have not yet become a specific controversy.

2. *Standing.* A case can be brought only by someone who has legal standing—that is, a person who is directly affected by the law or practice in question. For example, you may not like a new federal law, but if you are not affected by it, you do not have standing to bring suit challenging it.

3. *Getting to the Court.* A case may reach the Supreme Court by one of several routes: on appeal from one of the ten U.S. circuit courts of appeals; on appeal from a U.S. district court; on appeal from one of several special federal courts; or on direct appeal from a state supreme court. Article III of the Constitution spells out several types of cases in which the Supreme Court has original jurisdiction.

The formal process by which a case reaches the Court is diagramed by the Supreme Court Historical Society on its Web site *(www.supremecourthistory.org)*. The Web site's Learning Center has a page devoted to landmark cases (directly accessible at *www.landmarkcases.org*). Diagrams of how the cases moved through the court system are presented for *Brown v. Board of Education* (1954), *Mapp v. Ohio* (1961), *Tinker v. Des Moines* (1969), and other landmark civil liberties cases.

4. *Writ of certiorari.* To appeal to the Supreme Court one must file a writ of certiorari (file for "cert" in common parlance). The Court has tremendous discretion in whether to accept cases. It may choose to decline to hear a case, and it does not have to provide any reason for doing so. The Court refuses to accept the vast majority of cases that are appealed to it.

5. *The briefs.* The Supreme Court is presented with the facts of a case and the constitutional arguments in the main briefs filed by the two parties in the case. Other groups may also file amicus curiae briefs (Latin for "friend of the court"; amicus briefs in the legal vernacular). Amicus briefs play an important role in civil liberties cases. Public interest groups such as the American

Civil Liberties Union frequently file amicus briefs in cases in which a specific civil liberties issue is involved. Frequently, the group filing the amicus has no direct involvement with either of the parties in the case itself, but is only concerned with the civil liberties issue. A group filing an amicus brief does not care whether the main figure in the case is innocent or guilty, but it is very concerned with, for example, the Fourth Amendment search and seizure issue that the case raises. Amicus briefs are an important avenue by which new ideas about civil liberties reach the court. Some political scientists argue that public interest groups, because of their expertise, resources, and experience from prior court cases, play an especially important role in shaping Supreme Court decisions (Epstein and Kobylka, 1992).

The rules for filing amicus briefs are spelled out in rule 37 of the *Rules of the Supreme Court:* "An *amicus curiae* brief that brings to the attention of the Court relevant matter not already brought to its attention by the parties may be of considerable help to the Court. An *amicus curiae* brief that does not serve this purpose burdens the Court, and its filing is not favored."

6. *Oral arguments.* Each side is allowed 30 minutes to present an oral argument on behalf of its side in a case. One attorney presents the argument for each side. Supreme Court justices frequently ask questions from the bench, often posing hypothetical questions related to the issue being argued.

7. *Sources of ideas.* The Court is presented with ideas in the briefs filed with a case. The briefs, however, contain ideas that originate elsewhere. Many new ideas originate through social and political change. For example, at some point in the 1950s and 1960s people began to believe that there is a right to privacy. New ideas are discussed and debated in the political arena and among scholars at colleges and universities. Law schools play a particularly important role in formulating new ideas into the specific terms of constitutional law. Law review articles contribute to the debate over civil liberties issues and are often cited by the Court as sources in making decisions.

8. *The decision.* The nine-member Court decides cases by majority rule. Many important cases are decided by a vote of 5–4. Because of the need to put together a majority, final decisions are often the result of compromises among the justices. A justice who represents a potential fifth vote, for example, may insist that the other four make some changes in order to gain his or her vote. In some cases, even the majority is divided, with several members writing separate opinions, disagreeing on certain parts of the case. When this happens, the Court's decision is binding only for those points in which a majority agree.

9. *Majority and dissenting opinions.* The chief justice of the Supreme Court assigns justices to write the opinion or opinions. In a unanimous decision, the chief justice may assign himself or some other justice. In split opinions, the chief justice assigns the senior justice on each side to write the majority and minority opinions (although some other justice may eventually write an opinion). Justices who are not chosen to write the majority or minority opinions may write a concurring opinion. A justice might express agreement with part of the majority opinion while disagreeing with part of it, for example. A justice might agree with the majority opinion but disagree with the legal rationale for it, or a justice may feel it important to express an important point in writing (Stern, 1993).

Dissenting opinions have often exerted an important influence in the history of civil liberties. Early in the twentieth century, for example, dissents by Justices Oliver Wendell Holmes Jr. and Louis Brandeis set forth ideas in free speech cases that eventually became First Amendment law (Polenberg, 1987).

The Dynamics of Change on the Supreme Court

Generally, the Supreme Court's interpretation of constitutional law is characterized by stability and continuity. The Court does not like to change abruptly or to reverse itself. Holding to precedent is known as the principle of stare decisis. Important changes in constitutional law do occur, however. A decision may expand, contract, or modify the existing law of civil liberties. A good example is the 2003 *Lawrence v. Texas* decision reversing *Bowers v. Hardwick* (1986) and ruling that sexual relations between people of the same sex is constitutionally protected.

Political scientists offer three basic explanations for changes in the Supreme Court's position of issues (Epstein and Kobylka, 1992). Some scholars argue that it is the result of change in the personnel of the Court itself: the replacement of judges who are not sympathetic to civil liberties with justices who are. Other scholars argue that the Court responds to the external environment, as expressed in public opinion or political trends (Marshall, 1989). A third interpretation holds that the Court responds to the legal arguments presented to it in both the main and the amicus briefs.

Civil Liberties, Culture, and Politics

Most civil liberties issues are highly controversial: Can public schools require students to recite a prayer each morning? Does the First Amendment protect the right of Nazis to hold marches and demonstrations? (Strum, 1999). Does the Eighth Amendment prohibit capital punishment as "cruel and unusual"? Does the constitution guarantee the right to an abortion? Civil liberties issues touch on fundamental issues involving cultural values, and they frequently generate intense controversy and political conflict.

Civil Liberties and U.S. Culture

The United States is an exceedingly diverse society. It includes a wide range of religions, cultural values, and lifestyles. Inevitably the different points of view inherent in this diversity come into conflict. Since the 1960s, U.S. society has been characterized by what some observers call the "culture wars": deep political divisions over issues of morality such as sexuality, the family, and the arts. Yet, as historian James Davison Hunter (1991) persuasively argues, similar disputes over cultural issues and moral standards have been present throughout U.S. history.

Religion is an excellent example of these conflicts. Many people want the government to support religious values as a way of promoting moral values and respect for law. Others, however, believe that the government should remain neutral in all matters of religion, not sponsoring any religious practices and certainly not supporting certain religious beliefs at the expense of others (Frankel, 1994).

Abortion is another good example. U.S. society includes a wide range of religious traditions that have different views on the question of when life begins, whether or not abortion is a sin, and whether it should be illegal (Tribe, 1990). Gun ownership is a third example. Many Americans believe that they have a right to own guns and that the Second Amendment to the Constitution guarantees them that right. Others believe that given the Second Amendment's reference to "a well regulated militia," the amendment refers only to the militia—today, the national guard—and does not guarantee individuals an unconditional right to own guns.

The Constitution provides *a framework for resolving conflicts* of this sort. The Supreme Court has interpreted the Establishment Clause of the First Amendment, for example, to require a strict separation of church and state, and it has ruled that prayers or other officially sponsored religious exercises in public schools are unconstitutional. Those who believe the government should support religious values disagree strongly with this position and believe the Court has gone too far in barring religion from public life. Many others, however, agree with the Court's position. Because of the prestige of the Court and a deeply ingrained respect for the law, Americans generally accept Court decisions—even ones they do not like (Lasser, 1988).

Civil Liberties and U.S. Politics

When people and groups are unhappy with a Supreme Court decision, they often try to reverse it, which in effect makes it a political issue. The twentieth century has witnessed several periods characterized by a political "storm over the Court" (O'Brien, 2003; Lasser, 1988). The first occurred in the mid-1930s, when a conservative Court struck down New Deal legislation sponsored by the Roosevelt administration (Irons, 1999). A second occurred in the 1950s after the Court ruled that racially segregating schools was unconstitutional (Kluger, 1975). A third occurred in the 1960s as a result of pro–civil liberties decisions related to prayer in schools and the rights of criminal suspects. A fourth was prompted by the *Roe v. Wade* decision establishing a constitutional right to abortion (Lasser, 1988).

There are several different strategies for seeking to change a Supreme Court decision: bringing new cases to the Court with new arguments; attempting to amend the Constitution; organizing politically to elect presidents who will appoint sympathetic judges to the Court; enacting federal legislation that will overrule the Court's decision.

Numerous attempts have been made to overturn Supreme Court decisions through constitutional amendments. After the Court banned school prayer in 1962 (*Engel v. Vitale*), more than 100 proposed amendments allowing prayer in schools were introduced in Congress. None of these proposals has ever been approved, however. Similarly, prolife groups have made an effort to overturn the 1973 *Roe v. Wade* decision through a constitutional amendment. This effort also has not succeeded.

Many presidential candidates have promised to appoint justices who will reverse existing Court decisions. In 1968, Richard Nixon campaigned for the presidency on a promise to appoint "strict constructionists" to the Court. By that he meant that he would appoint conservative justices who did not agree with the recent pro–civil liberties decisions of the Earl Warren Court on such issues as prayer in schools and the rights of criminal suspects. To a certain extent, Nixon's efforts succeeded. As president, he did appoint conservative justices who reversed some of the Warren Court's decisions on criminal procedure, but not on other issues (Irons, 1999).

In another important controversy, the U.S. Senate in 1987 rejected the nomination of Robert Bork to the Court because of his views on privacy, abortion, and some other issues. Bork's nomination provoked a major and ultimately successful political effort by civil liberties groups to block his appointment (Pertschuk and Schaetzel, 1989).

There have also been efforts to reverse Court decisions through federal legislation. In 1993, for example, Congress passed the Religious Freedom Restoration Act in an attempt to overturn a 1990 Court decision limiting the right of some Native American groups to use peyote in their religious ceremonies. Peyote is a naturally occurring substance that has a hallucinogenic effect when ingested and has been declared illegal (Long, 2000). In 1989, Congress passed the Flag Protection Act, making it a crime to burn the American flag. This law was a response to a 1989 Court decision (*Texas v. Johnson*) that had overturned the conviction of a person who burned the flag. The Court, however, ruled the new federal law unconstitutional in 1990, also on First Amendment grounds (*United States v. Eichman*) (Goldstein, 2000).

In short, controversial civil liberties issues are never completely settled by a Supreme Court decision. The underlying cultural and political conflicts continue as Americans wrestle with the meaning of the Constitution. As Lasser (1988) argues, the role of the Court in modern times has been one of "crisis as usual."

Conclusion

Civil liberties are the rights that the individual enjoys over and against the government. Civil liberties are primarily protected by the Bill of Rights and other amendments to the U.S. Constitution. They are also protected by state bills of rights and federal, state, and local laws. The U.S. Supreme Court is the final authority on the meaning of particular provisions of the Bill of Rights and the precise scope of particular rights such as freedom of speech. Chapter 2 examines specific civil liberties issues in detail.

References

Bork, Robert H. 1990. *The Tempting of America*. New York: Free Press.

Bradley, David, and Shelley Fisher Fishkin, eds. 1998. *The Encyclopedia of Civil Rights in America*. Armonk, NY: Sharpe Reference.

Brant, Irving. 1965. *The Bill of Rights: Its Origin and Meaning*. Indianapolis: Bobbs-Merrill.

Brownlie, Ian, and Guy S. Goodwin-Gill, eds. 2002. *Basic Documents on Human Rights*, 4th ed. Oxford, England: Clarendon Press.

Casper, Jonathan D. 1972. *The Politics of Civil Liberties*. New York: Harper and Row.

Cleary, Edward J. 1994. *Beyond the Burning Cross: The First Amendment and the Landmark R.A.V. Case*. New York: Random House.

Curry, Thomas J. 1986. *The First Freedoms: Church and State in America to the Passage of the First Amendment*. New York: Oxford University Press.

Epstein, Lee, and Joseph F. Kobylka. 1992. *The Supreme Court and Legal Change: Abortion and the Death Penalty*. Chapel Hill: University of North Carolina Press.

Etzioni, Amitai. 1993. *The Spirit of Community: Rights, Responsibilities, and the Communitarian Agenda*. New York: Crown.

Fliter, John A. 2001. *Prisoners' Rights: The Supreme Court and Evolving Standards of Decency*. Westport, CT: Greenwood Press.

Frankel, Marvin E. 1994. *Faith and Freedom: Religious Liberty in America*. New York: Hill and Wang.

Glasser, Ira. 1991. *Visions of Liberty: The Bill of Rights for All Americans*. New York: Arcade.

Glendon, Mary Ann. 1991. *Rights Talk: The Impoverishment of Political Discourse*. New York: Free Press.

Goldstein, Robert J. 2000. *Flag Burning and Free Speech: The Case of Texas v. Johnson*. Lawrence: University Press of Kansas.

Grossman, Joel B. 2003. "The 200th Anniversary of *Marbury v. Madison*: The Reasons We Should Still Care About the Decision, and The Lingering Questions It Left Behind." Arlington, VA: Freedom Forum.

Hall, Timothy L. 1998. *Separating Church and State: Roger Williams and Religious Liberty*. Urbana: University of Illinois Press.

Handler, Jack G. 1994. *Ballentine's Law Dictionary*. Albany, NY: Lawyer's Cooperative Publishing Co.

Hentoff, Nat. 1980. *The First Freedom: The Tumultuous History of Free Speech in America*. New York: Delacorte Press.

Human Rights Watch. 1998. *Shielded from Justice: Police Brutality and Accountability in the United States*. New York: Human Rights Watch.

Hunt, James W., and Patricia K. Strongin. 1994. *The Law of the Workplace: Rights of Employers and Employees*. Washington, DC: Bureau of National Affairs.

Hunter, James Davison. 1991. *Culture Wars: The Struggle to Define America*. New York: Basic Books.

Irons, Peter. 1983. *Justice at War: The Story of the Japanese American Internment Cases*. New York: Oxford University Press.

———. 1999. *A People's History of the Supreme Court*. New York: Viking.

Karst, Kenneth L. 1989. *Belonging to America: Equal Citizenship and the Constitution*. New Haven, CT: Yale University Press.

Kluger, Richard. 1975. *Simple Justice: The History of* Brown v. Board of Education *and Black America's Struggle for Equality*. New York: Knopf.

Lasser, William. 1988. *The Limits of Judicial Power: The Supreme Court in American Politics*. Chapel Hill: University of North Carolina Press.

Levy, Leonard. 1988. *Original Intent and the Framers' Constitution*. New York: Collier Macmillan.

Long, Carolyn N. 2000. *Religious Freedom and Indian Rights: The Case of* Oregon v. Smith. Lawrence: University Press of Kansas.

Maddex, Robert L. 1998. *State Constitutions of the United States.* Washington, DC: Congressional Quarterly.

Marshall, Thomas R. 1989. *Public Opinion and the Supreme Court.* Boston: Unwin Hyman.

Nieman, Donald G. 1991. *Promises to Keep: African Americans and the Constitutional Order, 1776 to the Present.* New York: Oxford University Press.

O'Brien, David M. 2003. *Storm Center: The Supreme Court in American Politics,* 6th ed. New York: W. W. Norton.

Pertschuk, Michael, and Wendy Schaetzel. 1989. *The People Rising: The Campaign against the Bork Nomination.* New York: Thunder's Mouth Press.

Peters, Shawn Francis. 2000. *Judging Jehovah's Witnesses: Religious Persecution and the Dawn of the Rights Revolution.* Lawrence: University Press of Kansas.

Polenberg, Richard. 1987. *Fighting Faiths: The Abrams Case, The Supreme Court, and Free Speech.* New York: Viking.

Repa, Barbara Kate. 2000. *Your Rights in the Workplace.* Berkeley, CA: Nolo.

Schwartz, Bernard. 1977. *The Great Rights of Mankind: A History of the American Bill of Rights.* New York: Oxford University Press.

Schwartz, Bernard, ed. 1980. *The Roots of the Bill of Rights: An Illustrated Source Book of American Freedom.* 5 vols. New York: Chelsea House.

Simon, James F. 2002. *What Kind of Nation: Thomas Jefferson, John Marshall, and the Epic Struggle to Create a United States.* New York: Simon and Schuster.

Stern, Robert L. 1993. *Supreme Court Practice: For Practice in the Supreme Court of the United States.* Washington, DC: Bureau of National Affairs.

Strum, Philippa. 1999. *When the Nazis Came to Skokie: Freedom for Speech We Hate.* Lawrence: University Press of Kansas.

Tarr, G. Alan. 1998. *Understanding State Constitutions.* Princeton, NJ: Princeton University Press.

Tribe, Lawrence. 1990. *Abortion: The Clash of Absolutes.* New York: W. W. Norton.

Urofsky, Melvin I. 1991. *A Conflict of Rights: The Supreme Court and Affirmative Action.* New York: Scribner's.

Walker, Samuel. 1999. *In Defense of American Liberties: A History of the ACLU,* 2nd ed. Carbondale: Southern Illinois University Press.

Walzer, Lee. 2002. *Gay Rights on Trial: A Reference Handbook.* Santa Barbara, CA: ABC-CLIO.

2

Issues and Controversies

The purpose of this chapter is to describe the major civil liberties issues and controversies. It identifies all of the major subject areas and provides a brief discussion of the core issues for each one. This chapter is by no means exhaustive. Each of the subjects identified here can be covered in a long and detailed textbook. This chapter is designed to provide a basic introductory overview.

Civil liberties issues are divided into five basic categories:

1. First Amendment rights: freedom of speech, press, and assembly; religious liberty
2. Equal protection of the law
3. Due process of law
4. Privacy
5. National Security and the War on Terrorism

First Amendment Issues

Freedom of Speech, Press, and Assembly
The Right to Criticize the Government
The core civil liberties issue in a democratic society is the right of citizens to criticize the government. Before the development of modern free speech law, citizens who criticized the government could be prosecuted for the crime of seditious libel (Levy, 1963). Under the Alien and Sedition Acts of 1798, critics of President John Adams were prosecuted and imprisoned. The Sedition Act

made it a crime to "write, print, utter or publish, or . . . cause or procure to be written, printed, uttered or publishing . . . any false, scandalous and malicious writing or writings against the government of the United States. . . ." (The Sedition Act is reprinted in Chapter 5.) The punishment for those convicted under this law was a fine of up to $2,000 and two years' imprisonment. Individuals prosecuted included Thomas Cooper, a scientist, educator, and political philosopher, and eventually president of what later became the University of South Carolina (Smith, 1956). A supporter of the Jeffersonian opposition to the Federalists, Cooper was convicted, fined $400, and imprisoned. Another victim was Benjamin Franklin Bache, grandson of Benjamin Franklin and editor of the Philadelphia *Democrat-Republican Aurora* (Rosenfeld, 1997). After being elected president in 1800, Thomas Jefferson pardoned everyone who had been convicted under the law.

The modern body of free speech law in the United States grew out of the crisis of World War I, when the federal government suppressed all criticism of the war. Federal agencies banned from the mail publications that were critical of the government and prosecuted prominent war critics. Socialist Party leader Eugene V. Debs, for example, was convicted and imprisoned for giving a speech in Canton, Ohio, opposing war in general, without even criticizing the government itself (Murphy, 1979). (An excerpt from the 1917 Sedition Act is presented in Chapter 5.) Both the federal and the state governments prosecuted dissenters. In the most important case to reach the U.S. Supreme Court, the Court upheld the conviction of a radical activist and articulated the *clear and present danger test* that dominated the law of free speech for many decades thereafter (Chafee, 1941). In one of the most famous passages in Court history, Justice Oliver Wendell Holmes Jr. wrote:

> But the character of every act depends upon the circumstances in which it is done. The most stringent protection of free speech would not protect a man in falsely shouting fire in a theatre and causing a panic. It does not even protect a man from an injunction against uttering words that may have all the effect of force. The question in every case is whether the words used are used in such circumstances and are of such a nature as to create clear and present danger that they will bring about the

substantive evils that Congress has a right to prevent (*Schenk v. United States*, 1919).

Later the same year, however, Justice Holmes's view had changed. Dissenting in the case of *Abrams v. United States* (and joined by Louis Brandeis) he argued that "the ultimate good desired is better reached by free trade in idea [and that] the best test of truth is the power of the thought to get itself accepted in the competition of the market. . . ." (Polenberg, 1987). The Supreme Court eventually accepted Holmes's basic idea and expanded the First Amendment protections of speech. This development of First Amendment law culminated in the 1964 *New York Times v. Sullivan* decision (Lewis, 1991), in which the Court articulated what is now regarded as the basic philosophy of freedom of speech in a free society. The Court concluded that freedom of speech involved "a profound national commitment to the principle that debate on public issues should be uninhibited, robust, and wide-open, and that it may well include vehement, caustic, and sometimes unpleasantly sharp attacks on government and public officials."

Speech versus Acts One of the most important distinctions regarding free speech is the difference between *speech or expression*, which is protected by the First Amendment, and *acts*, which are not. Basically, you can say that you hate someone (expression), but you cannot hit them (act). Deeply offensive statements about certain groups are protected (e.g., "They all have low IQs"), but actually harming a person or his or her property is a crime and is not protected by the First Amendment (Haiman, 1993).

Burning the American Flag The issue of speech versus action is illustrated by the highly volatile question of whether the First Amendment protects the right to criticize the government by burning the American flag (Goldstein, 2000). Burning or otherwise desecrating the flag—the symbol of the country—outrages most Americans. Civil libertarians, however, believe that burning the flag is an act of symbolic speech protected by the First Amendment.

Surprisingly, the Supreme Court did not address the flag burning issue until 1989. Gregory Lee Johnson was convicted

**Sidebar 2.1   Civil Liberties in Conflict: The Case of Hate Speech—
Freedom of Speech versus Equal Protection**

Some of the most difficult civil liberties issues in recent years involve conflicts between competing civil liberties principles. The issue of pornography discussed in a later section, for example, represents a conflict between free speech and women's rights. One of the most difficult conflicts involves hate speech, defined as any form of expression that is offensive to a distinct group (e.g., racial or ethnic minority groups, religious groups, women, gay and lesbian people, disabled persons, etc.) (Walker, 1994). The hate speech issue represents a conflict between the principle of First Amendment protection of free speech and the Fourteenth Amendment guarantee of equal protection of the law.

In 1977 the hate speech issue emerged as a national controversy when a small American Nazi group sought to hold a demonstration in the largely Jewish community of Skokie, Illinois. Understandably, the residents of Skokie were deeply offended by the anti-Semitic views of the Nazis, and the town refused to grant a permit for the demonstration. When the controversy finally reached the courts, the Seventh Circuit Court of Appeals upheld the First Amendment rights of the Nazi group. It went out of its way to distinguish between the *content* of the speech in question ("we nevertheless feel compelled once again to express our repugnance at the doctrines which the appellees desire to profess publicly.") and the basic principle of free speech: "The result we have reached is dictated by the fundamental proposition that if these civil rights are to remain vital for all, they must protect not only those society deems acceptable, but also those whose ideas it quite justifiably rejects and despises" (Neier, 1979; Strum, 1999).

under a Texas flag protection law of burning the American flag. The Supreme Court overturned his conviction, ruling that burning the flag is a form of political expression protected by the First Amendment (*Texas v. Johnson*, 1989). The *Johnson* decision provoked a national uproar, and some members of Congress proposed amending the First Amendment to specifically exempt flag burning from its protection. As an alternative, Congress passed a law, the Flag Protection Act, which provided that "Whoever knowingly mutilates, defaces, physically defiles, burns, maintains on the floor or ground, or tramples upon any flag of the United States shall be fined under this title or imprisoned for not

---

Sidebar 2.1 (continued)

In the 1980s, in response to a rash of racist incidents on college campuses, a number of colleges and universities developed campus speech codes that penalized speech or expression that offended or degraded people on the basis of race, ethnicity, gender, or sexual preference. Advocates of campus speech codes argue that offensive speech creates a hostile climate on campus, which impinges on the right of people of color, women, or lesbian and gay students to an education. This rationale for censorship is very different from the traditional rationales based on moral grounds, because it is based on the civil libertarian principle of equal opportunity, grounded in the Fourteenth Amendment (Walker, 1994; Heumann, Church, and Redlawsk, 1997).

Eventually, the speech codes from the University of Michigan and University of Wisconsin were challenged as violations of free speech. In both cases the federal district courts struck down the speech codes on First Amendment grounds. The speech codes in question impermissibly punished speech on the basis of content, and in addition the terms in the codes regarding what kind of speech was prohibited were impermissibly vague. (The original Wisconsin speech code is reprinted in Chapter 5.)

---

more than one year, or both." (The Flag Protection Act is reprinted in Chapter 5.)

Predictably, some people immediately challenged the law by burning the flag to force a constitutional test of the law. In the case of *United States v. Eichman* (1990), the Court reiterated its position in the *Johnson* case, declaring, "If there is a bedrock principle underlying the First Amendment, it is that the Government may not prohibit the expression of an idea simply because society finds the idea itself offensive or disagreeable. Punishing desecration of the flag dilutes the very freedom that makes this emblem so revered, and worth revering" (Goldstein, 2000).

Advocating Illegal Activity Another important free speech issue is whether the First Amendment protects the right to advocate illegal activity. Does it, for example, protect political radicals who advocate revolution and the overthrow of the government? Under the clear and present danger test that Justice Holmes articulated in 1919, the Supreme Court held that the First Amendment did not protect advocacy of illegal activity. However, the Court gradually expanded the scope of First Amendment protections, and finally in 1969, in *Brandenburg v. Ohio*, it held that the First Amendment protected the advocacy of illegal action except where it involves *incitement to imminent lawless action*. The Court held that "the principle that the constitutional guarantees of free speech and free press do not permit a State to forbid or proscribe advocacy of the use of force or of law violation except where such advocacy is directed to inciting or producing imminent lawless action and is likely to incite or produce such action."

In short, the First Amendment protects the right to discuss Communism or anarchism as revolutionary political philosophies but does not protect the right to incite someone to bomb a government building. Similarly, with regard to hate speech (see the full discussion later in this chapter), it protects the right to say offensive things about a particular racial or religious group (as in, "they all are . . ."), but it does not protect the right to urge people to attack someone who is a member of one of those groups (as in, "let's get . . .).

Freedom of Speech for Students in Public Schools   The Supreme Court has created a number of exceptions to First Amendment protection of free speech in the context of special institutions: public schools, prisons, and the military. In these situations, the Court has often ruled in favor of restrictions on speech that officials feel are necessary to maintain order within the institution.

One of the most famous cases of the 1960s involved the free speech rights of children in public schools. The Court upheld the right of Mary Beth Tinker, of Des Moines, Iowa, to wear an armband to school to protest the Vietnam War. The Court ruled that public school students are guaranteed certain constitutional rights (Johnson, 1997). The Court's opinion declared, "In our system, state-operated schools may not be enclaves of totalitarianism. School officials do not possess absolute authority over their students. Students in school as well as out of school are "persons" under our Constitution. They are possessed of fundamental rights which the State must respect" (*Tinker et al. v. Des Moines*).

The First Amendment rights of public school students are not absolute, however. In 1988, the Court upheld the right of the Hazelwood, Missouri, public school officials to censor the student newspaper. The Hazelwood East paper in this case published a story about students' experiences with pregnancy and the impact of parents' divorce. The Court held that the school paper was part of the curriculum over which school officials had legitimate authority, and also that the paper could reasonably be perceived to represent the official views of the school itself. Thus, the facts of the case were different from those in the *Tinker* case, which involved the right of individual students to free expression (*Hazelwood v. Kuhlmeier*).

The Supreme Court has fairly consistently found that in certain institutions, such as schools, prisons, and the military, constitutional rights can be limited because of the needs of the institution. In a 1995 case involving drug testing of student athletes, Justice Antonin Scalia wrote, "We have found . . . 'special needs' to exist in the public-school context" (*Vernonia School District v. Acton*). These special needs include the right of officials to maintain order and discipline. Civil libertarians generally disagree with this position and argue that officials in schools and prisons often overreact to behavior that may be embarrassing but does not pose a real threat to the maintenance of order.

Offensive Speech and Expression

Speech or expression that is offensive to other people raises particularly sensitive First Amendment issues. The two main categories of offensive speech involve sexually oriented material (Strossen, 1995) and "hate speech" that offends people on the basis of race, ethnicity, religion, gender, or sexual preference (Walker, 1994).

Obscenity, Pornography, and Sexually Explicit Material   Censorship of sexually oriented material has long raised some of the most controversial First Amendment issues. Historically, the federal government outlawed sexually oriented material. The 1873 Comstock Act, for example, banned from the U.S. mails any material related to birth control (Boyer, 1968). Many states and cities censored movies, requiring each film to obtain a license, until the 1950s. (See Chapter 4 for a description of the famous "Banned in Boston" censorship controversy that began in the 1920s.)

The courts began to extend First Amendment protection to literature with sexual themes in the 1930s. The most famous case involved James Joyce's novel *Ulysses,* now widely regarded as one of the greatest novels in the English language. (A collection of documents related to this case is available in Moscato and LeBlanc, 1984). In a 1957 case, *Roth v. United States,* the Supreme Court addressed the issue of whether or not the First Amendment protects obscenity. It applied the clear and present danger test and concluded that forms of expression that had "even the slightest redeeming social importance" were protected by the First Amendment but that "obscenity is not within the area of constitutionally protected speech or press."

Having decided that obscenity was not protected by the First Amendment, the Supreme Court then had to wrestle with the problem of defining obscenity. This proved to be extremely difficult. As free speech advocates have always argued, definitions of "obscenity," "pornography," or "offensive" materials suffer from extreme vagueness. It is typically not clear what a law covers and does not cover. For example, does a law banning graphic images of genitalia also cover anatomy texts and discussions of medical issues?

In 1973, the Court developed the "Miller test," which serves as the basic framework for judging individual works. Under the Miller test, to be obscene, material must meet three tests: (1) the "average person" would agree that work as a whole "appeals to prurient interest"; (2) the work depicts or describes in a "patently offensive way" sexual conduct specifically defined by applicable state law; (3) the work as a whole lacks "serious literary, artistic, political, or scientific value"(*Miller v. California*).

Attempts to censor sexually explicit material continue to arise. In 1978 the U.S. Supreme Court upheld the right of the Federal Communications Commission to ban seven words used by comedian George Carlin in one of his routines. (An excerpt from the Supreme Court opinion in *Federal Communications Commission v. Pacifica Foundation* is presented in Chapter 5.)

Censorship of the Internet   One of the most important recent censorship controversies involved the 1996 Communications Decency Act (CDA), which was an effort to protect children from "indecent" material on the Internet (Lipschultz, 2000). The law prohibited "the knowing transmission of obscene or indecent messages to any recipient under 18 years of age . . . by means of a telecommunications device." Another section prohibited "the knowing sending or displaying of patently offensive messages in a manner that is available to a person under 18 years of age" using "any interactive computer service." Offensive material was defined to include "any comment, request, suggestion, proposal, image, or other communication that, in context, depicts or describes, in terms patently offensive as measured by contemporary community standards, sexual or excretory activities or organs." Anyone convicted of violating the law could be fined and sentenced to up to two years in prison. As Marjorie Heins (2001a) points out, there is a long history of censorship efforts designed to protect children from allegedly "indecent" material.

The CDA was immediately challenged in court by a coalition of twenty organizations led by the American Civil Liberties Union (ACLU) and including Human Rights Watch, the Electronic Privacy Information Center, Computer Professionals for Social Responsibility, and Planned Parenthood Federation of America. These groups argued that the law was a sweeping attack on freedom of expression and was particularly dangerous because the terms it used (e.g., "indecent") were extremely vague and subject to a wide range of interpretations. Additionally, they argued that the prohibition on sexual material would inevitably censor discussions of health issues as well as artistic works (Lipschultz, 2000).

A year later, in the case of *Reno v. ACLU,* the U.S. Supreme Court unanimously ruled the CDA unconstitutional as a violation of the First Amendment. The Court's opinion addressed many of the issues that had arisen in previous censorship cases, including the restriction of speech based on content, the vagueness of terms such as "indecent," and the impact any attempt to restrict communication to children would have on adult-to-adult communication.

First and most important, the Court found that the law regulated speech and expression on the basis of its content. It has consistently ruled that the First Amendment permits content regulation only in certain very limited situations. A second problem was that the terms "indecent" and "patently offensive" were impermissibly vague. The Court found that they "cover large amounts of nonpornographic material with serious educational or other value." The Court added that "[i]n evaluating the free speech rights of adults, we have made it perfectly clear that "[s]exual expression which is indecent but not obscene is protected by the First Amendment." The Court also reiterated its position that ("where obscenity is not involved, we have consistently held that the fact that protected speech may be offensive to some does not justify its suppression"). It reiterated its conclusion from an earlier case that "the fact that society may find speech offensive is not a sufficient reason for suppressing it" (*Reno v. ACLU,* 1997).

Protecting children from harm was one of the main purposes of the law (Heins, 2001a). The Court acknowledged Congress's desire to protect children from offensive material on the Internet but concluded that "[i]n order to deny minors access to potentially harmful speech, the CDA effectively suppresses a large amount of speech that adults have a constitutional right to receive and to address to one another."

Pornography and Women Some feminists argue that pornography should be censored because it violates the rights of women (MacKinnon, 1993). Catharine MacKinnon and Andrea Dworkin proposed a law that would give women a right to sue the producers of pornography for violating their civil rights on the grounds that pornography "subordinates" women and causes them actual harm. The city of Indianapolis enacted the ordinance in the early 1980s, and it was immediately challenged as a violation of the First Amendment (Downs, 1989). The Seventh Circuit Court of Appeals declared the law unconstitutional in the 1985 case of *American Booksellers Association v. Hudnut*, holding that the law establishes an "approved" view of women and of female sexuality. This represents a content-based form of censorship that the First Amendment prohibits. Or, as the court put it bluntly, "This is thought control." The Supreme Court declined to hear the case and let the lower court decision stand.

Nadine Strossen (1995), president of the ACLU, argues that censoring pornography and other forms of sexually explicit expression would actually harm women. She points out that historically censorship has been a weapon to limit women's freedom. The most important example of this application was the old federal Comstock Law that banned material about birth control from the U.S. mails (Boyer, 1968). Measures such as the Indianapolis antipornography ordinance embody a particular view of women and of women and sexuality, and thus represent content-based censorship. Also, censorship measures view women as weak and in need of protection. Strossen argues forcefully that "[w]omen do not need the government's protection from words and pictures" (p. 14).

Pornography and Violence One of the major issues related to pornography is whether it incites or encourages individuals to commit acts of violence. Many advocates of censoring pornography believe that it does. There has been considerable research on this topic by psychologists. Civil libertarians believe that there is no convincing evidence of a link between pornography and violence. A related issue is whether media portraying violence, such as video games, lead young people to commit violent acts. The 1999 shooting at Columbine High School in Colorado, in which two students shot and killed thirteen students and teachers and then themselves, brought this issue to the fore, because the two students who did the shooting played a lot of violent video games. A good summary of the issues is the report *Violence and the Media*, written by Marjorie Heins (2001b) and published by the First Amendment Center. As the report points out, attempts at censorship raise a number of difficult issues. How is "violent media" to be defined? Also, there is an important distinction between violence and aggression. Not all aggressive behavior is socially disapproved—sports, for example. The report is available on the Center's Web site *(www.firstamendmentcenter.org)*.

Academic Freedom

The principle of academic freedom encompasses a number of First Amendment issues (Aby and Kuhn, 2000). First and most important, it protects the free speech rights of faculty and students in colleges and universities. A public university, for example, cannot fire a faculty member or deny recognition to a student group because it does not like the ideas the person or the group has expressed. To do so would involve a *content-based* restriction of freedom of speech. Academic freedom also includes the freedom to teach, including teaching ideas that are controversial.

The most famous academic freedom case in U.S. history is the 1925 *Scopes* case (see the discussion later in this chapter and in Chapter 4), which arose after the state of Tennessee outlawed the teaching of evolution (Ginger, 1974; Larson, 1997). The First Amendment prohibits any restriction on teaching certain subjects because the content of that subject is offensive to some people. At the same time, the government cannot require the teaching of a subject that advances a particular religious point of view. This issue has arisen in the controversy over the teaching of creationism (Withman, 2002), which is discussed later in this chapter, in the section on church and state.

Academic freedom also involves certain due process rights for both students and teachers. A college or university may dismiss a faculty member or suspend a student for unprofessional conduct but must grant the individual a fair hearing, including the opportunity to rebut the charges (Rubin and Greenhouse, 1984).

Scientific Research: Stem Cell Research and Cloning   A current academic freedom issue involves the new medical advances in stem cell research (Leone, 2003). Stem cells are derived from embryos at the blastocyst stage. The importance of stem cells is that they can transform into any more developed cell type. Current research focuses on the possibility of treating certain illnesses such as Parkinson's disease by injecting healthy new cells into a patient's body to replace diseased or damaged cells. Some researchers believe that it might be possible to treat spinal cord injuries by injecting healthy spinal cord cells into a patient.

Some people are opposed to stem cell research on religious grounds. In particular, they object to the use of embryos derived from abortions as a source of stem cells. In 2001, President George W. Bush banned the use of federal funds in most stem cell research. Civil libertarians and most scientists oppose religious-based restrictions on stem cell research as a violation of the separation of church and state (discussed in a later section, Religious Liberty).

Freedom of Assembly

The First Amendment guarantees the freedom of assembly. Central to freedom of assembly under U.S. law is the concept of the *public forum:* areas that are considered public—streets, sidewalks, parks—are places where citizens have a right to be and to gather with other people (Gora et al., 1991). They enjoy the right to assemble there as long as they do not interfere with the rights of other people or commit a crime. The right of assembly includes the right to speak, picket, distribute leaflets, and parade. In 1939, the Supreme Court defined the crucial relationship between the right of freedom of assembly in a public forum and the right of freedom of speech: "Wherever the title of streets and parks may rest, they have immemorially been . . . used for purposes of assembly, communicating thoughts between citizens, and discussing political questions" (*Hague v. CIO*).

The right of assembly is not absolute. Those exercising it cannot interfere with the rights of other people. Blocking the streets or the entrance to a house or building is not protected by the First Amendment. A federal law prohibits blocking the entrance to an abortion clinic (see the discussion later in this chapter). Trespass on private property is also not protected. Even in public areas such as streets and sidewalks, government officials can require reasonable regulations about the *time, place, and manner* of assembly. They can, for example, impose some restrictions on a march in order to ensure the free flow of traffic or other activities. If two groups want to have big demonstrations on the same day, meanwhile, officials can impose regulations to ensure that they do not conflict with each other and create chaos. Officials can require permits for public demonstrations. Regulations related to time, place, and manner, however, cannot be so burdensome that they restrict freedom of assembly and speech (Gora et al., 1991).

What the First Amendment forbids, however, is restricting assembly on the basis of the *content* of the message being expressed by a person or group. Many freedom of speech and assembly cases involve attempts to ban demonstrations or meetings by groups such as the Ku Klux Klan that some members of the community regard as offensive. In the Skokie affair (see earlier discussion and Chapter 4), the heavily Jewish village of Skokie, Illinois, tried to keep a Nazi group from holding a demonstration. The courts rejected the village's efforts. One of these efforts involved requiring a very high insurance bond. The courts ruled that the amount required was so high that it unreasonably restricted freedom of speech and assembly. In some other cases, cities have tried to charge groups holding demonstrations for the cost of extra police protection. The courts have ruled that this is also an unconstitutional restriction on freedom of assembly (Strum, 1999).

Freedom of Assembly in Shopping Malls   The modern shopping mall presents a special problem with regard to freedom of assembly. The mall has become an extremely important part of American life. It is where large numbers of people shop and congregate. If someone wants to communicate a message (about a political candidate, abortion, gun control, or the like), the mall is a good place to find an audience. Malls are private property, however, owned by private business corporations. In this respect they are different from the traditional shopping area where stores are found along streets and sidewalks that are public property (Freedman, 1988).

Courts across the country have made different rulings on freedom of speech and assembly in shopping malls. The New Jersey courts have ruled that the state constitution guarantees freedom of speech on private property that is open to the public for commerce. (This does not include private homes that are not otherwise open to the public.) The U.S. Supreme Court ruled in a California case that a state law specifically granted free speech rights in shopping malls and other locations where the owners have invited the public in to shop. (Thus, a shopping mall is distinguished from the headquarters of a private corporation.) But the Minnesota Supreme Court ruled that the state constitution did not guarantee freedom of speech at the Mall of America (Gora et al., 1991).

Abortion Clinic Demonstrations Demonstrations by antiabortion protesters in front of abortion clinics pose a particularly difficult problem in freedom of speech and assembly. Many of these demonstrations have been loud, with offensive words directed at people entering and leaving the clinics (Jacoby, 1998). Abortion rights advocates argue that such demonstrations constitute a form of harassment and interfere with a woman's constitutionally protected right to an abortion as secured in *Roe v. Wade* (American Civil Liberties Union, 1986). Consequently, they have sought to have laws enacted to create protected "buffer zones" around abortion clinics. (Of course, blockading abortion clinics or trespassing on clinic property are clearly illegal acts unrelated to First Amendment rights.) This issue is another example of a conflict between competing civil liberties principles: freedom of speech versus the right to an abortion.

In 1993, Colorado passed a law creating a 100-foot-radius zone around a health care facility. Within this "fixed buffer zone" no person could knowingly come closer than 8 feet to another person for the purpose of displaying a sign, engaging in oral protest, educating, counseling, or passing leaflets or handbills, unless that other person consented to such an approach. This 8-foot-radius area was called a "floating buffer zone." The U.S. Supreme Court upheld that Colorado law by a vote of 6–3, holding that it was narrowly drafted and content neutral (*Hill v. Colorado*, 2000). In short, the Court struck a balance between the two competing civil liberties principles. It protected the free speech rights of antiabortion protesters but placed some limited restrictions on them in order to protect the rights of clinic patients. Congress, meanwhile, passed the Freedom of Access to Clinic Entrances (FACE) law in 1994, making it illegal to obstruct access to health facilities. (Excerpts from the FACE law are reprinted in Chapter 5.)

Sidebar 2.2   Civil Liberties in Conflict: Fair Trial versus Freedom of the Press

The Sixth Amendment guarantee of a fair trial sometimes clashes with the First Amendment protection of freedom of the press. Sensational crimes are usually accompanied by tremendous coverage in the news media. Inevitably, most people will have heard about the crime and the suspect. This pretrial publicity can bias potential jurors against the defendant, who will be denied a fair trial as a result. To deal with the problem, the courts allow trials to be moved to other jurisdictions (referred to as a change of venue) where there has not been as much publicity about the crime.

In some cases, however, judges have tried to limit pretrial publicity by placing restrictions on the press. Such restrictions are often referred to as "gag orders." The most important case of this conflict to reach the U.S. Supreme Court involved a gruesome murder of several people in Nebraska in the early 1970s. In an effort to ensure a fair trial for the defendant the trial judge issued an order restraining the news media from publishing or broadcasting any reports of confessions the defendant made to the police or other persons, along with any "other facts 'strongly implicative' of the accused." The Supreme Court acknowledged that the case involved "a confrontation between prior restraint imposed to protect one vital constitutional guarantee and the explicit command of another that the freedom to speak and publish shall not be abridged." The Court overturned the trial judge's gag order, holding that "the barriers to prior restraint remain high and the presumption against its use continues intact" (*Nebraska Press Association v. Stuart*, 1976).

Freedom of the Press

The core issue related to First Amendment protection of freedom of the press is that the government cannot impose a *prior restraint* on a publication (Ingelhart, 1997)—that is, officials cannot prevent it from being published. If a publication is libelous, then the person libeled can sue for damages after publication.

The first Supreme Court decision affirming freedom of the press was in the 1931 case of Jay Near, a Minneapolis journalist with an unsavory reputation who published a small scandal sheet with exposés of local politicians. Among other things, he was a notorious anti-Semite. The Minnesota legislature responded by passing a law that allowed authorities to ban publications as a "public nuisance." A state court subsequently banned one of Near's papers on these grounds. The Supreme Court overturned the judgment in *Near v. Minnesota,* ruling that the law imposed a prior restraint on the press. In this case the Court linked rights from the First and Fourteenth Amendments: "Liberty of the press is within the liberty safeguarded by the due process clause of the Fourteenth Amendment from invasion by state action" (Friendly, 1981).

One of the most dramatic legal and political confrontations of the Vietnam War years involved the *Pentagon Papers* case. The *New York Times* (and later, other papers) obtained and published parts of a secret Pentagon report on how the United States became involved in the war in Vietnam. The Pentagon Papers, as they became known, were highly embarrassing because they clearly indicated that several presidents had lied to the American public. Under President Nixon, the Department of Justice immediately went to court to secure an order to stop publication of the Pentagon Papers—in short, to restrain the *New York Times* from publication (*New York Times Co. v. United States,* 1971). The Court overruled the government, holding that "[a]ny system of prior restraints of expression comes to this Court bearing a heavy presumption against its constitutional validity" (Goodale, 1971; Ungar, 1972).

Restrictions on Campaign Contributions and Spending

One of the most hotly debated political issues today involves the question of whether the government can limit contributions to and spending by political candidates (Corrado, 1997; Slabach, 1998). Advocates of campaign finance reform believe that large contributions by wealthy individuals and organizations undermine the democratic process, giving the rich too much influence over who runs for office and what issues they raise. The basic question is whether money spent in a political campaign is a form of speech or expression. To put it another way, if you restrict someone's spending, are you also restricting that person's freedom of speech rights (Corrado, 1997)? Advocates of campaign finance reform argue that money is not speech and that the government can and should limit campaign contributions and spending. The ACLU and other free speech advocates argue that limiting spending inevitably leads to limits on free speech. (Current position papers in favor of campaign finance reform can be found at Common Cause's Web site, *www.commoncause.org;* materials opposing campaign finance reform on First Amendment grounds can be found at the ACLU's site, *www.aclu.org.)*

To limit the effect of money on politics, Congress passed the Federal Election Campaign Act in 1971. After the law had undergone several amendments, the Supreme Court considered whether it restricted freedom of speech. The Court's decision in *Buckley v. Valeo* (1976) was extremely complicated, upholding part of the law and ruling other parts unconstitutional. The Court upheld limits on contributions by individuals to political candidates, along with the requirements that contributions be disclosed and reported, but it struck down the limitations on campaign expenditures by candidates.

The system of political campaign spending resulting from the *Buckley* decision satisfied almost no one, and the debate over campaign finance reform raged for another twenty-five years. In 2002, Congress passed the Bipartisan Campaign Reform Act, known as the McCain-Feingold campaign finance reform law. The law contained many complex provisions on both contributions and spending in political campaigns. With respect to free speech, one of the important provisions of the law holds that political issue advertisements that are broadcast on radio and television within 30 days of a primary election or 60 days of a general election are subject to the overall campaign spending limits. One important aspect of modern political campaigns is that much advertising involves *issue ads* (e.g., for or against gun control; for or against environmental regulation; for or against privatizing Social Security; and so on) that are paid for by issue organizations and not political parties and do not necessarily mention any specific candidates.

In December 2003, the Supreme Court upheld the constitutionality of the key provisions of the Bipartisan Campaign Reform Act (the McCain-Feingold Act). In *McConnell v. Federal Election Commission,* the Court upheld the ban on large contributions to political parties, including donations by corporations, labor unions, or wealthy individuals. It also upheld the ban on broadcast advertisements (radio, broadcast television, cable television) that support or oppose candidates for federal office within sixty days before a general election or thirty days before a primary election in the candidate's district or state.

Writing for the majority, Justices Sandra Day O'Connor and John Paul Stevens held that "The question for present purposes is whether large soft-money contributions to national party committees have a corrupting influence or give rise to the appearance of corruption." They concluded that there is "substantial evidence . . . that large soft-money contributions to national political parties give rise to corruption and the appearance of corruption."

Civil libertarians criticized the decision. Justice Antonin Scalia, a conservative who generally does not support civil liberties issues, began his dissenting opinion with the declaration "This is a sad day for the freedom of speech." He and civil libertarians argue that the decision upholds government restrictions on how people can express themselves on political issues. Scalia added, "Given the premises of democracy, there is no such thing as too much speech."

Freedom of Association

Although the First Amendment does not contain the word *association*, the Supreme Court has created a very broad freedom of association under the First Amendment. The most important application of this right involves membership in unpopular groups such as the Ku Klux Klan and the Communist Party. A person should not be penalized because of his or her membership in a group or be subject to some kind of penalty through government exposure of such membership.

The Supreme Court first established a constitutionally protected freedom of association in a 1950s case involving the National Association for the Advancement of Colored People (NAACP). The state of Alabama, which still had segregation laws in effect, passed a law requiring schoolteachers to disclose the groups of which they were members. Enactment of the law was an obvious attempt to publicly identify African American teachers who were members of the NAACP. Such identification in that context would expose them to retaliation by segregationists and possibly cause them to lose their jobs. The Supreme Court declared the law unconstitutional, holding that "[e]ffective advocacy of both public and private points of view, particularly controversial ones, is undeniably enhanced by group association, as this Court has more than once recognized by remarking upon the close nexus between the freedoms of speech and assembly" (*NAACP v. Alabama*, 1958). The legal scholar Harry Kalven (1965) points out that in this case and many others, the civil rights movement made enormous contributions to the growth First Amendment rights that have benefited all Americans.

Religious Liberty

The First Amendment contains two clauses related to freedom of religion. The Establishment Clause prohibits the government from establishing a religion. The Free Exercise Clause guarantees citizens the right to practice their religion without any government restrictions (Frankel, 1994).

The Establishment Clause: Separation of Church and State

The Establishment Clause of the First Amendment forbids the government from supporting or endorsing religious beliefs or activity (Drakeman, 1991). The first important case to reach the Supreme Court involved a New Jersey law that allowed local school districts to reimburse parents for bus fares for students attending private religious schools. In the 1947 *Everson v. Board of Education* decision, the Court framed the issue in terms of a "wall of separation" between church and state. Justice Hugo Black wrote, "The First Amendment has erected a wall between church and state. That wall must be kept high and impregnable. We could not approve the slightest breach." But he then concluded that the state of New Jersey had not violated the wall in this instance. In a series of subsequent decisions, however, the Court found that different forms of support for religious activities by public schools were unconstitutional under the Establishment Clause (Souraf, 1976). One of the most important of these activities, prayer in public schools, is discussed in the next section.

Prayer in Public Schools

Whether or not public schools can sponsor organized prayers continues to be the most controversial church-state issue. Before the 1960s, public schools typically began the day with a prayer that all students were required to recite. Many Americans—perhaps even a majority—believe that daily prayer or some other religious exercise helps instill moral values in schoolchildren. They also argue that the majority of a community has a right to control its local schools, including the decision of whether organized prayers are appropriate. Some also argue that forbidding all religious expression in schools discriminates against people on the basis of religion (Ravitch, 1999). Opponents of prayer in public schools, on the other hand, believe that it represents an official endorsement of religion by the government, that students are coerced into a religious exercise because they are required to attend school, and that it imposes a particular religious creed (e.g., Christianity) on students who are members of other religions (Judaism, Islam, etc.), or who are agnostics or atheists (Fenwick, 1989; Jurinski, 1998).

In 1962, the Supreme Court ruled that an official New York state prayer, composed by state officials and recited each morning by students, was unconstitutional. The entire prayer read: "Almighty God, we acknowledge our dependence upon Thee, and we beg Thy blessings upon us, our parents, our teachers and our country." Ruling it unconstitutional, the Court held that "[w]hen the power, prestige and financial support of government is placed behind a particular religious belief, the indirect coercive pressure upon religious minorities to conform to the prevailing officially approved religion is plain" (*Engel v. Vitale*, 1962). The following year, the Court ruled that the daily reading of the Bible also violated the wall of separation between church and state (*Abington v. Schempp*, 1963).

The issue of school prayer dramatizes the tension between the democratic principle of majority rule and the role of the Bill of Rights in protecting the rights of the minority. Advocates of school prayer believe that the majority of any community, acting through their elected school boards, have a right to prescribe school practices. Civil libertarians argue that compulsory religious exercises infringe on the rights of members of other religions groups (e.g., Jews or Muslims when schools have a Christian prayer), as well as of nonbelievers. There are also many Christians who oppose government-supported religious activity. They not only believe that the government should not favor one religion over another, but they also worry that government support of religion could eventually lead to government control of religious organizations.

Instead of a prayer, some states have sought to allow a "moment of silence" in the school day during which students can think about whatever they want (meditate, think about their homework, or pray). Alabama enacted a moment of silence law in the early 1980s. The law was challenged by the ACLU, and the Supreme Court found that the clear intent of the law was to promote religion. In *Wallace v. Jaffree* (1985), it ruled that the law was enacted "for the sole purpose of expressing the State's endorsement of prayer activities for one minute at the beginning of each school day. The addition of 'or voluntary prayer' indicates that the State intended to characterize prayer as a favored practice.

Such an endorsement is not consistent with the established principle that the government must pursue a course of complete neutrality toward religion." The story of Ishmael Jaffree's challenge to the Alabama moment of silence law is recounted in Peter Irons's 1988 book, *The Courage of Their Convictions.*

The Establishment Clause does not prohibit all forms of religious activity in public schools. Students have a right to say private prayers, to wear T-shirts with religious symbols or sayings, and to talk to other students about religion. The basic difference is between actions by individuals, which are protected by the First Amendment, and actions by school officials themselves, which are prohibited because they represent an official endorsement of religion by the state (Frankel, 1994). The U.S. Department of Education clarified these rights in 1995 in a statement on religious expression in schools (see Chapter 5).

School Vouchers A relatively new church-state issue involves government vouchers to help parents pay to send their children to private schools (Weil, 2002). Because many—and perhaps most—of those schools will be parochial schools, civil libertarians argue that voucher programs violate the separation of church and state (Doerr, Menendez, and Swomley, 1996). Advocates of vouchers support the idea on the grounds of parental choice: Parents, they argue, should be free to choose where to send their children to school. However, since those who send their children to private schools nevertheless pay local taxes that support the public schools, the government should offset their tax contribution with school vouchers to facilitate that choice.

The vouchers issue finally reached the Supreme Court in a case involving the voucher program in Cleveland, Ohio. Under the Ohio Pilot Project Scholarship Program, low-income families are eligible for up to $2,250 in tuition assistance for private schools, and other families may receive up to $1,875. In 2002, the Supreme Court upheld the constitutionality of the Cleveland vouchers program in a 5–4 decision *(Zelman v. Simmons-Harris).* In the majority opinion, Justice Sandra Day O'Connor argued that the Ohio law did not violate the separation of church and state because it was neutral with regard to religious and nonreligious schools. The funds did not go directly to religious schools but to parents, who then chose where to send their children to school. In the wake of the Court's decision, some other states enacted school voucher laws. A number of states, however, had previously rejected such laws, because they believed it violated the separation of church and state and also because of concern that voucher programs would reduce funds for public schools.

Religious Symbols in Public Places   Another set of controversial church-state issues involves the placing of religious symbols on public property, such as parks and government buildings. At Christmastime, for example, some Christians want to erect Nativity scenes in front of courthouses or city halls. Similarly, private groups have donated monuments with the Ten Commandments (Hester, 2003), crosses, or other religious symbols to cities or counties to be placed in public parks. (A statement by the Anti-Defamation League opposing religious displays on public property is reprinted in Chapter 5.)

Civil libertarians oppose displays of religious symbols on public property—schools, courthouses, public parks—because they not only endorse religion, and usually a particular religion, but also send a message that other people are less than full citizens. In *Lynch v. Donnelly,* Justice Sandra Day O'Connor explained that "[e]ndorsement [of religion] sends a message to nonadherents that they are outsiders, not full members of the political community, and an accompanying message to adherents that they are insiders, favored members of the political community."

In one of the most highly publicized cases in 2003, the chief justice of the Alabama Supreme Court defied a federal court order to remove a 2-ton monument displaying the Ten Commandments from the state courthouse. Chief Justice Roy Moore argued that the Ten Commandments are the basis for U.S. law. The federal courts consistently held that placing the Ten Commandments in the courthouse was an establishment of religion. In the end, the monument was removed and Judge Moore was suspended by the Alabama Judicial Council.

The Alabama controversy highlighted the fact that there are actually several different versions of the Ten Commandments (Hester, 2003). The Protestant, Catholic, and Jewish versions are all slightly different. These variations dramatize the theological hornet's nest that arises when people try to have the government display some kind of religious symbol. It results in the government endorsing a *particular* set of religious beliefs, and the result is to divide the community along religious lines. (The different versions of the Ten Commandments, along with other related material, may be read at *www.positiveatheism.org).*

The Establishment Clause does not prohibit religious displays that are on private property. In fact, the Free Exercise Clause protects the right of a person to place a religious symbol in front of his or her home. An individual or a group can rent space on a billboard to present a religious message. The distinction in such religious displays is between private behavior, which the First Amendment protects, and action by government agencies, which it prohibits.

Teaching Evolution in Public Schools The famous *Scopes* case in 1925 involved a challenge to a Tennessee law that outlawed the teaching of evolution. (The text of the law is reproduced in Chapter 5.) The law reflected the views of the Christian majority in Tennessee. John T. Scopes, a biology teacher, challenged the law, arguing that by outlawing an idea, the state had both established a religion and infringed on his academic freedom (the case is described in Chapter 4) (Ginger, 1974; Larson, 1997).

In the 1980s, opponents of evolution fought back by seeking state laws requiring the teaching of creationism. Creationism is a theory that explains the origins of the universe and mankind in a way consistent with the teachings of the Christian Bible. Advocates of creationism argue that it is a scientific theory of creation and therefore should be taught along with other scientific theories, including Darwin's theory of evolution. (Information about creationism is available at *www.creationism.org* and *www.creation-science.org*) (Moore, 2002; Withman, 2002). Almost all scientists, however, argue that it is not supported by scientific evidence and is in fact a matter of religious doctrine.

In 1982, the state of Louisiana passed a law requiring the "balanced treatment" of evolution and creationism (Smout, 1998; Withman, 2002). Supporters of the law argued that it would result in the presentation of both sides of the controversy in the schools without seeming to favor one or the other. The Supreme Court, however, ruled the law unconstitutional on the grounds that it was clearly designed to advance a particular religious viewpoint—that is, creationism. The Court held that the law "advances a religious doctrine by requiring either the banishment of the theory of evolution from public school classrooms or the presentation of a religious viewpoint that rejects evolution in its entirety" *(Edwards v. Aguillard,* 1987).

The Free Exercise Clause

The Free Exercise clause of the First Amendment guarantees people the right to engage in religious activities without government interference (Frankel, 1994). This guarantee includes beliefs or practices that the majority of the community might find strange or offensive. Throughout U.S. history, small and unpopular religious groups have been persecuted because their beliefs or practices offended the majority. In one of the most famous chapters in early U.S. history, Roger Williams fled religious persecution in the colony of Massachusetts and founded Rhode Island, where he instituted the principle of free exercise of religion (Morgan, 1967). Also, in the early years of the Massachusetts Bay Colony, Puritan leaders persecuted Quakers because they regarded Quakerism as heresy.

The Jehovah's Witnesses Cases   In the late 1930s and 1940s, the Jehovah's Witnesses were one of the most hated groups in the United States (Peters, 2000). Many Americans found their beliefs and practices highly offensive. The Jehovah's Witnesses believed that theirs was the only true religion. Among other things, they made vicious attacks against the Catholic Church (which many people today would regard as hate speech). The Jehovah's Witnesses were also extremely aggressive in their efforts to recruit new members. Members would descend en masse on local communities, going door to door or broadcasting their message on portable record players. Many people regarded these tactics as offensive.

Across the country, communities tried many different measures to suppress the activities of the Jehovah's Witnesses, and many of these measures resulted in Supreme Court cases that are now landmarks in the history of the First Amendment. One Georgia town passed an ordinance forbidding the distribution of any kind of literature without a permit. The clear purpose of the law was to limit the Jehovah's Witnesses' activities. The Supreme Court declared the law unconstitutional because it was not narrowly limited to controlling littering, which the Court recognized as a legitimate public order issue (*Lovell v. Griffin*, 1938). In a West Virginia case, the Court struck down an ordinance that outlawed door-to-door canvassing (*Martin v. Struthers*, 1943).

In all, between the late 1930s and the early 1950s, the Supreme Court decided more than twenty cases involving the Jehovah's Witnesses (Peters, 2000). The long-term impact of the Jehovah's Witnesses cases was similar to that of the many cases arising from the civil rights movement (Kalven, 1965). In both instances, the Supreme Court not only affirmed constitutional protection for a group that had been denied basic constitutional rights but established broad principles of constitutional law that applied to all people.

Native Americans' Religious Liberty   A recent controversy involving the free exercise of religion involves Native American sects that use peyote, a hallucinogen, as part of their traditional religious exercise (Long, 2000). The Supreme Court ruled that the state of Oregon was justified in not allowing this practice. The decision provoked a strong response from religious leaders across the country who thought it represented a serious threat to the right of all religious groups to practice their religions without government interference. In response, Congress passed the Religious Freedom Restoration Act (RFRA) in 1993. The law declared that "[g]overnment shall not substantially burden a person's exercise of religion" unless there is some "compelling state interest." Even then, the government must use the "least restrictive alternative" to achieving its ends.

In 1997, however, the Supreme Court, in a 6–3 decision, declared the Religious Freedom Restoration Act of 1993 unconstitutional as applied to the states. Since then, ten states have enacted their own RFRA laws: Alabama, Arizona, Connecticut, Florida, Idaho, Illinois, New Mexico, Rhode Island, South Carolina, and Texas. In short, the struggle of religious freedom continues. (Information about RFRA and other religious liberty issues can be found at *www.religious-freedom.org*.)

Conscientious Objection to War   Many religious groups and individuals are opposed to participating in war on grounds of religious conscience. The free exercise clause of the First Amendment protects the right of conscientious objection to participating in either war or military service. Although it is not a major issue today because there is no military draft, it was a major controversy during earlier wars. During World War I, the federal government accepted the conscientious objector claims of some young draftees who belonged to religious denominations with a strong pacifist tradition (e.g., the Quakers), although many of them were abused in military camps because of their beliefs (Walker, 1999). By the time the United States became involved in World War II, the government had liberalized the law of military conscription to accept claims of conscientious objection on the basis of "religious training and belief." Nonetheless, 6,000 young men went to prison. Most were Jehovah's Witnesses; the government refused to accept their claim that all members of the faith are ministers (Peters, 2000). Others were men who refused on religious grounds to cooperate in any way with the selective service system (Eller, 2001).

In 1959, Daniel Seeger applied for conscientious objector status, citing his moral convictions, but not in traditional religious terms and without claiming to believe in a Supreme Being. The Supreme Court upheld his claim, holding that Seeger's views were similar to religious belief (*Seeger v. United States*, 1965) (Irons, 1988). A few years later, the Court backtracked and accepted only religious belief as grounds for conscientious objector status. During the Vietnam War, the courts rejected "selective" conscientious objection in which people object only to participating in a particular war (Moskos and Chambers, 1993).

The Second Amendment: The Right of Individuals to Own Guns

Great controversy exists over whether the Second Amendment to the Constitution confers a right of individuals to own guns without any government restrictions. Advocates of the rights of gun owners argue that it does. Gun control advocates, on the other hand, argue that the Second Amendment refers only to state militia, or the national guard (Cottrol, 1993). The debate turns on the meaning of the text of the Second Amendment, including what it meant at the time it was adopted. The Second Amendment in its entirety says, "A well regulated militia, being necessary to the security of a free state, the right of the people to keep and bear arms, shall not be infringed."

The courts have been unsympathetic to the argument advanced by gun owners. The controlling Supreme Court decision in a 1939 case holds that "[i]n reality, the Second Amendment applies only to firearm ownership in the context of a 'well-regulated militia,' and not individuals" (*United States v. Miller*, 1939). In 2001, however, the Fifth Circuit Court of Appeals ruled, "We have found no historical evidence that the Second Amendment was intended to convey militia power to the states . . . or applies only to members of a select militia. . . . All of the evidence indicates that the Second Amendment, like other parts of the Bill of Rights, applies to and protects individual Americans. We find that the history of the Second Amendment reinforces the plain meaning of its text, namely that it protects individual Americans in their right to keep and bear arms whether or not they are a member of a select militia or performing active military service or training" *(United States v. Emerson,* 2001). The meaning of the Second Amendment is still unresolved, and as with all other civil liberties issues, the debate continues.

Equal Protection of the Law

The Declaration of Independence expresses the principle of equality: "We hold these truths to be self-evident, that all men are created equal. . . ." Many people regard this as a statement of the core philosophy of the United States. The Declaration of Independence does not have the force of law, however. The principle of equality is embodied in the Fourteenth Amendment, which holds that no state shall "deny to any person within its jurisdiction the equal protection of the laws." The Equal Protection Clause has been the principal instrument in the modern civil rights movement and the struggle for equality for all groups in the United States (Curtis, 1986; Karst, 1989).

Race, Ethnicity, and National Origin

Historically, the greatest denial of equality in America has been race discrimination. De jure racial segregation—that is, segregation by law—existed in the southeastern states from the late nineteenth century until the 1960s (Lowery and Marszalek, 1992). The Supreme Court upheld the constitutionality of racial segregation in the famous 1896 case of *Plessy v. Ferguson.* In an eloquent dissent, Justice John Marshall Harlan wrote, "I am of opinion that the statute of Louisiana is inconsistent with the personal liberty of citizens, white and black, in that State, and hostile to both the spirit and letter of the Constitution of the United States" (Thomas, 1997). (Excerpts from the majority opinion in *Plessy* along with Justice Harlan's dissent are reprinted in Chapter 5.)

Beginning in the 1940s, and picking up momentum in the 1950s, the civil rights movement challenged both de jure segregation and other forms of racial discrimination (Grossman, 1993). The greatest achievement of that effort was the 1954 Supreme Court decision in *Brown v. Board of Education*, in which the Court ruled that maintaining racially segregated public schools was an unconstitutional violation of the Fourteenth Amendment. The *Brown* decision did more than just overrule the old *Plessy* decision. It established racial equality as a guiding national principle, and it paved the way for many other decisions affirming equality in subsequent years (Kluger, 1975; Martin 1998). (An excerpt from the *Brown* decision is presented in Chapter 5.)

Race discrimination in other areas of American life has also been declared illegal, either through Supreme Court rulings under the Fourteenth Amendment or through statutes. Title II of the 1964 Civil Rights Act outlaws segregation in public accommodations such as restaurants, hotels, swimming pools, buses, and other facilities. The Supreme Court upheld the constitutionality of Title II in *Heart of Atlanta Motel v. Atlanta* (Cortner, 2001).

Interracial Marriage

To preserve white supremacy, many southern states had "miscegenation" laws prohibiting marriage between people of different races. In 1958, Mildred Jeter, a black woman, and Richard Loving, a white man, both residents of the state of Virginia, married in Washington, D.C. When they returned to Virginia, they were charged with violating the state's antimiscegenation statute. The Supreme Court declared the Virginia law unconstitutional, holding that "[t]here can be no question but that Virginia's miscegenation statutes rest solely upon distinctions drawn according to race" and is therefore unconstitutional (*Loving v. Virginia*, 1967) (Wallenstein, 2002).

Employment: The Affirmative Action Controversy

Title VII of the 1964 Civil Rights Act outlaws discrimination in employment. The major civil liberties controversy today over employment involves the question of affirmative action. The concept of affirmative action means that employers take positive steps to correct past discrimination and to ensure a representative workforce. Affirmative action is a means to an end: a way of attempting to achieve equality. Most affirmative action steps are not controversial—for example, distributing job announcements widely and engaging in active outreach to encourage people to apply for jobs. The controversial aspects of affirmative action are those that involve specific preferences for racial minorities or women in hiring and quotas on the number of people from any particular group (Eisaguirre, 1999; Lawrence and Matsuda, 1997).

Affirmative action was introduced by President Lyndon Johnson in 1965 through Executive Order 11246, which states, "Each Government contractor with 50 or more employees and $50,000 or more in government contracts is required to develop a written affirmative action program (AAP) for each of its establishments." Executive Order 11246 does not require employers to use hiring quotas. However, some employers have adopted quotas, and some courts have ordered the use of quotas, as a means of fulfilling the goals of the order (Urofsky, 1991).

Advocates of affirmative action argue that the policy is necessary to overcome the legacy of past discrimination. Opponents, on the other hand, argue that it involves *reverse discrimination:* giving a preference on the basis of race, ethnicity, or gender in violation of the Fourteenth Amendment and Title VII of the 1964 Civil Rights Act (Eastland, 1996; Sowell, 1990).

Reflecting the very difficult issues raised by affirmative action, the U.S. Supreme Court wrestled with it for a quarter century, often making ambiguous rulings in cases involving employment and college admissions. The first important decision, *Regents of the University of California v. Bakke,* in 1978, held that the University of California could take race into consideration as one of many factors in admissions to the medical school but that it could not maintain a fixed quota for minority admissions (Ball, 2000). Over the next twenty-five years the Court issued a number of seemingly inconsistent rulings. Finally, in 2003, the Court decided two cases involving the University of Michigan that appear to resolve the issue for the foreseeable future. In a case involving admission to the Michigan Law School *(Grutter v. Bollinger),* the Court upheld the principle of affirmative action. A university can constitutionally take race into account in making admissions decisions as long as it is one of many factors. In a separate decision involving undergraduate admissions, however, the Court held that the university could not award extra points to all minority applicants *(Gratz v. Bollinger).* Justice Sandra Day O'Connor, in the law school case, explained that "[w]hen using race as a 'plus' factor in university admissions, a university's admissions program must remain flexible enough to ensure that each applicant is evaluated as an individual and not in a way that makes an applicant's race or ethnicity the defining feature of his or her application."

The Rights of Native Americans

The constitutional rights of Native Americans involve a complicated set of legal issues. Native American Indian tribes are semi-sovereign nations that have special legal status in the United States. Tribes that are officially recognized by the U.S. government have the right to govern their own affairs. As a result, tribes are not subject to many federal laws. With respect to civil liberties, the basic question is whether a tribe has the right to treat one of its members in a way that violates a provision of the U.S. Constitution. In any particular case, which principle should prevail: tribal autonomy or the U.S. Bill of Rights? As individuals, Native Americans are protected by the Bill of Rights against violations by either the federal government or a state government (Pevar, 2002; Wunder, 1994, 1996).

To protect the rights of individual Native Americans from violations by their own tribes, Congress passed the American Indian Civil Rights Act in 1968. In language that follows the Bill of Rights, the statute declares, "No Indian tribe in exercising powers of self-government shall (1) make or enforce any law prohibiting the free exercise of religion, or abridging the freedom of speech, or of the press, or the right of the people peaceably to assemble and to petition for a redress of grievances. . . ." Other sections follow the other provisions of the Bill of Rights related to searches and seizures, double jeopardy, speedy trial, and so on. The American Indian Civil Rights Act provides a basic framework but does not resolve all of the issues related to the competing claims of tribal autonomy and the Bill of Rights (Wunder, 1996).

The religious freedom rights of Native Americans are also extremely complex. The federal Religious Freedom Restoration Act (RFRA) and the right of Indians to engage in traditional practices that include the use of otherwise illegal substances are discussed in the section on religious liberty in this chapter.

The Rights of Latino and Hispanic Americans

Although the 1964 Civil Rights Act prohibits discrimination on the basis of race, ethnicity, or national origin, Latino and Hispanic Americans face many forms of unequal treatment.

The report, *Donde Esta la Justicia?* by Building Blocks for Youth (2002), found discrimination against Latinos and Hispanics in the criminal justice system. Police, courts, and correctional agencies do not employ sufficient numbers of Spanish-speaking employees. A police officer who does not speak Spanish or does not have quick access to a translator cannot provide quick and effective service to a crime victim or someone else in need of assistance. The report also found that, aside from language skills, agencies generally do not have staff members with the appropriate cultural competency—that is, employees who understand the culture and worldview of people for whom they are responsible. A juvenile probation officer, for example, needs to be able to relate to a probationer who is a recent immigrant, has a weak command of English, and does not fully understand U.S. culture and institutions.

The federal government is committed to a policy of overcoming barriers to equal treatment arising from language barriers. President Bill Clinton issued Executive Order 13166 in 2000, directing all organizations that receive federal funds to provide services in languages other than English where necessary. This includes providing written informational material and providing translators for individual clients or customers.

As part of a backlash against recent immigration, there has been a movement to make English the official language of states and the federal government (Tatalovich, 1995). By 2003, twenty-seven states had enacted "official English" laws. Some of these laws simply declare English to be the official language of the state. Others require that all business by state agencies be conducted in English (e.g., driver's license bureaus, welfare agencies, and public schools). Meanwhile, a federal "English only" law has been introduced in Congress. The English Language Unity Act of 2003 declares that "[t]he United States is comprised of individuals from diverse ethnic, cultural, and linguistic backgrounds, and continues to benefit from this rich diversity. . . . Throughout the history of the United States, the common thread binding individuals of differing backgrounds has been the English language" (*www.us-english.org*).

Civil libertarians oppose "English only" laws because they violate the Equal Protection Clause of the Fourteenth Amendment. Not providing translators in court, for example, threatens the right of defendants to receive a fair trial, since they cannot understand the proceedings. "English only" laws also interfere with the right to vote if a state does not provide bilingual ballots. Not providing bilingual education can jeopardize a child's right to an education.

Equal Protection for Women

Although the Fourteenth Amendment guarantees equal protection of the law to all people, the Supreme Court has not applied it as strictly to sex discrimination as it has in cases involving race discrimination. It wasn't until 1971 that the Court ruled that women are protected by the Equal Protection Clause of the Fourteenth Amendment (Cushman, 2000). In that case, the Court considered an Idaho state law requiring that males be preferred to females in the appointment of administrators of the estates of deceased persons. After their adopted son died, Sally and Cecil Reed, who were then divorced, both sought to be named the administrator of their son's estate. The Supreme Court ruled the Idaho law unconstitutional, holding that "[t]o give a mandatory preference to members of either sex over members of the other, merely to accomplish the elimination of hearings on the merits, is to make the very kind of arbitrary legislative choice forbidden by the Equal Protection Clause of the Fourteenth Amendment . . ." (*Reed v. Reed*, 1971).

The *Reed* case was brought by the ACLU Women's Rights Project, whose director at that time was Ruth Bader Ginsburg (Walker, 1999). Her brief in this and other cases influenced the decisions of the Court, and in 1993 she was appointed a justice of the Supreme Court. (For a biographical sketch of Ruth Bader Ginsburg, see Chapter 4.)

More recently, the Court ruled that the state of Virginia violated the Equal Protection Clause by operating the Virginia Military Institute (VMI) as an all-male college. As a result of the decision, VMI began to admit women students (*United States v. Virginia*, 1996). Justice Ginsburg wrote that "the question is whether the Commonwealth can constitutionally deny to women who have the will and capacity, the training and attendant opportunities that VMI uniquely affords." She then concluded that Virginia had shown no "exceedingly persuasive justification" for excluding all women from the citizen-soldier training afforded by VMI" (Brodie, 2000; Strum, 2002).

The Equal Rights Amendment   Because the Fourteenth Amendment has not been applied to women as strictly as it has to racial minorities, women's rights groups have advocated an Equal Rights Amendment (ERA) to the Constitution. An ERA was first introduced in Congress in 1923, but it never received significant support. In the 1970s, the women's movement revived the idea.

Congress passed the ERA as a proposed 27th amendment to the Constitution in 1972, and it was ratified by thirty-five states, three short of the thirty-eight necessary for ratification. In the mid-1970s, however, conservative groups organized strong opposition to the ERA and successfully blocked final ratification. The time period for ratification finally expired in 1979 (Feinberg, 1986). The full text of the ERA is reprinted in Chapter 5.

Legislative Protection of Women's Rights Title VII of the 1964 Civil Rights Act prohibits employment discrimination on the basis of sex, along with race, religion, and national origin. (Excerpts from Title VII of the 1964 Civil Rights Act are reproduced in Chapter 5.) This law has been as important for women as for racial minorities in fighting employment discrimination. Title VII has given rise to two subsidiary civil liberties issues. The first is sexual harassment as a form of employment discrimination, and the second is affirmative action as a remedy for past employment discrimination.

Women have also been helped by the Equal Pay Act of 1963, a federal law that requires that people performing the same job receive the same pay. One traditional form of sex discrimination in employment has been to pay women less than men who are doing the same job.

Sexual Harassment of Women An important recent application of Title VII involves sexual harassment in the workplace. Historically, women have been subject to harassment on the job in the form of demands for sexual favors, offensive sexually oriented jokes in their presence, and attempts to drive them out of their jobs because they are women (Stein, 1999). Law professor Catharine MacKinnon (1978) is generally credited with developing the idea that sexual harassment constitutes a form of employment discrimination under Title VII of the 1964 Civil Rights Act. The demand that a woman provide sexual favors in order to keep her job or to gain a promotion (referred to as a *quid pro quo*) is clearly a form of sexual harassment. Some people, however, argue that any attempt to limit sexually oriented expression at the workplace represents a restriction on free speech. For example, is it sexual harassment if a male employee hangs a poster in his office depicting a woman in a sexually provocative pose? How sexually explicit does a picture have to be to qualify as creating a hostile work environment? Reconciling legitimate First

Amendment rights with the right of women to be free of harassment in the workplace represents a difficult problem in balancing competing civil liberties interests.

The Supreme Court has accepted the argument that sexual harassment constitutes a form of employment discrimination in violation of Title VII. In *Meritor v. Vinson*, it held that "a claim of 'hostile environment' sex discrimination is actionable under Title VII." The Court added that "[s]exual harassment which creates a hostile or offensive environment for members of one sex is every bit the arbitrary barrier to sexual equality at the workplace that racial harassment is to racial equality. Surely, a requirement that a man or woman run a gauntlet of sexual abuse in return for the privilege of being allowed to work and make a living can be as demeaning and disconcerting as the harshest of racial epithets." Subsequent court decisions have dealt with questions of what sort of actions or expressions qualify as sexual harassment.

Women and Military Service   Women are not required to register with the Selective Service System for possible induction into the military. Since men are required to register, this is a clear case of sex-based classification. When a challenge to the law came before the Supreme Court in 1981, the Court ruled that the law was constitutional *(Rostker v. Goldberg)*. The key principle in the decision was judicial deference to the military. The Court noted that "[t]he operation of a healthy deference to legislative and executive judgments in the area of military affairs is evident in several recent decisions of this Court" and cited a report of the Senate Armed Services Committee: "The principle that women should not intentionally and routinely engage in combat is fundamental, and enjoys wide support among our people. It is universally supported by military leaders who have testified before the Committee. . . . Current law and policy exclude women from being assigned to combat in our military forces, and the Committee reaffirms this policy."

Several points about the decision are noteworthy. First, the law was challenged under the Due Process Clause of the Fifth Amendment. There is no provision of the Constitution forbidding sex discrimination by the federal government, and the Fourteenth Amendment applies only to the states (as in the *VMI* case, above). Second, the principle of deference to the military is the same rationale that the Supreme Court used in the World War II

Japanese American internment cases (see Chapter 4). In both *Hirabayashi v. United States* and *Korematsu v. United States,* the Court explicitly chose not to question the judgment of military authorities with regard to the constitutionality of the government's evacuation and internment of Japanese Americans. The result was one of the greatest violations of civil liberties in U.S. history (Irons, 1983).

Title IX   Title IX of the 1972 Education Act requires that educational institutions provide equal opportunity to women in higher education. Specifically, it provides that "[n]o person in the United States shall, on the basis of sex, be excluded from participation in, be denied the benefits of, or be subjected to discrimination under any education program or activity receiving Federal financial assistance...." A 1998 report by the U.S. Department of Education noted the following progress in educational equity as a result of Title IX: "In 1971, 18 percent of female high school graduates were completing at least four years of college compared to 26 percent of their male peers. Today, that education gap no longer exists. Women now make up the majority of students in America's colleges and universities in addition to making up the majority of those receiving master's degrees. Women are also entering business and law schools in record numbers. Indeed, the United States stands alone and is a world leader in opening the doors of higher education to women" (U.S. Department of Education, 1998).

Most of the controversy over Title IX has focused on athletic programs, even though it covers all aspects of education. As a result of Title IX, public schools and colleges have greatly expanded women's athletic programs. The number of women participating in intercollegiate athletics rose 81 percent between 1981 and 1999 (from 90,000 to 163,000), while participation by males increased only 5 percent (U.S. Department of Education, 1998). Most experts believe that Title IX accounts for most but not necessarily all of this increase. Title IX prohibits clearly discriminatory practices such as offering scholarships to male but not female athletes or not supporting an appropriate number of women's athletic teams. (A position statement by the Independent Women's Forum opposing Title IX is presented in Chapter 5.) In 2003, after a lengthy review prompted by criticisms of the program, the U.S. Department of Education decided to maintain Title IX as official federal policy.

Gender-Neutral Policies   Although laws and policies against sex discrimination are often thought of as protecting only women, in fact they are gender neutral in their purpose and effect, and hence they also prohibit discrimination against men on the basis of their sex. This principle was illustrated by a lawsuit brought by a Maryland state police officer who was denied the right to use the federal Family and Medical Leave Act to care for his and his wife's newborn child. The state police argued that only women could use the family leave law. A federal court ruled that the state police illegally discriminated against the officer on the basis of sex, and in a civil suit another court awarded him over $300,000 in damages.

Regulations issued by the Office of Personnel Management specifically state that the term "'Spouse' means an individual who is a husband or wife pursuant to a marriage that is a legal union between one man and one woman, including common law marriage between one man and one woman in States where it is recognized" (U.S. Office of Personnel Management, 2003).

Gay and Lesbian People

The constitutional rights of lesbians and gay men have been changing dramatically in recent years (Hunter, Joslin, and McGowan, 2004). The first important case to reach the Supreme Court involved Michael Hardwick, who was convicted of violating a Georgia law against sodomy after he had been caught, in his home, in bed with another man. He appealed his conviction but the Supreme Court rejected his claim of a right to privacy, holding that "[t]he Constitution does not confer a fundamental right upon homosexuals to engage in sodomy." The Court added than none of the prior decisions on the right to privacy applied in this case. The state of Georgia had a right to outlaw behavior that it regarded as immoral (*Bowers v. Hardwick*, 1986). Mr. Hardwick's personal account of the case is recounted in *The Courage of Their Convictions* (Irons, 1988).

In a remarkable turnaround, however, the Court reversed its *Bowers* decision in 2003, declaring unconstitutional a Texas sodomy law. Affirming a broad right to privacy, the Court held in *Lawrence v. Texas* that "[l]iberty protects the person from unwarranted government intrusions into a dwelling or other private places. In our tradition the State is not omnipresent in the home. And there are other spheres of our lives and existence, outside the home, where the State should not be a dominant presence. Freedom extends beyond spatial bounds. Liberty presumes an autonomy of self that includes freedom of thought, belief, expression, and certain intimate conduct."

The Court was very explicit about overturning *Bowers*: "*Bowers* was not correct when it was decided, and it is not correct today. It ought not to remain binding precedent. *Bowers v. Hardwick* should be and now is overruled" *(Lawrence v. Texas)*. The decision invalidated the Texas law and laws in some twenty other states criminalizing private sexual conduct between consenting adults. Most experts regard the decision as so sweeping that it is likely to be used to invalidate other restrictions on lesbian and gay people.

Previously, in 1996, the Court had affirmed protection of the rights of lesbian and gay people by declaring unconstitutional Colorado's Amendment Two, an amendment to the Colorado state constitution that barred local governments from passing laws protecting the rights of lesbian and gay people *(Romer v. Evans)*. Several Colorado cities had passed laws outlawing discrimination on the basis of sexual orientation. Anti–gay rights forces responded by sponsoring a referendum that added Amendment Two to the state constitution. The Supreme Court declared the amendment unconstitutional, on the grounds that it violated the Equal Protection Clause of the Fourteenth Amendment of the U.S. Constitution. Amendment Two prevented a distinct class of people from utilizing the political process to protect their rights. The decision did not overturn the *Hardwick* decision and did not confer a right of privacy on homosexuality, but said only that homosexuals could not be barred from using the political process.

Some of the most important victories for lesbian and gay rights have been First Amendment cases (Hunter, Joslin, and McGowan, 2004). In a number of decisions, for example, courts have ruled that a college or university cannot bar lesbian and gay rights groups from sponsoring activities on campus or being recognized as official student organizations. Barring groups from activities to which other groups are entitled constitutes a content-based discrimination in violation of the First Amendment.

Same-Sex Marriage

A current issue is whether people of the same sex can legally marry (Sherman, 1997). Not only do many same-sex couples wish to have their relationships confirmed in a symbolic fashion, but a legally recognized marriage has important implications for other practical aspects of life, such as child custody, adoption, inheritance, and other issues (Hunter, Joslin, and McGowan, 2004). A gay person, for example, has no legal right of child custody of his partner's child if the partner were to die. Nor does a gay or lesbian person have a right to inherit his or her partner's property.

In an important sign of change, the state of Vermont enacted a civil union law recognizing committed relationships. The law was a response to a Vermont Supreme Court decision holding that "the State is constitutionally required to extend to same-sex couples the common benefits and protections that flow from marriage under Vermont law." The court based its opinion on the Common Benefits Clause of the Vermont Constitution, which declares that "government is, or ought to be, instituted for the common benefit, protection, and security of the people, nation, or community, and not for the particular emolument or advantage of any single person, family, or set of persons, who are a part only of that community." (The Vermont Constitution may be found at *www.usconstitution.net/vtconst.html*). In the new Vermont law, "'civil union' means that two eligible persons have established a relationship . . . and may receive the benefits and protections and be subject to the responsibilities of spouses."

Congress responded by passing the Defense of Marriage Act, which allows states not to recognize same-sex marriages from other states (see Chapter 5). The Full Faith and Credit Clause of the U.S. Constitution (Article IV, Section 1) otherwise requires states to recognize laws from other states. A statement by the Human Rights Campaign in support of same-sex marriages is reprinted in Chapter 5. In 2000, the state of Nebraska passed a constitutional amendment prohibiting same-sex marriages. After the *Lawrence* decision, however, it is not clear whether these restrictions on same-sex marriages are constitutional.

The issue of same-sex marriage took a dramatic turn in late 2003. In a 4–3 ruling, the Supreme Judicial Court of Massachusetts ruled that the state marriage statute violated the rights of same-sex couples to due process and equal protection under the state constitution. The court remanded the case to a trial court, ordering it to remedy the constitutional violations in the statute. The court also gave the Massachusetts legislature 180 days to consider how it might bring state law into compliance with the decision.

The political reaction to the decision was quick and strong. Lesbian and gay rights activists hailed the decisions. Opponents of same-sex marriage, meanwhile, began discussing amendments to both the U.S. Constitution and individual state constitutions that would prohibit same-sex marriages.

Legislative Protection of the Rights of Lesbians and Gay Men

Lesbians and gay men have received increased protection against discrimination by legislation at the state and local levels. At the federal level, Title VII of the 1964 Civil Rights Act does not prohibit discrimination in employment on the basis of sexual orientation. By mid-2003, thirteen states had enacted laws prohibiting discrimination on the basis of sexual orientation. The laws vary in their coverage. The Illinois law covers only discrimination in employment by public agencies. The Connecticut law, on the other hand, also covers employment by private employers, housing, education, public accommodations, credit, and labor union membership. In addition, more than 100 cities and counties prohibit discrimination on the basis of sexual orientation. (Current information on antidiscrimination laws is available on the Web site of the Lambda Legal Defense Fund, *www.lambdalegal.org*).

Lesbians and Gay Men in the U.S. Military

The U.S. military services traditionally did not accept homosexuals and discharged any they discovered who were already in the military (Shilts, 1993). By the early 1990s the gay rights movement was increasingly pressing for a change in that policy. President Bill Clinton made a campaign promise in 1992 to admit gays into the military, but he did not follow through on this commitment when he became president in January 1993. Instead a compromise policy was implemented—the "don't ask, don't tell" policy. The military services are not to ask whether a person is a homosexual, and military personnel are not to tell whether they are.

The official Department of Defense policy states that "[h]omosexual conduct is grounds for separation from the Military Services. . . . Homosexual conduct includes homosexual acts, a statement by a member that demonstrates a propensity or intent to engage in homosexual acts, or a homosexual marriage or attempted marriage." At the same time, however, the department's policy says that "a member's sexual orientation is considered a personal and private matter, and is not a bar to continued service under this section unless manifested by homosexual conduct. . . ." The policy raises an important free speech issue, because openly discussing one's sexual orientation is regarded by the Defense Department as indicating a "propensity" toward conduct.

In *Able v. United States,* the Second Circuit Court of Appeals upheld the constitutionality of the "don't ask, don't tell" policy. As with the issue of women in the military, the Court acknowledged the traditional "deference by the courts to military-related judgments by Congress and the Executive" and refused to question that judgment on this issue. Lesbian and gay rights activists, however, argue that the "don't ask, don't tell" policy has not been enforced fairly and that discrimination against homosexuals in the military continues.

People with Disabilities

Persons with physical or mental disabilities are often the victims of discrimination, particularly in employment and public accommodations (Levy and Rubenstein, 1996; Pelka, 1997). Congress attempted to remedy this problem by passing the Americans with Disabilities Act (ADA) in 1990. The U.S. Justice Department explains that "[a]n individual is considered to have a 'disability' if s/he has a physical or mental impairment that substantially limits one or more major life activities, has a record of such an impairment, or is regarded as having such an impairment. Persons discriminated against because they have a known association or relationship with an individual with a disability also are protected (Department of Justice Web site *www.usdoj.gov*). Employers are also required to make "reasonable accommodations" for disabled persons. Doing so might involve modifying equipment or work schedules to facilitate work by a person with a disability. The ADA leaves many questions unanswered. The most important is that of what conditions count as a disability under the law. Is alcoholism, for example, a disability? What kind of limits are there on how far an employer must go to accommodate a disabled person? These questions are still being debated in ongoing litigation.

One important issue for disabled persons is access to buildings. Public facilities such as restaurants, educational institutions, and government buildings must be accessible to people who use in wheelchairs or whose mobility is limited in some other fashion. Private housing units, particularly apartment buildings, also must be accessible. In addition to the ADA, 1988 provisions of the Federal Fair Housing Act require that new construction provide accessibility, particularly for people in wheelchairs, through ramps or elevators. In the housing units themselves, facilities such as kitchens and bathrooms must be accessible to individuals in wheelchairs.

Age Discrimination

Discrimination against seniors is another problem, particularly in employment. Employers attempt to fire older workers and replace them with younger workers for a variety of reasons: because they can pay younger workers lower salaries, because of stereotypes about the abilities of older people, or because they want to have younger or more physically attractive employees dealing with the public. To remedy the problem, Congress passed the 1967 Age Discrimination in Employment Act. The law makes it illegal to "to fail or refuse to hire or to discharge any individual or otherwise discriminate against any individual with respect to his compensation, terms, conditions, or privileges of employment, because of such individual's age."

Older people face a variety of other problems that raise civil liberties issues (Brown, 1989). Many older people live in nursing homes. As is the case with other institutions, nursing homes can violate the liberties of their residents, for example, by physically abusing them, denying them freedom of speech (particularly the right to complain about their treatment), violating their right to privacy (for example, turning over personal information to commercial firms), denying them adequate medical care, and so on. In 1972, the federal government launched a Long-Term Elder Care Ombudsmen Program, a formal process for defending the rights of elderly people who are residents of nursing homes or other long-term care facilities. (Details of the program may be found on the Web site of the Administration on Aging, *www.aoa.dhhs.gov*.)

Equal Voting Rights

The right to vote is a fundamental right in a democratic society (Keyssar, 2000). Violations of voting rights have taken two basic forms. First, during the era of segregation (1890–1960s), African

Americans were denied the right to vote in the states of the South. This practice was ended by the civil rights movement and by the 1965 Voting Rights Act in particular. (An excerpt from the 1965 Voting Rights Act is reprinted in Chapter 5.) Second, by the early 1960s the votes of many people were "diluted" by the fact that state legislative districts were not apportioned on the basis of population.

By the early 1960s, as a result of population changes, the numbers of people in districts of state legislatures were very unequal. A rural district with a small population had the same number of representatives (one) as did urban districts with very large populations. Civil libertarians argued that unequal apportionment denied voters equal protection of the law. For decades, the Supreme Court rejected this view. Then, in the 1962 case of *Baker v. Carr*, the Court agreed that legislative apportionment did raise equal protection issues under the Fourteenth Amendment. The *Baker* decision set the stage for *Reynolds v. Sims* (1964) two years later, in which the Court enunciated the "one man, one vote" doctrine. Chief Justice Warren wrote that "[l]egislators represent people, not trees or acres. Legislators are elected by voters, not farms or cities or economic interests. As long as ours is a representative form of government, and our legislatures are those instruments of government elected directly by and directly representative of the people, the right to elect legislators in a free and unimpaired fashion is a bedrock of our political system." As a consequence of the *Reynolds* decision, states reapportioned their legislatures and congressional districts. The result was that urban and growing suburban areas gained greater political power at the expense of less-populated rural areas (Keyssar, 2000).

Disenfranchisement on the Basis of Race

During the segregation era in the South (1890–1960s), whites denied African Americans the right to vote. Several methods were used to exclude African Americans from the electoral process. Literacy tests eliminated illiterate people, although many illiterate whites were allowed to vote. The poll tax, which required a fee to register to vote, excluded poor people. Violence by the Ku Klux Klan intimidated many African Americans from even attempting to register and vote. Denial of the right to vote denies people of the most fundamental right in a democratic society. In addition to being unable to vote for candidates for office, disenfranchised people cannot serve on juries, thereby extending race discrimination to the criminal justice system (Karst, 1989).

The civil rights movement mounted an attack on the denial of African American voting rights. Civil rights organizations organized voter registration drives in southern states. Most important, the Voting Rights Act of 1965 suspended the use of literacy tests and provided for the appointment of federal voting examiners who had the power to register qualified citizens to vote. (These provisions applied only to jurisdictions that were covered by a formula defined in the text of the law.) The 1965 Voting Rights Act had a profound effect on American politics. African Americans were elected to office at all levels of government throughout the southeast: school boards, city councils, sheriffs' offices, mayoralties, and the U.S. Congress. Mississippi today has more African American elected officials than any other state.

Implementing some aspects of the Voting Rights Act of 1965 has been highly controversial, however. Under the law affected states cannot redraw congressional legislative districts without approval from the U.S. Department of Justice, a provision designed to ensure that the new district lines do not discriminate against African Americans. The design of some districts has been challenged on the grounds that they give a preference to African Americans. (This issue, and the cases surrounding it, raise the same questions about racial preferences that arise with regard to affirmative action in employment.) The U.S. Supreme Court, although generally sympathetic to the Voting Rights Act, has rejected some legislative districts on the grounds that they represent a racial preference (*Shaw v. Reno,* 1993) (Thernstrom, 1987).

Disenfranchisement of Ex-Offenders
An estimated 4 million Americans are not able to vote because they have been convicted of a felony. Forty-eight states and the District of Columbia deny the vote to people currently in prison. Thirty-two states do not allow offenders on parole to vote, and twenty-nine states deny the vote to offenders on probation. Fourteen states strip convicted felons of their right to vote for the rest of their lives. The Sentencing Project estimates that about 1 million people are disenfranchised for life. Disenfranchisement has a disproportionate racial impact, denying about 1.4 million African American men the right to vote—about 13 percent of all African American men (Sentencing Project, 1998).

Civil libertarians argue that denying someone the right to vote, particularly for life, violates one of the most basic rights of citizenship. For persons on probation and parole, it contradicts the goal of those programs of reintegrating offenders into law-abiding lives in the community. At the same time, many of these same laws deny offenders the right to obtain licenses for certain professions (e.g., driving school buses), which also serves to prevent offenders from establishing law-abiding lives.

All states have some procedure for allowing ex-offenders to regain their right to vote, but these procedures are typically extremely cumbersome or hostile to offenders. In Florida, the Department of Corrections is required by law to assist offenders in regaining their civil rights. But a lawsuit on behalf of ex-offenders alleged that between 1992 and 2001, nearly 125,000 ex-offenders in the state did not receive the required assistance.

The Rights of Poor People

Poor people are among the least powerful groups in the United States, and as a result many are not able to fully enjoy their civil liberties. Discrimination against the poor occurs in many ways. One of the most serious is access to the legal system. Because they have little if any money, poor people usually cannot afford a lawyer and consequently cannot effectively contest illegal actions by landlords or commercial vendors or seek a divorce settlement that would guarantee child support or visitation rights.

The federal Legal Services Corporation (LSC) provides federal funds for state and local legal services agencies to provide free legal assistance to poor people. Yet, conservative forces in Congress have made several attempts to sharply reduce or even eliminate the Legal Services Corporation. The American Bar Association has joined civil rights groups in preventing the elimination of the LSC. Nonetheless, opponents of the LSC have secured laws that prohibit legal services agencies from bringing class action suits on behalf of poor people. Class action suits would be a means of challenging a law or practice on behalf of all poor people or a large group of poor clients. The result of the prohibition is that poor persons have to fight their cases individually.

Poor people also suffer unequal treatment as criminal defendants. The Sixth Amendment guarantees all people the right to "effective counsel" in criminal cases, and the 1963 *Gideon v. Wainwright* decision requires states to provide legal counsel to all defendants facing felony charges (i.e., the possibility of being sentenced to prison). In practice, however, many public defender agencies are seriously underfunded and understaffed. Excessive caseloads mean that public defenders do not have sufficient time to meet with their clients and prepare their cases; in particular, they do not have adequate time to study the records of the case and to locate potential witnesses. Professional standards recommend that each public defender have an annual caseload not exceeding 150 felonies, or 400 misdemeanors, or 200 juvenile cases. A 1996 ACLU suit in Pittsburgh, Pennsylvania, however, charged that public defenders in that city were handling 600 and 1,100 cases a year. The suit was settled with an agreement that the staff of the public defender's office would be doubled.

Due Process of Law

The Fifth Amendment protects citizens' rights against denial of due process by the federal government; the Fourteenth Amendment protects against denial of both due process and equal protection by state governments. Due process is a *procedural* right, rather than a substantive one. The distinction is important. The government can arrest, prosecute, convict, and imprison you for committing a crime. Loss of liberty is a substantive right. The right to due process, however, means that the government can deprive you of your liberty only if it does so in a procedurally correct manner. The Bill of Rights enumerates the specific procedural rights that people are guaranteed. These include protection against unreasonable searches and seizures (Fourth Amendment) and against self-incrimination (Fifth Amendment), the right to a fair trial (Sixth Amendment), and protection against excessive bail and cruel and unusual punishment (Eighth Amendment).

The most heated civil liberties controversies over due process of law have generally involved criminal suspects. Often, a person is arrested and convicted of a crime, but the conviction is overturned because the police or the courts denied the person a specific due process right. Critics of civil liberties argue that excessive concern for the rights of criminal suspects and defendants limits the ability of criminal justice officials to fight crime effectively. Civil libertarians reply that due process rights are fundamental and that police and other officials can effectively fight crime even while complying with constitutional requirements regarding suspects and defendants.

The Fourth Amendment: Unreasonable Searches and Seizures

The Fourth Amendment protects people against "unreasonable searches and seizures." In the 1961 decision in *Mapp v. Ohio*, the Supreme Court ruled that evidence gained through an illegal search in violation of the Fourth Amendment could not be used in court. This decision established the "exclusionary rule" in police search cases. An important aspect of *Mapp* is that it imposes the rule on state and local police by linking the Fourth Amendment to the Fourteenth Amendment ("no state shall deny . . ."), creating a penalty for violating this right, ruling that evidence obtained through an unconstitutional search could not be used against a defendant. The exclusionary rule is extremely controversial. Critics argue that it allows criminals to go free because of legal "technicalities" (Horwitz, 1998).

Drug Testing

One of the most important current search and seizure issues involves drug testing. As part of the "war on drugs," many government agencies and private employers require employees and job applicants to take tests to detect illegal drug use. Schools have also required drug tests of students (Hinchey, 2001). These practices raise the question of whether a drug test is a search and seizure under the law. Civil libertarians argue that an involuntary drug test of a student, when there is no suspicion that a particular student is using drugs, is a violation of the Fourth Amendment. They argue that individualized drug tests are both reasonable and constitutional. The basic standard is that there is some *individualized suspicion* that a person is engaged in some illegal activity—in this case, illegal drug use. The same standard applies to other searches and seizures, including traffic stops and other police actions. If an employer has a specific reason to suspect that an employee is on drugs, such as slurred speech or erratic behavior, it is legitimate to ask that person to submit to a drug test. It is also reasonable to have a policy specifying that persons using illegal drugs can be fired.

The Supreme Court has upheld the constitutionality of requiring student athletes to take drug tests. The main rationale is that public schools are a special context, where the expressed needs of school administrators carry extra weight. Justice Antonin Scalia explained that "Fourth Amendment rights, no less than First and Fourteenth Amendment rights, are different in public schools than elsewhere . . ." (*Vernonia School District v. Acton*, 1995).

The Fifth Amendment: Self-Incrimination

Protection against self-incrimination is one of the most fundamental rights in Anglo-American law (Levy, 1968). In the distant past, officials would force people to confess, often through torture. The underlying principle of Anglo-American law is that a person is innocent until proven guilty and that the government must prove guilt through a fair procedure.

In *Miranda v. Arizona* (1966), one of the most controversial decisions of the Warren Court, the Supreme Court held that in order to secure criminal suspects' Fifth Amendment protection against self-incrimination, the police must advise suspects who are in custody, before any questioning takes place, of their right to remain silent (see Chapter 4). Ernesto Miranda had been convicted of kidnapping and rape in part on the basis of his confession. The Court overturned the conviction on the grounds that he had been denied his Fifth and Sixth Amendment rights. This decision established the famous "Miranda warning," which requires that the police advise suspects before questioning that they have the right to remain silent, that anything they say can be used against them, that they have a right to an attorney, and that if they cannot afford an attorney one will be provided.

The *Miranda* decision was as controversial as the earlier *Mapp* decision, because the Supreme Court probed deeply into police practices that had previously been hidden from public view and free from scrutiny by the courts (Baker, 1983). Conservative critics of the *Miranda* decision argue that the Supreme Court went too far in writing rules for the police; nothing in the Fifth or Sixth Amendments specifically refers to advising suspects of their rights. Civil libertarians reply that the Court acted properly in spelling out what is required in order to give practical meaning to specific provisions of the Bill of Rights. (An excerpt from the *Miranda* decision with the section on the required warning is reprinted in Chapter 5.)

The Sixth Amendment: Fair Trial

The Sixth Amendment guarantees criminal defendants a fair trial (Bodenhamer, 1992). The amendment specifies the right to "a speedy and public trial" and the right to the assistance of counsel, among others. The right to an attorney is particularly important. In the *Miranda* decision, the Supreme Court held that police must advise criminal suspects of their right to an attorney before any questioning can begin.

Three years earlier, in 1963, the Court ruled that all persons charged with a felony had a constitutional right to an attorney at trial *(Gideon v. Wainwright)*. Before that ruling, many people had been convicted and sentenced to prison without ever having had a lawyer. At the time of Clarence Gideon's trial for the felony crime of breaking and entering, a Florida court told him that, under the law, it could appoint an attorney for him only if he was charged with a capital crime (that is, one that carries the death penalty, such as murder). In *Gideon,* the Supreme Court held that "reason and reflection require us to recognize that in our adversary system of criminal justice, any person haled into court, who is too poor to hire a lawyer, cannot be assured a fair trial unless counsel is provided for him. This seems to us to be an obvious truth" (Lewis, 1964).

The current "war on terrorism" has introduced a new set of fair trial issues. The federal government is holding immigrants in secret detention, which violates the Sixth Amendment guarantee of a "public trial." The government is also using secret evidence against them. The government's claims of protecting national security are the justification behind the Foreign Intelligence Surveillance Act, which operates secret court proceedings against alleged spies. The civil liberties aspects of the war on terrorism are discussed in more detail later in this chapter.

Due Process Rights of Students and Teachers

Students and teachers who face disciplinary charges in their schools, colleges, or universities enjoy certain due process rights. The basic rights include notice of the charges against them, the right to confront their accusers, the right to a hearing, and the right to appeal a disciplinary action (Bryan and Mullendore, 1992).

Historically, public school students had no rights whatsoever. School officials had complete authority to suspend or expel students. (This situation was similar to the one that prevailed in prisons, where inmates had no rights and prison officials had unlimited authority.) In the 1960s, the Supreme Court began to establish constitutional standards for school discipline. The first important case, *Tinker v. Des Moines,* involved First Amendment issues, and the Court ruled that school officials could not suspend Mary Beth Tinker for exercising her right of free speech. The courts also began to establish procedural rights regarding student discipline. Some of these cases were related to the civil rights movement. Schools were found to be suspending or expelling African American students at higher rates than white students (Hinchey, 2001).

Teachers in public schools and colleges and universities also enjoy due process rights regarding discipline. An educational institution cannot arbitrarily fire a teacher without a hearing and offering a right to an appeal. Many of these due process rights are spelled out in collective bargaining agreements negotiated by teachers' unions. Teachers in public institutions are also protected by the First Amendment. A school or college cannot fire a teacher because of his or her beliefs or associations (American Library Association, 2002).

The Eighth Amendment

The Eighth Amendment to the Constitution prohibits "cruel and unusual punishments" and "excessive bail." The Cruel and Unusual Clause has had two important applications: the death penalty and prison conditions.

Capital Punishment

The merits of the death penalty can be argued on three different grounds: whether it is morally justified, whether it deters crime, and whether it is constitutional (Banner, 2002). With respect to civil liberties, the first issue is whether, by modern standards, the capital punishment is inherently a cruel and unusual punishment. Opponents of the death penalty believe that it is. The Supreme Court, however, has never accepted this argument. In the 1972 case of *Furman v. Georgia* (1972), only two justices—Thurgood Marshall and William Brennan—argued that the death penalty was inherently unconstitutional under the Eighth Amendment. No other Supreme Court justices have ever accepted this argument.

Race and the Death Penalty The other constitutional question is whether the death penalty *as applied* is unconstitutional. In the *Furman* case, a majority of the Court held that because the selection of people for execution had been so arbitrary and "freakish," the death penalty was unconstitutional under the Due Process Clause of the Fourteenth Amendment, and executions in the United States were halted. The basic problem was that there were no standards to guide the decision of whether to use the death penalty. As a result, states revised their death penalty statutes, with new provisions to guide discretion in imposing death sentences. These new laws were upheld by the Supreme Court four years later in *Gregg v. Georgia,* and executions resumed in 1976 (Banner, 2002).

Research on capital punishment has consistently found that African Americans are more likely to receive the death penalty than white defendants who are charged with similar kinds of murders. The most consistent pattern is that African Americans who are charged with murdering a white person are the most likely to receive sentences of death, whereas whites who murder African Americans are the least likely to be sentenced to death. In a major test case, Robert McCleskey challenged his death penalty, relying primarily on a study of executions in Georgia conducted by law professor David Baldus and his colleagues. The Baldus study was consistent with other studies finding that African Americans were more likely to receive the death penalty. The Supreme Court, however, did not accept the use of this statistical evidence to overturn the death sentence in McCleskey's case (*McCleskey v. Kemp*). The decision had broad implications regarding the Court's willingness to consider statistical studies about general patterns and practices.

Juveniles and the Death Penalty The United States is one of the few countries that allow the execution of juveniles. Iran is the only other country that officially allows it, and four other countries have in fact executed juveniles.

The United States is out of step with virtually the entire

world on the issue of allowing the death penalty for juveniles. All of the major international human rights declarations oppose it (Brownlie and Goodwin-Gill, 2002). In the United States, the American Bar Association passed an official resolution opposing "in principle, the imposition of capital punishment upon any person for any offense committed while under the age of eighteen (18)" (American Bar Association, 1983). Opponents of executing juveniles argue that young people are not always fully responsible for their actions. They cite medical research indicating that the cognitive powers of young people have not fully developed until around age twenty. Finally, many opponents argue that young people are most likely to be rehabilitated and, with treatment, to develop a mature sense of responsibility.

By 2003, about 2.3 percent of all death row inmates in the United States committed their crimes when they were juveniles (a total of eighty-two in mid-2003). Twenty-two states permit the execution of juveniles, and a total of 160 juveniles have been executed since 1973. The U.S. Supreme Court has held that executing juveniles does not violate the Cruel and Unusual Clause of the Eighth Amendment. For the Court, Justice Antonin Scalia argued that there is mixed evidence regarding public opinion about executing juveniles, and the fact that many states allow the practice indicates that it is not clearly out of step with prevailing standards of justice (*Stanford v. Kentucky*, 1989)

In 2003, however, the Missouri Supreme Court overturned the death sentence of a juvenile offender, arguing that "a national consensus has developed against the execution of juvenile offenders."

People with Mental Disabilities and the Death Penalty   Civil libertarians believe that persons who are mentally retarded should not be subject to the death penalty. People with diminished mental capacity often do not fully understand the legal consequences of their actions. In addition, they are often more willing to confess than people with full mental capacity and are less able to work effectively with their lawyers in their own defense. Moreover, the deterrent effect of capital punishment is unlikely to work on someone with diminished mental capacity. In 2002, the U.S. Supreme Court reversed an earlier 1989 decision and held that executing a mentally retarded person was a "cruel and unusual punishment" (*Atkins v. Virginia*).

Executing the Innocent   One of the major objections to the death penalty is that there is no way of correcting mistakes that might be discovered after a person has been executed. Miscarriages of justice do occur. Some people are convicted because of police misconduct, including coercive tactics that lead people to confess to crimes they did not convict. Others are convicted on the basis of faulty eyewitness testimony. Some people are convicted because they did not have a competent lawyer to challenge weaknesses in the prosecution's case (Banner, 2002).

Between 1973 and mid-2003, 111 people were released from death row because it was established that they were innocent of the crimes for which they were convicted. Because so many people on death row in Illinois were found to have been falsely convicted, the governor declared a temporary moratorium on the death penalty. Other states have considered similar moratoriums. Recent advances in the scientific analysis of DNA have made it possible, where the necessary evidence is available, to reopen some criminal cases and conclusively determine whether the person who was convicted did in fact commit the crime. (Information on miscarriages of justice may be found at *www.deathpenaltyinfo.org*).

Conditions of Confinement: The Rights of Prisoners

Until the 1960s, prisoners had virtually no legal rights. Convicted criminals were considered to be in a condition of "civil death," with no rights, allowed only those privileges that prison officials were willing to grant them (Rudovsky et al., 1992).

As part of the revolution in constitutional law in the 1960s, prisoners began to gain some constitutional rights. The first changes occurred with respect to the free exercise of religion. In some prisons, officials denied African American prisoners who had converted to Islam the right to read the Koran and engage in religious practices. Gradually, the courts began to grant these prisoners protection under the First Amendment.

By the late 1960s, prisoners began to challenge other conditions of their confinement, including denial of mail privileges, denial of visitors, long terms in solitary confinement, and other administrative punishments without due process of law. Soon, a coherent prisoners' rights movement developed, and the American Civil Liberties Union organized a National Prison Project to challenge prison conditions in states across the country (Walker, 1999). The project addressed extreme overcrowding; inadequate food, ventilation, and medical care; denial of the right to have visitors; and excessive punishments such as sentences to solitary confinement. Prisoners were also denied due process with regard to punishment for violating prison rules.

By the 1980s, the courts established a body of prisoners' rights law. One court, for example, held that a disciplinary punishment of two years in solitary confinement constituted cruel and unusual punishment. Prisoners have a right to medical care, and any "deliberate indifference" to a medical problem constitutes a violation of the Eighth Amendment. In a number of states, federal courts have held that prison conditions as a whole represented cruel and unusual punishment. In some of these cases, for example, the complete lack of recreational, educational, and vocational programs resulted in complete idleness among prisoners, conditions that courts found to be cruel and unusual punishment. In *Wolff v. McDonnell* (1974), the Supreme Court ruled that prisoners are entitled to certain minimal due process rights when faced with discipline for violating prison rules. They are entitled to 24 hour notice of the charges, an impartial hearing, and a right to call witnesses and present other evidence in their own defense (Fliter, 2001).

Many of the prisoners' rights issues that were deemed radical or controversial when first raised in the 1960s and early 1970s have become established standards. The American Correctional Association (ACA), a professional association of correctional officials, publishes a series of standards for correctional institutions and uses them to accredit prisons and other facilities. The ACA standards incorporate many once-radical ideas about prison conditions.

The Right to Bail

The Eighth Amendment also prohibits "excessive bail" (Thomas, 1976). It does not guarantee an absolute right to bail—that is, release from jail pending trial. Traditional practice in the United States has been that a person has a presumption of bail except in capital crimes (crimes that carry the death penalty).

In the 1970s and 1980s, almost every state and the federal government passed *preventive detention* laws, which authorize judges to deny bail to defendants they believe to be dangerous to the community. The constitutionality of preventive detention was upheld by the U.S. Supreme Court in *United States v. Salerno* (1987). The Court ruled that the denial of bail under the conditions of the law was a reasonable "regulatory" measure and was not unconstitutional.

The Right to Privacy

The right to privacy is a special civil liberties case, because the Bill of Rights does not specifically mention privacy. Nonetheless, a legal right to privacy has been established by the U.S. Supreme Court, several state supreme courts, and federal and state laws (Alderman and Kennedy, 1991; Strum, 1998).

Individual rights to privacy fall into two broad areas. The first involves private sexual behavior, including access to birth control information and products, the right to abortion, and the right to engage in sexual activity with a person of the same sex. The second involves the collection and possible use of information about peoples' private lives, both by the government and by private organizations.

The Bill of Rights and the Right to Privacy

A constitutional right to privacy was established by the U.S. Supreme Court in the case of *Griswold v. Connecticut* (1965). The decision declared unconstitutional a Connecticut law that prohibited both the use contraceptives and assisting another person to use them (Garrow, 1994). Justice William O. Douglas's opinion held that a constitutional right to privacy is guaranteed by the "penumbra and emanations" of other amendments to the Constitution. "Zones of privacy" are created by, for example, "[t]he right of association contained in the penumbra of the First Amendment" and the Fourth Amendment's guarantee of the "right of the people to be secure in their persons, houses, papers, and effects, against unreasonable searches and seizures." In the case of *Eisenstadt v. Baird* (1972), the Supreme Court extended the right to privacy to all individuals and not just those who are married, as was the case in the *Griswold* decision.

Griswold remains one of the most controversial decisions in the history of the Supreme Court and is heavily criticized by conservative legal scholars. They argue that in this decision and many others that advance civil liberties, Supreme Court justices substituted their own personal social and political values for the specific language of the Constitution. They point out that the word "privacy" does not appear in the Constitution or the Bill of Rights (Bork, 1990). On the Court today, Justice Antonin Scalia is the leading advocate of this point of view (Scalia, 1998). He and fellow conservatives argue that the Supreme Court should not go beyond the "original intent" of the framers of the Constitution (see the discussion of original intent in Chapter 1, in the subsection Interpreting the Constitution, under The Role of the Courts).

Reproductive Rights

The right to privacy articulated in *Griswold* laid the foundation for the even more controversial decision in *Roe v. Wade* (1973) establishing a legal right to an abortion (Faux, 1988). Before that ruling, abortion was a crime under state laws, although several states had liberalized their laws in the years just before *Roe*. The Court did not create an absolute right to abortion. It held that "the right of personal privacy includes the abortion decision, but that this right is not unqualified and must be considered against important state interests in regulation." It then developed a trimester framework. During the first three months of pregnancy, women have an almost absolute right to an abortion. But as a pregnancy continues, the interest of the state in protecting the fetus steadily becomes greater. Restrictions on abortion may be greater in the second trimester, and greater still in the third trimester. (An excerpt from the *Roe* decision is reprinted in Chapter 5)

Since *Roe*, the Court has heard many other cases involving abortion rights. One of the basic principles in these decisions is that government cannot place an "undue burden" on a woman's right to an abortion. That is, it can regulate the medical practice of abortion but cannot, for example, impose unduly long waiting periods before a woman could actually have an abortion. With respect to public funding of abortion for poor people, the Court has held that the right to abortion is protected by the constitution, there is no constitutional right to public funding. The Court has upheld the constitutionality of the Hyde Amendment, which prohibits the use of federal funds for abortion services. Since this law applies only to the use of federal funds, a number of states make state funds available to poor women (Hull and Hoffer, 2001).

Another particularly contentious issue involves the right of minors to have abortions without the consent of their parents.

The Supreme Court has upheld this right but has also upheld the constitutionality of state laws that require parental notification or some form of judicial bypass (allowing a girl to receive approval from a judge in cases where notifying her parents might pose some kind of obstacle or risk).

The Collection and Use of Personal Information

Government Agencies

The collection of personal information about individuals has become increasingly important because of modern computer technology, which makes it possible for an organization (government or private) to collect, store, analyze, and quickly retrieve vast amounts of information. Such information includes medical records, financial records, employment histories, criminal histories, and so on (Raul, 2002).

In the absence of any explicit right to privacy in the Bill of Rights, the basic framework for a legal right to privacy in this context was established by the 1974 Privacy Act. The law states, "No [government] agency shall disclose any record which is contained in a system of records by any means of communication to any person, or to another agency, except pursuant to a written request by, or with the prior written consent of, the individual to whom the record pertains." Federal agencies are also directed to collect only such information as is "necessary."

An important companion to the Privacy Act is the 1966 Freedom of Information Act (FOIA). The FOIA states that, apart from certain exceptions, "each [government] agency, upon any request for records which (i) reasonably describes such records and (ii) is made in accordance with published rules stating the time, place, fees (if any), and procedures to be followed, shall make the records promptly available to any person." The FOIA has been extremely important in holding government agencies accountable to the public. For example, the law helped in exposing the long history of FBI spying on individuals (Gentry, 1991).

Private Organizations

Private organizations, especially commercial firms, also collect enormous amounts of information about individuals. Banks, credit card companies, and other financial institutions, for example, have a great deal of information about private financial activities, which can be used to create a detailed profile of any individual: purchases, travel, lifestyle, political beliefs and associations, and so on. This information can potentially be sold to other organizations or individuals for profit or other purposes. Similarly, medical institutions and insurance companies have detailed information about individuals' personal health issues, such as history of cancer treatment, mental health problems, and so on (Raul, 2002).

One of the first attempts to regulate private organizations was the Fair Credit Reporting Act of 1970. This law gives individuals the right to see their own credit reports and to challenge any inaccurate information in them. Certain kinds of information that is more than seven years old is not permitted in credit reports. Under the law, a creditor or employer can receive medical information contained in a credit report only with the approval of the individual.

Genetic Privacy

Advances in medical science have created a potential new privacy issue involving genetic information (Laurie, 2002). It is increasingly possible to conduct a genetic "screening" of an individual and, for example, identify that person's risk of developing certain diseases. Employers and insurance companies could use such information to deny jobs or insurance coverage. Genetic information is different from standard medical information. A person can change his or her weight or cholesterol level through lifestyle modification, but genetic characteristics are immutable. Moreover, as recent developments in the use of DNA in criminal cases demonstrate, genetic information is unique, capable of specifically identifying an individual, unlike other data such as sex, race, height, weight, and so on, which would apply to many people.

Civil libertarians argue that obtaining genetic information without permission is a violation of a person's privacy and that denial of employment or insurance on the basis of such information would represent a form of discrimination. To guard against abuse of this sort, President Bill Clinton issued Executive Order 13145 in 2000, barring federal agencies from discriminating against employees or job applicants on the basis of genetic information. Executive Order 13145 is reproduced in Chapter 5.

Personal Health Information

To protect the privacy of individuals' personal health information, Congress passed the Health Information Portability and Accountability Act (HIPAA) in 1996. The law took effect in April 2003. (The delay in implementation was designed to give health care agencies time to establish compliance procedures for the law's complex requirements.) Health care agencies include not only individual doctors and hospitals but also insurance companies and employers.

With respect to privacy, HIPAA limits the ability of a health care agency to disclose personal health information about an individual without that person's consent. One danger, for example, is that an insurance agency might disclose information about someone's medical condition to a prospective employer, resulting in the denial of a job. Also, there is the danger that insurance companies might sell information about all people who have a certain medical condition to commercial firms that want to sell them medicines, equipment, or services.

HIPAA does allow the disclosure of personal health information in certain circumstances. If a person is incapacitated and unable to make decisions about care, the doctor or organization may disclose information to family members. Information can also be disclosed as part of a legal proceeding (e.g., by subpoena). Also, information about many individuals can be aggregated for purposes of research, for example, the prevalence of a particular condition among women or older men. (Information about HIPAA can be found on the Web site of the U.S. Department of Health and Human Services, *www.hhs.gov*).

Privacy Rights in the Workplace

An emerging issue related to privacy rights involves the question of the extent to which employers can regulate what their employees do outside the workplace on their own time (Repa, 2000). Many employers, for example, have attempted to prohibit their employees from smoking. They argue that smoking affects their employees' health, which has an impact on their productivity and on health insurance costs. Civil libertarians argue that off-the-job behavior is a private matter that employers have no right to control. The ACLU refers to regulation of off-work behavior as "lifestyle discrimination." If employers have the right to prohibit smoking for health reasons, can they also regulate consumption of high cholesterol foods?

A more common threat to employees' privacy is drug testing. Employers have a legitimate right to ensure that their employees are not impaired in any way, particularly by drug or alcohol abuse. Civil libertarians argue that no person should be subject to an intrusive search, such as a compulsory urinalysis, without some individualized suspicion that the person's behavior is impaired (for example, by slurred speech or inability to perform tasks). A major problem with workplace drug testing is the unreliability of many tests. They often incorrectly indicate that a person is using drugs and in some cases fail to identify those who in fact are using drugs.

National Security and the War on Terrorism

The "war on terrorism" has raised a number of important civil liberties issues (Hentoff, 2003). None of these issues is new. Past wars and conflicts, including the Cold War, have raised issues related to freedom of speech, religious liberty, due process of law, and privacy (Walker, 1999). During World War I, for example, the federal government engaged in a massive suppression of the free speech rights of opponents of the war (Murphy, 1979). World War II witnessed the violation of the rights of over 100,000 Japanese Americans through their evacuation from the West Coast and their confinement in internment camps (Irons, 1983). The Cold War included measures that violated the rights of freedom of speech and association of many people on the basis of their actual or alleged political beliefs. The war on terrorism has revived many of these issues, often in somewhat new forms (Cole and Dempsey, 2002; Hentoff, 2003).

The Patriot Act

The Patriot Act was passed by Congress after the September 11, 2001, terrorist attacks on the World Trade Center and the Pentagon. Intended to protect the country against terrorism, the law includes many provisions that civil libertarians believe violate or threaten the rights of Americans. For example, the law expands the power of law enforcement agencies to conduct secret searches of individuals, including wider powers of telephone wiretapping and internet surveillance. The Patriot Act does not completely abolish any civil liberties, but it relaxes existing protections against government surveillance. Advocates of the law argue that the government will use these new powers sparingly and only in the case of suspected terrorists. Civil libertarians, however, argue that past history indicates that government officials often abuse such powers and that the label "terrorist" can be used to justify investigations against a wide range of people and organizations the government does not like (American Civil Liberties Union, 2003).

One part of the Patriot Act that especially disturbs civil libertarians is Section 213, which allows the government to conduct searches of homes or other locations without informing the individuals who are the subjects of the search. Civil libertarians call these "sneak and peek" searches. Specifically, Section 213 grants the government "authority for delaying notice of the execution of a [search] warrant." A court may authorize such a search if it "finds reasonable cause to believe that providing immediate notification of the execution of the warrant may have an adverse result" on the government's investigation. Civil libertarians argue that this standard is a very low one and that it is likely to lead to a broader pattern of evasion of the normal requirements for a search warrant.

The Patriot Act also includes new restrictions on the rights of noncitizens. It allows the government to hold them in jail on mere suspicion and also to be denied reentry into the United States for engaging in free speech. Particularly important is that the law limits the role of the courts in examining government conduct. Noncitizen suspects who have not been convicted of any crime may be held in jail indefinitely in 6 month increments without meaningful judicial review.

Profiling Suspects on the Basis of National Origin or Religion

The war on terrorism has also introduced a new form of profiling, similar to the racial profiling that has affected African Americans (Harris, 2002). A 2003 report by the Leadership Conference on Civil Rights (2003), *Wrong Then, Wrong Now: Racial Profiling before and after September 11,* found that a new pattern of discriminatory profiling had developed since the terrorist attacks. The

FBI questioned thousands of people specifically because they were from a Middle Eastern country or were Muslim and not because of any suspected criminal activity. Although individuals have a right not to cooperate with such questioning, the FBI's request for interviews was widely regarded as intimidating.

In 2003, the federal government launched a program to profile airline passengers. The Computer Assisted Passenger Prescreening System II (CAPPS II) is designed to identify potential terrorists on the basis of certain characteristics. Civil libertarians protested that the nature of the program was secret, including the factors to be used in developing the profile of suspected terrorists.

Attorney-Client Privilege

The federal government has also claimed the right to monitor communications between people being held on federal charges and their lawyers. Civil libertarians argue that this practice violates the historic right to attorney-client privilege and threatens the Sixth Amendment right to counsel.

Freedom of Speech

During past national security crises, serious assaults were made on freedom of speech (Walker, 1999), particularly during World War I and the Cold War. The war on terrorism raises similar dangers. In an address to Congress on December 6, 2001, Attorney General John Ashcroft said, "We need honest, reasoned debate; not fearmongering. To those who pit Americans against immigrants, and citizens against noncitizens; to those who scare peace-loving people with phantoms of lost liberty; my message is this: Your tactics only aid terrorists—for they erode our national unity and diminish our resolve. They give ammunition to America's enemies, and pause to America's friends."

In a similar vein, on September 9, 2003, Secretary of Defense Donald Rumsfeld stated that critics of the war in Iraq were aiding the enemy. He said that criticism of the war gave Iraqi enemies hope that the United States would abandon the war effort in Iraq. He said, "The United States is not going to . . . [acquiesce]. President Bush is not going to do that. Now, to the extent terrorists are given reason to believe he might, or if he is not willing to, the opponents might prevail in some way . . . and they take heart in that, and that leads to more recruiting . . . that leads to more encouragement, or that leads to more staying power. Obviously that does make it more difficult."

Civil libertarians were horrified by these statements. During World War I, the federal government used precisely the same argument to suppress freedom of speech and press (Murphy, 1979; Walker, 1999). Although the attorney general's remarks were not followed by any new laws or actions directly censoring critics of the war on terrorism, civil libertarians feared that such remarks from some of the highest-ranking government officials created a climate that would "chill" free speech (American Civil Liberties Union, 2003; Hentoff, 2003).

Surveillance

The federal government has also increased its efforts to maintain surveillance of people. Perhaps the most controversial idea was a plan called Total Information Awareness (TIA). Under TIA, the federal government would develop a massive computerized database on people, including all the possible information that could be collected about their finances, education, travel, health care, housing, and so on. The planners of the system argued that it would allow federal agents to identify terrorists on the basis of suspicious patterns of activity—for example, travel to and from certain places; travel patterns that match those of certain other people; financial transactions; and education or training that could be related to a planned terrorist activity.

Civil libertarians charged that TIA represented a plan for massive spying on all American citizens. Members of Congress also expressed serious objections to the plan, and it was dropped by the government.

Government Secrecy

The war on terrorism has included a dramatic increase in secret policies and actions by the federal government. Historically, the federal government has expanded secret activities during times of war or threats to national security (Melanson, 2001). There was a tremendous increase in secret government activities during the Cold War, for example (see Chapter 4).

As part of the war on terrorism, the federal government has introduced a number of secrecy initiatives. First, the government created a secret "no fly" list that bars certain individuals from flying on commercial airliners. Officials do not have to give a reason why someone is not allowed to fly, and the standards used to identify such people are secret. Second, the Foreign Intelligence Surveillance Act created a system of secret courts that hold hearings and try people accused of being spies for foreign governments. Third, immigrants are being detained and deported on the basis of secret evidence. Noncitizens are held without charge for undefined periods of time.

Civil libertarians argue that secret proceedings violate fundamental standards of individual rights, including the right of defendants to public trials, the right of other citizens to know what their government is doing, and the right to know what standards are used to hold people or otherwise deprive them of their liberty (e.g., prevent them from flying).

Conclusion

Civil liberties cover an exceedingly broad range of issues. It is safe to say that virtually every area of American life involves at least some civil liberties issues. This chapter has discussed only some of the more important issues. Each individual right, such as freedom of speech, includes a large number of issues, impossible to cover in detail in a single chapter.

Many civil liberties issues are old and enduring ones, such as the First Amendment right to criticize the government. Some, however, are relatively new issues, such as the rights of two people of the same sex to marry. Some of the most difficult controversies today involve conflicts between competing civil liberties issues, such as the First Amendment right of free speech, which includes "hate speech," and the Fourteenth Amendment guarantee of equal protection of the law.

The scope of civil liberties today is very different from what it was twenty-five years ago, and the list of prominent civil liberties issues will very likely be different again twenty-five years from now.

References

Aby, Stephen H., and James C. Kuhn IV, comps. 2000. *Academic Freedom: A Guide to the Literature.* Westport, CT: Greenwood Press.

Alderman, Ellen, and Caroline Kennedy. 1991. *In Our Defense: The Bill of Rights in Action.* New York: Morrow.

American Bar Association. 1983. *Policy against Executing Juveniles.* Available at *www.abanet.org.*

American Civil Liberties Union. 1986. *Preserving the Right to Choose: How to Cope with Violence and Disruption at Abortion Clinics.* New York: American Civil Liberties Union.

———. 2003. *Freedom under Fire: Dissent in Post-9/11 America.* New York: American Civil Liberties Union.

American Library Association, Office for Intellectual Freedom. 2002. *Intellectual Freedom Manual.* Chicago: American Library Association.

Baker, Liva. 1983. *Miranda: The Crime, the Law, the Politics.* New York: Atheneum.

Ball, Howard. 2000. *The Bakke Case: Race, Education, and Affirmative Action.* Lawrence: University Press of Kansas.

Banner, Stuart. 2002. *The Death Penalty: An American History.* Cambridge, MA: Harvard University Press.

Bodenhamer, David J. 1992. *Fair Trial: Rights of the Accused in American History.* New York: Oxford University Press.

Bork, Robert. 1990. *The Tempting of America.* New York: Free Press.

Boyer, Paul S. 1968. *Purity in Print: The Vice-Society Movement and Book Censorship in America.* New York: Scribner.

Brodie, Laura Fairchild. 2000. *Breaking Out: VMI and the Coming of Women.* New York: Pantheon Books.

Brown, Robert N. 1989. *The Rights of Older Persons.* Carbondale: Southern Illinois University Press.

Brownlie, Ian, and Guy S. Goodwin-Gill, eds. 2002. *Basic Documents on Human Rights,* 4th ed. Oxford, England: Clarendon Press.

Bryan, William A., and Richard H. Mullendore, eds. 1992. *Rights, Freedoms, and Responsibilities of Students.* San Francisco: Jossey-Bass.

Building Blocks for Youth. 2002. *Donde Esta la Justicia?* East Lansing: Michigan State University.

Chafee, Zechariah Jr. 1941. *Free Speech in the United States.* Cambridge, MA: Harvard University Press.

Cole, David, and James X. Dempsey. 2002. *Terrorism and the Constitution: Sacrificing Civil Liberties in the Name of National Security.* New York: New Press.

Corrado, Anthony. 1997. *Campaign Finance Reform: A Sourcebook.* Washington, DC: Brookings Institution.

Cortner, Richard C. 2001. *Civil Rights and Public Accommodations: The Heart of Atlanta Motel and McClung Cases.* Lawrence: University Press of Kansas.

Cottrol, Robert J. 1993. *Gun Control and the Constitution: Sources and Explorations on the Second Amendment.* New York: Garland.

Curtis, Michael Kent. 1986. *No State Shall Abridge: The 14th Amendment and the Bill of Rights.* Durham, NC: Duke University Press.

Cushman, Clare, ed. 2000. *Supreme Court Decisions and Women's Rights: Milestones to Equality.* Washington, DC: CQ Press.

Doerr, Edd, Albert J. Menendez, and John M. Swomley. 1996. *The Case against School Vouchers.* Amherst, NY: Prometheus Books, 1996.

Downs, Donald A. 1989. *The New Politics of Pornography.* Chicago: University of Chicago Press.

Drakeman, Donald L. 1991. *Church-State Constitutional Issues: Making Sense of the Establishment Clause.* Westport, CT: Greenwood Press.

Eastland, Terry. 1996. *Ending Affirmative Action: The Case for Colorblind Justice.* New York: Basic Books.

Eisaguirre, Lynne. 1999. *Affirmative Action: A Reference Handbook.* Santa Barbara, CA: ABC-CLIO.

Faux, Marian. 1988. Roe v. Wade. New York: New American Library.

Feinberg, Renee, comp. 1986. *The Equal Rights Amendment: An Annotated Bibliography of the Issues, 1976–1985.* Westport, CT: Greenwood Press.

Fenwick, Lynda Beck. 1989. *Should the Children Pray? A Historical, Judicial, and Political Examination of Public School Prayer.* Waco, TX: Baylor University Press.

Fliter, John A. 2001. *Prisoners' Rights: The Supreme Court and Evolving Standards of Decency.* Westport, CT: Greenwood Press.

Frankel, Marvin E. 1994. *Faith and Freedom: Religious Liberty in America.* New York: Hill and Wang.

Freedman, Warren. 1988. *Freedom of Speech on Private Property.* New York: Quorum Books.

Friendly, Fred W. 1981. *Minnesota Rag: The Dramatic Story of the Landmark Case that Gave New Meaning to Freedom of the Press.* New York: Random House.

Garrow, David. J. 1994. *Liberty and Sexuality: The Right to Privacy and the Making of* Roe v. Wade. New York: Macmillan.

Gentry, Curt. 1991. *J. Edgar Hoover: The Man and the Secrets.* New York: W. W. Norton.

Ginger, Ray. 1974. *Six Days or Forever? Tennessee v. John Thomas Scopes.* New York: Oxford University Press.

Goldstein, Robert J. 2000. *Flag Burning and Free Speech: The Case of* Texas v. Johnson. Lawrence: University Press of Kansas.

Goodale, James C., comp. 1971. The New York Times Company v. United States; *a Documentary History [of] the Pentagon Papers Litigation.* New York: Arno Press.

Gora, Joel M., David Goldberger, Gary Stern, and Morton H. Halperin. 1991. *The Right to Protest.* Carbondale: Southern Illinois University Press.

Grossman, Mark. 1993. *The ABC-CLIO Companion to the Civil Rights Movement.* Santa Barbara, CA: ABC-CLIO.

Haiman, Frank. 1993. *"Speech Acts" and the First Amendment.* Carbondale: Southern Illinois University Press.

Harris, David. 2002. *Profiles in Injustice: Why Racial Profiling Won't Work.* New York: New Press.

Heins, Marjorie. 2001a. *Not in Front of the Children: "Indecency," Censorship, and the Innocence of Youth.* New York: Hill and Wang.

———. 2001b. *Violence and the Media: An Exploration of Cause, Effect, and the First Amendment.* Arlington, VA: First Amendment Center.

Hentoff, Nat. 2003. *The War on the Bill of Rights and the Gathering Resistance.* New York: Seven Stories Press.

Hester, Joseph P. 2003. *The Ten Commandments: A Handbook of Religious, Legal, and Social Issues.* Jefferson, NC: McFarland.

Heumann, Milton, and Thomas W. Church, with David P. Redlawsk. 1997. *Hate Speech on Campus: Cases, Case Studies, and Commentary.* Boston: Northeastern University Press.

Hinchey, Patricia H. 2001. *Student Rights: A Reference Handbook.* Santa Barbara, CA: ABC-CLIO.

Horwitz, Morton J. 1998. *The Warren Court and the Pursuit of Justice.* New York: Hill and Wang.

Hudson, David L. 2002. *Balancing Act: Public Employees and Free Speech.* Arlington, VA: First Amendment Center. Available at *www.firstamendmentcenter.org.*

Hull, N. E. H., and Peter Charles Hoffer. 2001. Roe v. Wade: *The Abortion Rights Controversy in American History.* Lawrence: University Press of Kansas.

Hunter, Nan D., Courtney G. Joslin, and Sharon M. McGowan. 2004. *The Rights of Lesbians, Gay Men, Bisexuals, and Transgender People,* 4th ed. Carbondale: Southern Illinois University Press.

Ingelhart, Louis Edward. 1997. *Press and Speech Freedoms in America, 1619–1995: A Chronology.* Westport, CT: Greenwood Press.

Irons, Peter. 1988. *The Courage of Their Convictions.* New York: Free Press.

———. 1983. *Justice at War: The Story of the Japanese American Internment Cases.* New York: Oxford University Press.

Jacoby, Kerry N. 1998. *Souls, Bodies, Spirits: The Drive to Abolish Abortion Since 1973.* Westport, CT: Praeger.

Johnson, John W. 1997. *The Struggle for Student Rights:* Tinker v. Des Moines *and the 1960s.* Lawrence: University Press of Kansas.

Jurinski, James John. 1998. *Religion in the Schools: A Reference Handbook.* Santa Barbara, CA: ABC-CLIO.

Kalven, Harry. 1965. *The Negro and the First Amendment.* Chicago: University of Chicago Press.

Karst, Kenneth L. 1989. *Belonging to America: Equal Citizenship and the Constitution.* New Haven, CT: Yale University Press.

Keyssar, Alexander. 2000. *The Right to Vote: The Contested History of Democracy in the United States.* New York: Basic Books.

Kluger, Richard. 1975. *Simple Justice: The History of* Brown v. Board of Education *and Black America's Struggle for Equality.* New York: Knopf.

Larson, Edward J. 1997. *Summer for the Gods: The Scopes Trial and America's Continuing Debate over Science and Religion.* New York: Basic Books.

Laurie, Graeme. 2002. *Genetic Privacy: A Challenge to Medico-Legal Norms.* New York: Cambridge University Press.

Lawrence, Charles R. III, and Mari J. Matsuda. 1997. *We Won't Go Back: Making the Case for Affirmative Action.* Boston: Houghton Mifflin.

Leadership Conference on Civil Rights. 2003. *Wrong Then, Wrong Now: Racial Profiling before and after September 11, 2001.* Washington, DC: Leadership Conference on Civil Rights.

Leone, Bruno, ed. 2003. *Cloning.* San Diego, CA: Greenhaven Press, Thomson/Gale.

Levy, Leonard W. 1963. *Jefferson and Civil Liberties: The Darker Side.* Cambridge, MA: Harvard University Press.

———. 1968. *Origins of the Fifth Amendment: The Right against Self-Incrimination.* New York: Oxford University Press.

Levy, Robert M., and Leonard S. Rubenstein. 1996. *The Rights of People with Mental Disabilities.* Carbondale: Southern Illinois University Press.

Lewis, Anthony. 1964. *Gideon's Trumpet.* New York: Random House.

———. 1991. *Make No Law: The Sullivan Case and the First Amendment.* New York: Random House.

Lipschultz, Jeremy Harris. 2000. *Free Expression in the Age of the Internet: Social and Legal Boundaries.* Boulder, CO: Westview Press.

Long, Carolyn N. 2000. *Religious Freedom and Indian Rights: The Case of Oregon v. Smith.* Lawrence: University Press of Kansas.

Lowery, Charles D., and John F. Marszalek. 1992. *Encyclopedia of African American Civil Rights: From Emancipation to the Present.* Westport, CT: Greenwood.

MacKinnon, Catharine A. 1993. *Only Words.* Cambridge, MA: Harvard University Press.

———. 1978. *Sexual Harassment of Working Women: A Case of Sex Discrimination.* New Haven, CT: Yale University Press.

Martin, Waldo E., ed. 1998. Brown v. Board of Education: *A Brief History with Documents.* Boston: Bedford/St. Martin's.

Melanson, Philip H. 2001. *Secrecy Wars: National Security, Privacy, and the Public's Right to Know.* Washington, DC: Brassey's.

Moore, Randy. 2002. *Evolution in the Courtroom: A Reference Guide.* Santa Barbara, CA: ABC-CLIO.

Morgan, Edmund S. 1967. *Roger Williams: The Church and the State.* New York: Harcourt, Brace and World.

Moscato, Michael, and Leslie LeBlanc. 1984. The United States of America v. One Book Entitled Ulysses by James Joyce: *Documents and Commentary: A 50-Year Retrospective.* Frederick, MD: University Publications of America.

Moskos, Charles C., and John Whiteclay Chambers II, eds. 1993. *The New Conscientious Objection: From Sacred to Secular Resistance.* New York: Oxford University Press.

Murphy, Paul L. 1979. *World War I and the Origin of Civil Liberties in the United States.* New York: W. W. Norton.

Neier, Aryeh. 1979. *Defending My Enemy: American Nazis, the Skokie Case, and the Risks of Freedom.* New York: E. P. Dutton.

Pelka, Fred. 1997. *The ABC-CLIO Companion to the Disability Rights Movement.* Santa Barbara, CA: ABC-CLIO.

Peters, Shawn Francis. 2000. *Judging Jehovah's Witnesses: Religious Persecution and the Dawn of the Rights Revolution.* Lawrence: University Press of Kansas.

Pevar, Steven L. 2002. *The Rights of Indians and Tribes,* 3rd ed. Carbondale: Southern Illinois University Press.

Polenberg, Richard. 1987. *Fighting Faiths: The Abrams Case, the Supreme Court, and Free Speech.* New York: Viking.

Raul, Alan Charles. 2002. *Privacy and the Digital State: Balancing Public Information and Personal Privacy.* Boston: Kluwer Academic Publishers.

Ravitch, Frank S. 1999. *School Prayer and Discrimination: The Civil Rights of Religious Minorities and Dissenters.* Boston: Northeastern University Press.

Repa, Barbara Kate. 2000. *Your Rights in the Workplace.* Berkeley, CA: Nolo, 2000.

Rubin, David, and Steven Greenhouse. 1984. *The Rights of Teachers.* New York: Bantam Books.

Rudovsky, David, Alvin Bronstein, Ed Koren, and Julia Cade. 1992. *The Rights of Prisoners,* 4th ed. Carbondale: Southern Illinois University Press.

Scalia, Antonin. 1998. *A Matter of Interpretation: Federal Courts and the Law.* Princeton, NJ: Princeton University Press.

Sentencing Project. 1998. *Losing the Vote: The Impact of Felony Disenfranchisement Laws in the United States.* Washington, DC: The Sentencing Project.

Sherman, Suzanne, ed. 1997. *Lesbian and Gay Marriage: Private Commitments, Public Ceremonies.* Philadelphia: Temple University Press.

Shilts, Randy. 1993. *Conduct Unbecoming: Gays and Lesbians in the U.S. Military.* New York: St. Martin's Press.

Slabach, Frederick G., ed. 1998. *The Constitution and Campaign Finance Reform: An Anthology.* Durham: Carolina Academic Press.

Smith, James Morton. 1956. *Freedom's Fetters: The Alien and Sedition Laws and American Civil Liberties.* Ithaca, NY: Cornell University Press.

Souraf, Frank J. 1976. *The Wall of Separation: The Constitutional Politics of Church and State.* Princeton, NJ: Princeton University Press.

Sowell, Thomas. 1990. *Preferential Policies: An International Perspective.* New York: William Morrow.

Stein, Laura W. 1999. *Sexual Harassment in America: A Documentary History.* Westport, CT: Greenwood Press.

Strossen, Nadine. 1995. *Defending Pornography: Free Speech, Sex, and the Fight for Women's Rights.* New York: Scribner's.

Strum, Philippa. 1998. *Privacy: The Debate in the United States since 1945.* Fort Worth, TX: Harcourt Brace.

———. 1999. *When the Nazis Came to Skokie: Freedom for Speech We Hate.* Lawrence: University Press of Kansas.

———. 2002. *Women in the Barracks: The VMI Case and Equal Rights.* Lawrence: University Press of Kansas.

Tatalovich, Raymond. 1995. *Nativism Reborn? The Official English Language Movement and the American States.* Lexington: University Press of Kentucky.

Thernstrom, Abigail M. 1987. *Whose Votes Count? Affirmative Action and Minority Voting Rights.* Cambridge, MA: Harvard University Press.

Thomas, Brook. 1997. Plessy v. Ferguson: *A Brief History with Documents.* Boston: Bedford Books.

Thomas, Wayne H., Jr. 1976. *Bail Reform in America.* Berkeley: University of California Press.

Ungar, Sanford J. 1972. *The Papers and the Papers: An Account of the Legal and Political Battle over the Pentagon Papers.* New York: Dutton.

U.S. Department of Education. 1998. *Title IX: Twenty-five Years of Progress.* Washington, DC: U.S. Department of Education.

U.S. Office of Personnel Management. 2003. Final Regulations on Family and Medical Leave. Available at *www.opm.gov.*

Urofsky, Melvin I. 1991. *A Conflict of Rights: The Supreme Court and Affirmative Action.* New York: Scribner's.

Walker, Samuel. 1994. *Hate Speech: The History of an American Controversy.* Lincoln: University of Nebraska Press.

———. 1999. *In Defense of American Liberties: A History of the ACLU,* 2nd ed. Carbondale: Southern Illinois University Press.

Wallenstein, Peter. 2002. *Tell the Court I Love My Wife: Race, Marriage, and Law: An American History.* New York: Palgrave.

Weil, Danny. 2002. *School Vouchers and Privatization: A Reference Handbook.* Santa Barbara, CA: ABC-CLIO.

Withman, Larry A. 2002. *Where Darwin Meets the Bible: Creationists and Evolutionists in America.* New York: Oxford University Press.

Wunder, John R., ed. 1996. *The Indian Bill of Rights, 1968.* New York: Garland.

Wunder, John R. 1994. *"Retained by the People": A History of American Indians and the Bill of Rights.* New York: Oxford.

3

Chronology

1902   Free Speech League organized by Theodore Schroeder; the first national civil liberties organization. It has little impact on the law and eventually fades away.

1907   Chicago passes the first film censorship law.

1909   National Association for the Advancement of Colored People (NAACP) founded; the first national African American civil rights organization.

1914   World War I begins in Europe.

Margaret Sanger arrested in New York City for distributing birth control information.

1917   United States enters World War I.

The federal government suppresses free speech and refuses to recognize the right of conscientious objection to military service.

Federal Bureau of Investigation (FBI) begins spying on political groups.

Civil Liberties Bureau formed. Organized effort to defend free speech and the rights of conscientious objectors.

1918   American Jewish Congress founded; Jewish civil rights organization with strong civil liberties orientation.

1919   *Schenck v. United States:* Supreme Court upholds the conviction of antiwar activist and enunciates the "clear and present danger" test for the First Amendment.

Abrams v. United States: dissent by Justices Holmes and Brandeis marks beginning of modern law of free speech.

"Red Scare": the federal government arrests and deports thousands of suspected radicals and immigrants in a major violation of civil liberties.

1920   American Civil Liberties Union (ACLU) founded; the first national organization devoted to defending civil liberties. Organized and led by Roger Baldwin.

Zechariah Chafee publishes *Freedom of Speech;* the first important book on free speech, very influential on subsequent development of First Amendment law.

Nineteenth Amendment to the U.S. Constitution adopted, allowing women to vote.

American Fund for Public Service ("Garland Fund") established; private foundation supports civil rights and civil liberties causes in the 1920s.

1921   NAACP sponsors first antilynching legislation in Congress.

Margaret Sanger founds American Birth Control League.

1923   Equal Rights Amendment (ERA) to the U.S. Constitution proposed.

Meyer v. Nebraska: Supreme Court rules that parents have a right to control the education of their children. Decision is a precursor of a broader right to privacy.

1924 Harlan Fiske Stone appointed U.S. attorney general. Orders end to FBI spying on political groups.

1925 *Scopes* "Monkey" Trial: ACLU challenges Tennessee law prohibiting teaching of evolution. Raises enduring issues of academic freedom and separation of church and state.

Gitlow v. New York: Supreme Court rules that the Fourteenth Amendment binds the Bill of Rights to the states. Principle serves as the legal foundation for much of the subsequent civil liberties and civil rights law.

Pierce v. Society of Sisters: Supreme Court invalidates Oregon statute outlawing private parochial schools, holding that parents have right to control education of their children. Early right to privacy decision.

1926–ﾠ
1929 "Banned in Boston" censorship crisis: Margaret Sanger banned from giving a speech on birth control in December 1926. Other speakers and birth control advocates also banned.

1927 *Whitney v. California:* concurring opinion by Justice Louis Brandeis has a major influence on the subsequent development of First Amendment law.

Buck v. Bell: Supreme Court upholds involuntary sterilization of mentally retarded woman.

1929 Japanese American Citizens League (JACL) founded; most important national Japanese American civil rights organization.

1931 *Near v. Minnesota:* first Supreme Court decision upholding freedom of press under the First Amendment. Court rules that prior restraint of the press is unconstitutional.

Stromberg v. California: Supreme Court overturns conviction of Stromberg for displaying a red flag; invalidates part of California Criminal Syndicalism law. Court expands First Amendment protection of political speech.

1931
cont.
Scottsboro case begins; nine young African American men in Alabama accused of raping white woman. Case becomes national civil rights issue and results in several landmark Supreme Court cases.

Fish Committee Investigation; the first congressional committee to investigate alleged un-American activities. Named after Representative Hamilton Fish.

1932
Oliver Wendell Holmes Jr. retires from Supreme Court.

Powell v. Alabama: case involving one of the Scottsboro defendants. Supreme Court overturns convictions on grounds that defendants were denied effective counsel as guaranteed by the Sixth Amendment. Decision marked first time constitutional standards were applied to state criminal proceedings.

1933
Ulysses case: U.S. district court overturns U.S. Customs Bureau ban on the famous James Joyce novel. Decision represents a major expansion of First Amendment protection for sexually oriented literature.

1934
Motion Picture Production Code: movie industry strengthens production code to prohibit allegedly offensive material. Launches a thirty-year period of self-censorship by the industry.

1934
Domestic Nazi groups appear—American sympathizers of German Nazis. Marches and publications raise issue of whether the First Amendment protects hate speech.

1935
Antilynching legislation reintroduced into Congress, but NAACP unable to secure passage of federal law.

National Labor Relations Act (Wagner Act) passed; guarantees freedom of speech and association to workers in their efforts to form labor unions.

1936
U.S. v. One Package: Supreme Court strikes down U.S. Customs Bureau restrictions on importing contraceptives.

President Roosevelt gives FBI Director J. Edgar Hoover a verbal directive to investigate "subversive activities." Spying on political groups resumes.

1937 *De Jonge v. Oregon:* Supreme Court overturns conviction of a Communist for organizing a political rally. Case marks important expansion of First Amendment protection for unpopular political views.

Roosevelt's "Court-packing" plan: president proposes to expand size of Supreme Court. Plan fails in the face of strong public opposition.

Hugo Black appointed to Supreme Court; becomes one of the great civil libertarians to serve on the Court.

1938 House Un-American Activities Committee (HUAC) created; investigates political beliefs and associations, raising issue of scope of legislative inquiry into speech and association.

National Organization for Decent Literature (NODL) founded; leads national campaign to censor literature with sexual content.

Carolene Products decision: Supreme Court explains its role in protecting political and civil liberties.

Missouri ex. rel. Gaines v. Canada: Supreme Court rules that state of Missouri must admit African American to state law school.

Lovell v. Griffin: first of many cases involving Jehovah's Witnesses. Court strikes down Georgia ordinance prohibiting the distribution of "literature of any kind" without a city manager's permit, ruling that the law is a violation of religious freedom.

1939 NAACP Legal Defense Fund (LDF) established; creates a tax-exempt organization to handle civil rights litigation. Directed by Thurgood Marshall, the group leads constitutional challenge to racial segregation.

1939
cont.
Hague v. CIO: Supreme Court invalidates repressive actions of Jersey City's Mayor Hague, establishing freedom of assembly in public forums.

American Library Association Library Bill of Rights: responding to Nazi suppression of free use of libraries in Germany, ALA adopts Bill of Rights for libraries.

Civil Liberties Unit created in U.S. Department of Justice; first effort by U.S. government to affirmatively defend civil rights. It is the forerunner of the present Civil Rights Division.

Louis Brandeis retires from Supreme Court; Brandeis was one of the first two civil libertarian Justices on the Supreme Court. Felix Frankfurter appointed to his seat.

1940
Smith Act: Congress passes law forbidding advocacy of overthrowing the government and membership in organizations that advocate government overthrow.

Cantwell v. Connecticut: Supreme Court upholds free speech rights of Jehovah's Witnesses on grounds of free exercise of religion.

American Association of University Professors issues Statement on Academic Freedom and Tenure; principles of academic freedom accepted by major colleges and universities.

1941
Zechariah Chafee publishes *Free Speech in the United States,* revised and expanded version of *Freedom of Speech* (1920), an extremely influential book on free speech.

Edwards v. California: Supreme Court declares unconstitutional a California law prohibiting indigents from moving into the state. Established First Amendment right to travel.

March on Washington Movement: African Americans threaten to march on Washington to protest racial discrimination in employment.

Committee on Fair Employment Practices; first federal effort to eliminate race discrimination in employment, created by President Roosevelt with Executive Order 8802.

"The four freedoms": President Roosevelt defines four freedoms in State of the Union Address: Freedom of Speech, Freedom from Want, Freedom of Religion, Freedom from Fear.

1942   Japanese American Evacuation and Internment: President Roosevelt issues Executive Order 9066 authorizing military to evacuate Japanese Americans from West Coast. Evacuees are interned in relocation centers.

Chaplinsky v. New Hampshire: Supreme Court rules that "fighting words" are not protected by First Amendment.

Congress of Racial Equality (CORE) founded; a national civil rights organization. In Chicago, CORE leads the first "sit-in" to protest segregation in public accommodations.

1943   *Hirabayashi v. United States:* first important Japanese American case. Supreme Court upholds curfew on Japanese Americans.

West Virginia Board of Education v. Barnette: Supreme Court upholds right of Jehovah's Witness schoolchildren to refuse to salute the American flag.

1944   *Korematsu v. United States:* Supreme Court upholds evacuation of Japanese Americans.

Gunnar Myrdal publishes *An American Dilemma,* the first comprehensive study of race relations in the United States.

Smith v. Allwright: early civil rights victory invalidates Texas's "white primary," which excluded African Americans from primary elections, as a violation of the right to vote under the Fifteenth Amendment.

1945   New York State creates the first permanent Fair Employment Practices Commission to investigate allegations of discrimination in employment.

        Massachusetts eliminates prohibition on married women as public school teachers.

        New York City Mayor Fiorello LaGuardia leads campaign against the play *Trio* because of its explicit treatment of homosexuality.

1946   U.S. District Court decision ends segregation of Mexican American public school students in California.

        Supreme Court overturns U.S. Post Office ban on the magazine *Esquire,* ruling that it cannot ban a publication from the mails without granting the publisher a formal hearing (*Hanegan v.* Esquire).

1947   *Everson v. Board of Education:* first important separation of church and state case. Supreme Court enunciates principle of "wall of separation" between church and state.

        Cold War anti-Communist hysteria begins. President Truman creates Federal Loyalty Program. Attorney General publishes list of subversive organizations. House Un-American Activities Committee investigates alleged Communist influence in Hollywood. Hollywood blacklist of suspected Communists begins.

        To Secure These Rights: report of the President Truman Committee on Civil Rights; advocates equality for African Americans.

        Journey of Reconciliation: first "freedom ride." CORE organizes bus ride to protest segregation in interstate travel through southern states.

        Shelley v. Kraemer: Supreme Court declares unconstitutional private covenants requiring racial discrimination in sale of housing.

Americans United for Separation of Church and State founded; public interest group advocating separation of church and state.

1948   Universal Declaration of Human Rights: United Nations adopts statement on human rights. Heavily influenced by U.S. Bill of Rights.

Alexander Meiklejohn publishes *Free Speech and Its Relation to Self-Government*, the first important theory of the First Amendment.

McCollum v. Board of Education: Supreme Court rules that Illinois "released time" law represents an unconstitutional establishment of religion.

1949   President Truman orders end to racial segregation in U.S. military forces.

Terminiello v. Chicago: Supreme Court overturns conviction of Chicago priest convicted of giving a racist, anti-Semitic speech, ruling that First Amendment protects provocative speech.

1950   Senator Joseph R. McCarthy launches anti-Communist crusade.

Internal Security Act (also known as McCarran Act): federal law requiring Communists and Communist organizations to register with the government. Also provides for emergency detention of alleged subversives in case of national emergency.

Sweatt v. Painter: Supreme Court requires Texas to admit African Americans to previously all-white law school despite creation of separate black law school.

United Nations Educational, Scientific and Cultural Organization (UNESCO) issues Statement on Race; UN statement by leading scientists challenging traditional racist views on differences among races.

1951   *Dennis v. United States:* Supreme Court upholds conviction of Communist Party leaders under Smith Act.

Mattachine Society founded; first organization to fight for civil rights of homosexuals.

1952   *Zorach v. Clauson:* Supreme Court upholds constitutionality of New York state law allowing public school students released time to study religion.

Beauharnais v. Illinois: Supreme Court upholds constitutionality of Illinois "group libel" law.

Burstyn v. Wilson: Supreme Court rules that motion pictures are protected by First Amendment.

1953   Earl Warren appointed chief justice of U.S. Supreme Court; leads Court in expansion of civil liberties.

1954   *Brown v. Board of Education:* Supreme Court declares racially "separate but equal" public schools unconstitutional.

Comics Code Authority: publishers of comic books create voluntary censorship system.

1955   Montgomery bus boycott begins; grassroots challenge to racial segregation in public transportation. Civil rights movement enters new militant phase. Martin Luther King emerges as national civil rights leader.

Samuel A. Stouffer publishes *Communism, Conformity, and Civil Liberties,* a study of public attitudes toward free speech and other civil liberties issues during the Cold War.

1956   William J. Brennan appointed to Supreme Court; emerges as intellectual leader of civil libertarian wing of Court.

1957   *Roth v. United States:* first important obscenity case in Supreme Court. Court attempts to define obscenity.

Citizens for Decency through Law (CDL) founded; national organization devoted to promoting censorship of indecent literature.

1957 Civil Rights Act creates U.S. Civil Rights Commission, agency empowered to investigate race discrimination.

1958   *NAACP v. Alabama:* Supreme Court enunciates principle of freedom of association under First Amendment.

Cooper v. Aaron: Supreme Court rules that government officials are required to enforce Court decisions. Rejects challenge to implementation of *Brown* decision.

Kent v. Dulles: Supreme Court rules that Constitution protects right to travel overseas.

Speiser v. Randall: Supreme Court overturns California law requiring veterans to sign a loyalty oath to qualify for a property tax exemption.

1960   Sit-ins begin in Greensboro, North Carolina. Civil Rights Movement enters new militant phase that raises many important civil liberties issues in following years.

1960 Civil Rights Act strengthens 1957 Civil Rights Act.

1961   President Kennedy appoints President's Commission on the Status of Women (report published 1963).

Freedom rides: civil rights activists travel on buses in southern states to protest racial segregation in interstate travel.

Mapp v. Ohio: Supreme Court rules that Fourth Amendment bars use of illegally seized evidence in a state criminal trial. Applies Fourth Amendment to states.

1962   *Baker v. Carr:* Supreme Court rules unconstitutional legislative districts with extremely unequal populations.

1962
cont.

Engel v. Vitale: Supreme Court rules that school-sponsored prayer in public schools is an unconstitutional violation of the separation of church and state.

Morris L. Ernst and Alan U. Schwartz publish *Privacy: The Right to Be Let Alone,* an important early book on the right to privacy.

1963

Gideon v. Wainwright: Supreme Court rules that all felony defendants are entitled to an attorney under the Sixth Amendment.

Abington School District v. Schempp: Supreme Court rules that school-sponsored Bible reading in public schools violates the First Amendment.

March on Washington: massive civil rights march on Washington, D.C., on August 23. Martin Luther King delivers "I Have a Dream" speech.

Betty Friedan publishes *The Feminine Mystique,* the book credited with launching the modern women's rights movement.

1964

Civil Rights Act: comprehensive federal law outlawing discrimination in public accommodations and employment.

Equal Employment Opportunity Commission (EEOC), an administrative agency to fight employment discrimination, is created by 1964 Civil Rights Act.

Heart of Atlanta Motel v. Atlanta: Supreme Court upholds public accommodations provision of 1964 Civil Rights Act.

New York Times *v. Sullivan:* major statement of the philosophy of the First Amendment. Court rules that public officials can sue for damages for defamation only if they can prove "actual malice." Major case arising from civil rights movement.

Reynolds v. Sims: Supreme Court holds that legislative districts must be apportioned on the basis of "one man–one vote."

Free speech movement: students at University of California, Berkeley, protest restrictions on political activity on campus. Beginning of 1960s campus protest movements.

1965   Voting Rights Act outlaws discrimination in election practices and procedures.

Executive Order 11246 requires employers receiving federal funds to undertake affirmative action to ensure equal employment opportunity.

Griswold v. Connecticut: Supreme Court invalidates Connecticut law prohibiting sale of contraceptives, enunciates constitutional right of privacy.

United States escalates involvement in Vietnam War. Protests against the war raise many civil liberties issues in the next ten years.

United States v. Seeger: Supreme Court establishes broad definition of religious belief and expands right of conscientious objection to military service.

Lamont v. Postmaster General: Supreme Court strikes down federal law requiring postmaster general to detain and destroy unsealed mail from abroad deemed to be "Communist political propaganda."

1966   National Organization for Women (NOW) founded; national organization to fight for rights of women. Beginning of new phase of women's rights movement.

Freedom of Information Act (FOIA): federal law guaranteeing public access to government records.

Miranda v. Arizona: Supreme Court expands Fifth Amendment rights of criminal suspects. Rules that police must

1966
cont.   advise suspects of their right to remain silent and their right to an attorney.

Lawrence Lader publishes *Abortion,* the first book to study the abortion issue and advocate legalized abortion.

1967   *Loving v. Virginia:* Supreme Court rules unconstitutional a Virginia law banning marriage between people of difference races.

Thurgood Marshall appointed to the Supreme Court; former legal director of the NAACP Legal Defense Fund becomes the first African American justice of the Supreme Court.

In re Gault: Supreme Court rules that defendants in juvenile court have a right to basic due process guarantees.

Keyishian v. Board of Regents: Supreme Court invalidates law requiring public school teachers to sign a loyalty oath; holds that public employment is not a "privilege" to which government can attach whatever conditions it pleases.

Office of Intellectual Freedom created by American Library Association to fight censorship.

Allen F. Westin publishes *Privacy and Freedom,* the first comprehensive study of privacy in the United States.

Whitus v. Georgia: Supreme Court invalidates systematic exclusion of African Americans from local grand juries and trial juries.

1968   Kerner Commission Report: report of the National Advisory Commission on Civil Disorders, appointed in response to urban racial disorders. Recommends actions to eliminate race discrimination.

United States v. O'Brien: Supreme Court upholds the conviction of antiwar protester for burning his draft card.

Rejects the argument that draft card burning is symbolic expression protected by First Amendment.

Epperson v. Arkansas: Supreme Court declares unconstitutional a state law banning the teaching of evolution.

Terry v. Ohio: Supreme Court rules that police may frisk suspects without a warrant to find weapons.

Fair Housing Act: federal law prohibits discrimination in private housing transactions.

National Abortion Rights Action League (NARAL) founded; abortion providers create organization to defend reproductive rights.

Americans for Effective Law Enforcement (AELE) founded; organization opposes Supreme Court rulings protecting rights of criminal suspects.

American Indian Movement (AIM) founded; militant national American Indian civil rights organization.

Indian Civil Rights Act; confers civil rights on persons subject to tribal jurisdiction and authorizes federal courts to intervene in certain intertribal disputes.

National Council of La Raza founded; national Hispanic/Latino civil rights organization.

Mexican American Defense Fund founded; Hispanic/Latino legal defense organization.

Washington v. Lee: Supreme Court declares racially segregated prisons unconstitutional.

1969 Earl Warren retires as chief justice. Warren Burger appointed chief justice. Court enters more conservative phase.

Stonewall riot: New York City police raid Stonewall, gay

1969
cont.
bar (night of June 27–28). Beginning of modern gay and lesbian rights movement.

Brandenburg v. Ohio: Supreme Court rules that First Amendment protects offensive speech except where it is an incitement to "imminent lawless action."

Tinker v. Des Moines School District: Supreme Court rules that the First Amendment guarantees right of public school students to wear armbands protesting war in Vietnam.

1970
Thomas I. Emerson publishes *The System of Freedom of Expression,* a comprehensive theory of the First Amendment.

Report of the Commission on Obscenity and Pornography: federal commission rejects censorship as response to sexually oriented forms of expression.

Fair Credit and Reporting Act: federal law gives citizens right to copies of financial records maintained by private organizations and to request that inaccurate information be corrected.

Creation Science Research Center founded; organization created by opponents of evolution to promote scientific support for Biblical version of creation.

Mental Health Law Project created; nonprofit organization to defend the rights of mentally ill persons.

Walz v. Tax Commissioner: Supreme Court rules that tax exemptions for churches do not violate the Establishment Clause of the First Amendment.

Goldberg v. Kelly: Supreme Court rules that welfare recipients are entitled to due process, including notice and a hearing, before the state can terminate their benefits.

1971
Reed v. Reed: first Supreme Court decision upholding equality for women. Holds that a law giving a preference to males violates the Equal Protection clause. The first

ruling that sex-based classifications violate the Equal Protection Clause of the Fourteenth Amendment.

Lemon v. Kurtzman: Supreme Court defines test for determining whether state aid to public schools violates the Establishment Clause of the First Amendment.

New York Times *v. United States:* Supreme Court overturns federal government ban on *Times* publication of the *Pentagon Papers.*

Cohen v. California: Supreme Court reverses conviction of anti–Vietnam War protester; speech that is vulgar ("Fuck the Draft") it is protected by the First Amendment.

ACLU creates Women's Rights Project.

Native American Rights Fund (NARF) founded; legal defense organization for American Indians.

1972   *Furman v. Georgia:* Supreme Court declares that capital punishment laws, as applied, are unconstitutional under the Eighth Amendment, but does not declare capital punishment per se unconstitutional.

Wisconsin v. Yoder: Supreme Court upholds right of Amish parents not to be compelled to send their children to public school beyond the eighth grade under the Free Exercise clause of the First Amendment.

Eisenstadt v. Baird: Supreme Court declares unconstitutional a state law prohibiting distribution of contraceptives to unmarried persons.

Wyatt v. Stickney: federal court in Alabama establishes constitutional right to treatment for involuntarily committed mentally ill persons.

Title IX Amendment to Education Act; federal law bans sex discrimination in education. Plays important role in growth of women's athletic programs.

1972 Equal Rights Amendment (ERA) approved by Congress;
cont. proposed amendment to the Constitution to guarantee
equal rights for women. Not enough states ratify to
adopt it.

Watergate: burglary of Democratic Party offices by persons working for Nixon administration. Scandal exposes
abuses of powers by the president and other federal officials.

ACLU creates National Prison Project; leads concerted
effort to secure rights of prisoners.

Equal Employment Opportunity Act strengthens role of
EEOC in fighting employment discrimination.

First municipal ordinances outlawing discrimination on
the basis of sexual orientation are passed in Ann Arbor
and East Lansing, Michigan.

1973 *Roe v. Wade:* Supreme Court establishes constitutional
right to abortion under right to privacy principle.

National Right to Life Committee established; leading
organization opposed to legalized abortion.

Miller v. California: Supreme Court establishes three-part
test for defining obscenity.

Lambda Legal Defense and Education Fund established;
organization to defend legal rights of gay and lesbian
people.

National Gay Task Force established; national gay and
lesbian civil rights organization.

Holtzman v. Schlesinger: Representative Elizabeth Holtzman sues government to halt the bombing of Cambodia
as an unconstitutional presidential usurpation of Congress's authority to declare war.

War Powers Act: federal law designed to limit power of the president to wage war without approval of Congress.

Pacific Legal Foundation founded; conservative public interest group; opposes many civil liberties protections.

1974 *United States. v. Nixon:* Supreme Court orders President Nixon to turn over tapes recorded in his office on which the Watergate break-in is discussed; rejects president's claim of executive privilege.

Facing impeachment and probable conviction, President Nixon resigns.

Family Educational Rights and Privacy Act: first major federal law designed to protect individual privacy with regard to collection and use of data on individuals by federal agencies. Buckley Amendment to the law governs student records by colleges and universities.

National Coalition Against Censorship founded; national organization leads campaign against censorship.

Heritage Foundation established; conservative public interest group; opposes many civil liberties protections.

American Psychiatric Association removes homosexuality from its list of mental disorders.

1975 *Taylor v. Louisiana:* Supreme Court declares unconstitutional a state law excluding women from jury duty.

Eagle Forum founded; national organization opposed to passage of ERA.

U.S. Civil Service Commission eliminates ban on employment of homosexuals.

House Un-American Activities Committee (HUAC) abolished.

1975
cont. *O'Connor v. Donaldson:* Supreme Court establishes "right to treatment," ruling that state cannot hold a nonviolent mental patient.

1976 *Buckley v. Valeo:* Supreme Court invalidates part and upholds part of 1971 law regulating political campaign contributions and spending.

Hyde Amendment: federal law prohibits federal funds for abortion services.

Gregg v. Georgia: Supreme Court rules capital punishment constitutional provided sentencing decisions are guided by standards.

Sunshine Act: federal "open meetings" law guarantees public right to attend meetings of various federal governing boards.

Women Against Violence Against Women (WAVAW) holds first demonstration; beginning of feminist antipornography movement.

Washington Legal Foundation; conservative legal foundation fights many civil liberties protections.

1977 Skokie crisis: American Nazi group seeks to demonstrate in Skokie, Illinois, a predominantly Jewish community. Major controversy over First Amendment protection of offensive speech. Seventh Circuit Court of Appeals decisions affirming First Amendment rights of offensive speech upheld by U.S. Supreme Court.

1978 *Regents of University of California v. Bakke:* first important affirmative action case. Supreme Court rules that university may take race into account as one factor in admissions decisions.

Pregnancy Discrimination Act: federal law requires employers to treat pregnant women who are able to work the same as other workers.

American Indian Religious Freedom Act: federal law designed to protect religious freedom of Native Americans.

1979 Catharine MacKinnon publishes *Sexual Harassment of Working Women;* defines modern concept of sexual harassment as employment discrimination.

Moral Majority founded; Christian-based advocacy organization challenges many new civil liberties, including abortion rights, gay rights, First Amendment protection for pornography.

Women Against Pornography founded; feminist group opposed to pornography.

United States v. Progressive: *Progressive Magazine* prosecuted for publishing alleged "secret" of how to build a hydrogen bomb.

Harris v. McRae: Supreme Court upholds Hyde Amendment (1976) prohibiting federal funds for abortion services.

Disability Rights Education Fund founded; national civil rights organization for disabled persons.

1980s AIDS epidemic begins; raises new issues of privacy and equal treatment.

1980 People for the American Way founded; national organization to defend civil liberties, especially abortion rights and separation of church and state.

Civil Rights of Institutionalized Persons Act: federal law gives U.S. attorney general right to sue prisons and other institutions for violating rights of inmates or patients.

1981 Sandra Day O'Connor appointed to Supreme Court; first woman appointed to serve on the Court.

1981 Arkansas Balanced Treatment Law: state law requires
cont. teaching of creation science in addition to theory of evolution.

Rostker v. Goldberg: Supreme Court rules that male-only
military draft is constitutional.

1982 ERA expires; effort to amend U.S. Constitution to guarantee equality on the basis of sex fails to gain ratification.

Island Trees School District v. Pico: Supreme Court rules
that public schools cannot remove materials from school
library simply because they do not like the content of the
material.

Rutherford Institute founded; conservative public interest group; fights many civil liberties protection issues.

1983 A national survey of public attitudes about civil liberties,
*Dimensions of Tolerance: What Americans Believe About
Civil Liberties,* is published.

Wisconsin enacts first state law prohibiting discrimination on the basis of sexual orientation.

Bob Jones University v. United States: Supreme Court upholds revocation of tax-exempt status of the university
because of its policies of race discrimination.

1984 Indianapolis antipornography ordinance enacted; law
creates right of women to sue for harm by pornography.

Bail Reform Act: Congress authorizes federal courts to
deny bail to "dangerous" criminal defendants.

Berkeley, California, enacts the first ordinance recognizing domestic partnerships among gays and lesbians.

1980s– Campus hate speech code movement; college and uni-
1990s versity groups seek policies punishing hate speech.

1984   U.S. district court judge Marilyn Hall Patel vacates conviction of Fred Korematsu for refusing to relocate to a Japanese American internment camp during World War II.

Lynch v. Donnelly: Supreme Court upholds constitutionality of religious display in front of a public building.

1985   *American Booksellers Association v. Hudnut:* appeals court declares Indianapolis antipornography law unconstitutional.

Parent's Music Resource Center (PMRC) established; organization created to fight offensive recorded music.

Wallace v. Jaffree: Supreme Court invalidates Alabama "moment of silence" law as violation of Establishment Clause.

1986   *Bowers v. Hardwick:* Supreme Court refuses to extend right of privacy to private consensual homosexual acts.

Batson v. Kentucky: Supreme Court rules that potential jurors may not be excluded on the basis of race.

Meritor Savings Bank v. Vinson: Supreme Court rules that sexual harassment is a form of employment discrimination under Title VII of the 1964 Civil Rights Act.

Attorney general's Commission on Pornography *Final Report* recommends new laws and greater efforts to suppress production and distribution of sexually explicit materials.

1987   200th anniversary of the ratification of the U.S. Constitution.

Robert Bork nominated to Supreme Court. Major controversy over Bork's views on civil liberties issues, especially abortion rights; nomination rejected.

1987 ACLU Lesbian and Gay Rights Project established.
cont.

McCleskey v. Kemp: Supreme Court rules that statistical evidence of race discrimination in death penalty sentencing not sufficient to overturn death sentence of specific plaintiff.

1988 Civil Liberties Act: Congress votes compensation of $20,000 per person to interned Japanese Americans.

Hazelwood v. Kuhlmeier: Supreme Court upholds right of school officials to censor high school newspaper.

Hustler Magazine *v. Falwell:* Supreme Court upholds First Amendment protection for offensive expression.

1989 *Texas v. Johnson:* Supreme Court rules that the First Amendment protects the right to burn the American flag and declares state flag protection law unconstitutional. Congress passes Flag Protection Act; federal law punishing burning of the American flag declared unconstitutional.

Doe v. University of Michigan: U.S. district court declares University of Michigan campus speech code a violation of the First Amendment.

1990 Americans with Disabilities Act (ADA): federal law bans discrimination on the basis of a disability.

Cruzan v. Director: first important "right-to-die" case. Court upholds power of state to maintain medical treatment against wishes of parents.

Native American Graves Protection and Repatriation Act: federal law protects Native American grave sites and requires return of bones and other burial artifacts that are held by non–Native Americans.

United States v. Eichman: Supreme Court rules 1989 federal Flag Protection Act unconstitutional.

Employment Division v. Smith: Supreme Court rules that Free Exercise Clause of First Amendment does not protect right of Native American to use peyote.

Hodgson v. Minnesota: Supreme Court invalidates requirement that minors seeking an abortion must notify both parents but upholds one-parent requirement.

1991   200th anniversary of the adoption of the Bill of Rights.

Communitarian Platform adopted; statement of principles by Communitarian Network, seeking to balance individual rights with social responsibilities.

Rust v. Sullivan: Supreme Court upholds federal regulations forbidding doctors working in federally funded programs from discussing abortion with patients (so-called "gag order").

UWM Post v. University of Wisconsin: U.S. district court declares unconstitutional University of Wisconsin student code of conduct that punishes hate speech.

1992   *RAV v. City of St. Paul:* Supreme Court overturns conviction of juvenile charged with burning a cross.

Planned Parenthood v. Casey: Supreme Court upholds parts of Pennsylvania abortion restrictions but affirms "central holding" of *Roe v. Wade.*

1993   *Wisconsin v. Mitchell:* Supreme Court upholds state " hate crimes" law establishing harsher penalties for crimes motivated by bias.

Religious Freedom Restoration Act: Congress seeks to overturn 1990 Supreme Court decision in *Employment Division v. Smith* and to protect free exercise of religion.

Shaw v. Reno: Supreme Court invalidates North Carolina congressional redistricting plan designed to increase racial minority representation in Congress.

1993
cont.
"Don't ask, don't tell" policy: U.S. military branches refuse to accept homosexuals; adopt Clinton administration's compromise, "don't ask, don't tell" policy.

1994
Freedom of Access Act (FACE): federal law establishes penalties for interfering with access to abortion clinics.

1995
Nadine Strossen, president of ACLU, publishes *Defending Pornography*, advocating First Amendment protection for sexually oriented materials.

U.S. Department of Education issues *Religious Expression in Public Schools*, federal guidelines on religious activities by students in public schools.

1996
Proposition 209: California voters approve referendum ending use of racial preferences by state agencies, including University of California.

Romer v. Evans: Supreme Court overturns amendment to Colorado state constitution prohibiting local gay and lesbian rights ordinances.

Defense of Marriage Act (DOMA): federal law holds that states do not have to recognize same-sex marriages from other states.

United States v. Virginia: Supreme Court declares male-only policy of Virginia Military Institute (VMI), a state school, unconstitutional.

Communications Decency Act (CDA): Congress enacts law restricting "indecent" material directed toward children on the Internet.

1997
Reno v. ACLU: Supreme Court declares Communications Decency Act unconstitutional.

1999
ACLU issues report, *Driving while Black*, exposing problem of racial profiling—police stopping drivers because of their race or ethnicity.

Chicago v. Morales: Supreme Court invalidates Chicago antigang loitering law.

2000   Nebraska amends state constitution to prohibit same-sex marriages.

Vermont passes law recognizing civil unions between people of the same sex.

Stenberg v. Carhart: Supreme Court declares unconstitutional a Nebraska law prohibiting "partial birth abortion."

Governor of Illinois imposes moratorium on death penalty in the state.

2001   Terrorist attack on World Trade Center in New York City and Pentagon outside Washington, D.C.

Congress passes USA Patriot Act, which is intended to expand the power of the federal government to fight terrorism. Civil libertarians regard the law as a threat to civil liberties.

2002   *Zelman v. Simmons-Harris:* Supreme Court upholds constitutionality of Ohio law providing public funds (vouchers) for students to attend private schools, including religious schools.

2003   University of Michigan affirmative action cases: in two decisions, Supreme Court upholds constitutionality of affirmative action as long as race is only one of several factors used in college admissions cases. The Court declares unconstitutional an admission program that awards extra points to all minority applicants.

Lawrence v. Texas: Supreme Court declares Texas sodomy law unconstitutional under broad right to privacy; decision reverses 1986 ruling in *Bowers v. Hardwick.*

Massachusetts Supreme Court rules that marriages between people of the same sex are protected by the state constitution.

4

Key People and Concepts

Anti-Communist Hysteria in the Cold War

The Cold War is generally regarded as a period of one of the greatest assaults on civil liberties in American history. The Cold War was defined in terms of an anti-Communist movement that included both opposition to Communist governments abroad and attempts to suppress Communist activity in the United States. Civil libertarians generally believe the attacks on domestic Communism involved violations of the freedoms of speech and association of numerous law-abiding individuals who were neither Communists nor threats to national security.

The period of the Cold War cannot be defined by precise dates. Usually it is considered to have begun in 1947 and ended with the collapse of the Soviet Union in 1989. Anti-Communism, however, emerged as a strong force after the Russian Revolution of 1917 and continued through the 1920s and 1930s. Anti-Communism intensified with the creation of the House Un-American Activities Committee (HUAC) as a permanent committee in 1938 and passage of the Smith Act in 1940, which outlawed advocacy of the violent overthrow of the U.S. government.

The Cold War involved a number of specific laws and programs that threatened civil liberties. In 1947 President Harry Truman created the Federal Loyalty Program, designed to eliminate potential security risks from federal employment. Federal employees were investigated on the basis of their membership in certain political groups or because of certain views they held. One of the major abuses of the program was that people were often subject to anonymous allegations by accusers whom they did not have an opportunity to confront. As a part of the program, the attorney general published a "Guide to Subversive Organizations." Membership in any of these organizations was likely to cause a person to labeled disloyal, even if the membership had been only for a brief period and occurred many years earlier.

Individuals were often labeled disloyal or possible Communists because they advocated certain political views that coincided with those of the Communist Party. Thus, for example, advocates of "peace" or "civil rights" were attacked as Communists because the Communist Party also advocated these goals.

HUAC investigated the political beliefs and associations of individuals alleged to be Communists or associated with Communist issues or organizations. Persons called before the committee as witnesses were often stigmatized as Communists simply because they had been called to testify, and many people lost their jobs as a result. HUAC investigations of alleged Communist influence in Hollywood, for example, led to a movie industry "blacklist" that denied employment to actors, writers, and directors who were suspected of being Communists.

Several states enacted loyalty oaths that required public employees to swear that they were not members of the Communist Party. Many colleges and universities fired faculty members who refused to sign loyalty oaths or were accused of being Communists. As in the case of federal employees, often accusations were made secretly, and people had no opportunity to confront their accusers and rebut the allegations. Other colleges and universities refused to hire people because of their actual or alleged political beliefs. These policies had a serious impact on teaching and research. Many scholars, for example, shied away from research that might lead to criticism of U.S. foreign policy out of fear of being labeled "un-American." Such fears also prevented scholars from conducting any serious research on the Central Intelligence Agency (CIA) and the Federal Bureau of Investigation (FBI).

The Smith Act made it illegal to advocate the violent overthrow of the government or to belong to an organization that advocated it. In 1949 the federal government prosecuted and convicted the top leaders of the American Communist Party under the Smith Act. The Supreme Court upheld the convictions and the constitutionality of the Smith Act in the 1951 case of *Dennis v. United States*.

Accusations of disloyalty and Communist sympathies reached their highest degree of recklessness with the work of Senator Joseph McCarthy, a Republican from Wisconsin. McCarthy's career as an anti-Communist began in 1950 with a famous speech in which he claimed to have a list of Communists employed by the federal government. For almost five years, McCarthy was almost completely immune from criticism. The news media reported even his wildest accusations without any fact-checking. The demise McCarthy's career began in 1954. Journalist Edward R. Murrow broadcast a critical two-part report on his tactics early that year. Later that year the U.S. Senate officially censured him for bringing the Senate into disrepute because of his tactics. McCarthy then quickly faded into insignificance.

Initially, the Supreme Court upheld the constitutionality of most Cold War anti-Communist measures, as it had with the Smith Act. By the late 1950s, however, the Court began to limit the scope of many anti-Communist measures and to define broader First Amendment protections for unpopular ideas. The anti-Communist hysteria of the Cold War waned notably in the 1960s. The House of Representatives abolished the Un-American Activities Committee in the 1970s. Revelations by investigative journalists, often using the Freedom of Information Act (FOIA), along with some congressional investigations revealed a wide pattern of illegal activity by both the FBI and the CIA during the Cold War. Nonetheless, anti-Communist feeling never completely disappeared from U.S. politics.

Roger Baldwin (1884–1981)

Roger Nash Baldwin was the founder of the American Civil Liberties Union (ACLU) and served as its director from 1920 to 1950. During that time, Baldwin was widely regarded as the foremost spokesperson for civil liberties in the United States.

Baldwin was born in 1884 in Wellesley Hills, Massachusetts, to an upper-middle-class family that traced its heritage back to the earliest colonists in America. He graduated from Harvard College in 1905 and received a master's degree the following year. Instead of following his father into business, he moved to St. Louis to become a social worker. During his years in St. Louis he became a prominent social activist involved in many social justice causes, including establishing the city's first juvenile court.

In early 1917, as the United States was about to enter World War I, he moved to New York City to work with the American Union Against Militarism (AUAM). With Crystal Eastman, the organization's director, he created a Civil Liberties Bureau within the AUAM to defend the rights of conscientious objectors and critics of the war.

During the war Baldwin refused to register for the draft because of his philosophical opposition to military conscription. In 1918 he was convicted and sentenced to prison, where he served eight months. After he was released, he helped organize the ACLU. The Bureau soon became a separate organization, the National Civil Liberties Bureau, which in 1920 evolved into the American Civil Liberties Union (ACLU), with Baldwin as director.

Baldwin's most important contribution to civil liberties lay in his charismatic leadership. He inspired many people to commit themselves to the cause of civil liberties. Among them were many brilliant attorneys who argued civil liberties cases in court, writers who publicized civil liberties issues, and wealthy individuals who contribute funds to the ACLU. Baldwin often described himself as a philosophical anarchist, but he was always an activist rather than a systematic thinker. He never wrote a full statement of his views. His approach to civil liberties could be characterized as a strong distaste for seeing people pushed around by the government or powerful private interests. He was a tireless speaker and author of numerous magazine articles and pamphlets. In those capacities he was the most widely known proponent of civil liberties issues through the 1950s.

During the ACLU's first two decades, Baldwin and other leaders often engaged in direct action, personally challenging restrictions of free speech. Baldwin was himself arrested in Paterson, New Jersey, in 1924 at a demonstration for the rights of workers to form a labor union. He was convicted under an otherwise obsolete 1796 law against unlawful assembly. In 1928 the New Jersey Supreme Court overturned the conviction, which was an early free speech victory for the ACLU.

After stepping down as director of the ACLU in 1950, Baldwin devoted much of his time over the next thirty years to international human rights issues, which had always been one of his great concerns. Baldwin died in 1981.

"Banned in Boston"

The phrase "banned in Boston" originated in that city's long history of censorship of books, plays, movies, and public speakers. The most famous controversy erupted in 1926, when the city banned an issue of *The American Mercury*, H. L. Mencken's magazine, because of an allegedly offensive story. As the censorship struggle escalated, city officials banned books by some of America's greatest novelists, including Ernest Hemingway and Sinclair Lewis. In 1929 the city refused to allow birth control advocate Margaret Sanger to speak. Eventually she appeared at a protest rally organized by the ACLU, in which she sat on the stage with a gag over her mouth while someone else read some of her writings.

As the protest against official censorship continued, the ACLU organized its first national campaign against the censorship of literary works, and sexually oriented works in particular. Although the censorship issue in Boston generated the phrase "banned in Boston," which became nationally popular, the censorship of sexually oriented materials—books, poems, plays, comic books, and movies, was just as great in almost every U.S. city until the 1960s. Even San Francisco, which has long had a reputation as a liberal and tolerant community, prosecuted Lawrence Ferlinghetti, a poet and the owner of the City Lights Book Store in the late 1950s, for publishing Allen Ginsberg's famous Beat Generation poem "Howl." He was acquitted in a celebrated trial involving First Amendment issues.

The city of Boston maintained an active policy of censorship until 1982, when the city's Licensing Division was finally abolished. The last person to head the office, Richard Sinnott, served in that capacity from 1955 until 1982. He died in 2003.

Ruth Bader Ginsburg (1933–)

Ruth Bader Ginsburg is an associate justice of the U.S. Supreme Court, appointed in 1993. She made her greatest contributions to civil liberties earlier in her career as a pioneer in developing constitutional protection for the rights of women.

Justice Ginsburg was born in 1933 in Brooklyn, New York. She graduated from Cornell University in 1954 and received her law degree from Columbia University in 1959. She began teaching law at Rutgers University in 1963 and then at Columbia University in 1971. President Carter appointed her to the U.S. Court of Appeals for the District of Columbia Circuit in 1980, and President Clinton appointed her to the Supreme Court in 1993.

Ginsburg held several important positions with the ACLU, including as general counsel (1973–1980) and, most notably, as director of the ACLU Women's Rights Project in the 1970s. In that role she developed legal strategy, drafted court briefs, and argued the first important women's rights cases decided by the Supreme Court. Ginsburg argued and fought for the principle that women were guaranteed equal protection under the Fourteenth Amendment to the Constitution. The most important cases she was responsible for included *Reed v. Reed* (1971) and *Frontiero v. Richardson* (1973), the first decisions in which the Supreme Court acknowledged constitutional protection for women.

Ginsburg's concern with equality was in part a result of her experiences as a child, when she and her family experienced anti-Semitic prejudice. While on vacation, for example, they encountered hotels that refused to serve Jews. Early in her professional career, Ginsburg also experienced blatant sex discrimination in employment. When she was married and working for the U.S. Social Security System, she was demoted three pay levels after she informed her employer that she was pregnant. Finally, despite having graduated first in her law school class, she was not able to obtain a job with a major law firm.

As a member of the Supreme Court, Justice Ginsburg established a position as a judicial moderate. She usually voted with the liberal bloc on the Court and was generally a strong advocate of equal rights. She was the author of the Court's majority opinion in *United States v. Virginia*, which declared the male-only policy at Virginia Military Institute, a state school, to be unconstitutional. But she has also taken moderate positions on some other issues, which no doubt disappointed her former civil liberties allies.

Japanese American Internment

During World War II the U.S. government evacuated some 120,000 persons of Japanese descent, including about 90,000 Japanese American citizens, from the West Coast and interned them in remote inland camps for the duration of the war. The treatment of the Japanese Americans under this program is widely regarded as the greatest single violation of civil liberties in U.S. history.

President Franklin D. Roosevelt issued Executive Order 9066 on February 19, 1942, authorizing U.S. military authorities to declare certain areas military zones and to evacuate designated people from those areas. The president's order did not mention the Japanese Americans specifically, nor did it mention the detention of people who might be evacuated.

The evacuation of the Japanese Americans began in March 1942 and was completed by early June. Many Japanese Americans had to sell their farms, businesses, or other property under emergency conditions, and it is estimated that collectively they lost a total of $400 million in income and property.

To handle the evacuation, the government created the War Relocation Authority (WRA). Initially, the WRA planned simply to relocate evacuated Japanese Americans to areas away from the West Coast. When the governors of other states objected to receiving them, however, the WRA created ten Relocation Centers to house the Japanese Americans. WRA regulations made it a crime for a relocated person to leave one of the centers. The Relocation Centers thus became internment camps, or concentration camps.

Because of a deeply ingrained loyalty to the United States and fear of reprisals, only a handful of Japanese Americans challenged the evacuation and internment. The American Civil Liberties Union (ACLU) brought a series of challenges to the government's program to the U.S. Supreme Court. In the first important case, *Hirabayashi v. United States* (1943), the Court unanimously upheld the constitutionality of a curfew placed on Japanese Americans, justifying it as a legitimate wartime measure. In the key passage, Justice Harlan Fiske Stone wrote that "it is not for any court to sit in review of the wisdom of [military authorities] or substitute its judgment for theirs." Several justices were deeply disturbed by the program but chose not to dissent. In *Korematsu v. United States* (1944), by a 6–3 vote, the Court upheld the constitutionality of the evacuation of the Japanese Americans. Again the Court held that the program was justified by a "military imperative." This time, three justices dissented, however. Justice Frank Murphy argued that the evacuation "falls into the ugly abyss of racism." Also in dissent, Justice Robert Jackson warned that the extraordinary powers granted to the government by the majority opinion "lies about like a loaded weapon ready for the hand of any authority that can bring forward a plausible claim of an urgent need." The government decided to end the program in late 1944 and soon began releasing the surviving internees. In September 1945 all formal restrictions on Japanese Americans were ended (with the exception of some still held for alleged disloyalty or criminal behavior).

The evacuation and internment of the Japanese Americans was recognized as a shameful violation of civil liberties almost as soon as the program was ended. No legal scholar has written an article supporting the Supreme Court's decisions in *Hirabayashi* and *Korematsu*. In 1984, on the basis of newly discovered evidence that the federal government had deliberately withheld information from the Supreme Court in the original *Korematsu* case, U.S. District Court Judge Marilyn Hall Patel overturned the conviction of Fred Korematsu for refusing to relocate to an internment camp. In 1988, in an attempt to redress the harm done by the internment program, Congress enacted the Civil Liberties Act, which awarded $20,000 to each surviving person who had been interned.

Mildred and Richard Loving

Richard and Mildred Loving were an interracial couple who married in 1958. They married in Washington, D.C., because Virginia, where they lived, had an antimiscegenation law that prohibited interracial marriages. When they moved back to Virginia they were prosecuted and convicted for violating the law and sentenced to one year in jail. The state offered to suspend the sentence if they promised to leave the state. They moved back to Washington, D.C., and filed a suit challenging the Virginia law. In 1967, the U.S. Supreme Court unanimously ruled the law unconstitutional. The decision invalidated similar laws in fifteen other states.

Thurgood Marshall (1908–1993)

Thurgood Marshall, an attorney, spent the first half of his career as the chief legal official of the NAACP (1938–1961), arguing and winning many of the most important civil rights cases decided by the Supreme Court. Eventually Marshall himself was appointed to the Court, where he served as the first African American justice of the U.S. Supreme Court (1967–1991).

Marshall was born in 1908, the great-grandson of a slave. He graduated from Lincoln University in 1930 and received his law degree from Howard University in 1933, graduating first in his law school class. The following year, he went to work for the NAACP. In 1938 Marshall became the NAACP's chief legal official and in 1939 assumed the title of Director of the NAACP Legal Defense and Education Fund. In that capacity he was responsible for coordinating a legal assault on racial segregation. In a truly remarkable record, Marshall won twenty-nine of the thirty-two cases he argued before the Supreme Court.

The crowning achievement of Marshall's NAACP career was the landmark Supreme Court decision in *Brown v. Board of Education* (1954) declaring racially segregated public schools unconstitutional. The case was the culmination of many years of planning, including other cases challenging racial segregation. Marshall was principally responsible for selecting the cases to be brought into the courts, writing the briefs, and arguing the cases in court. Prior to the *Brown* decision, Marshall won landmark cases ending racial segregation in university law school admissions and eliminating the so-called "white primary," through which African Americans were barred from participating in Democratic Party primary elections in southern states.

In 1961 President John F. Kennedy appointed Marshall to the U.S. Circuit Court of Appeals. The appointment met strong opposition from southerners in the U.S. Senate and was delayed for many months. Marshall finally became a judge in 1962. In 1965 President Lyndon Johnson appointed him solicitor general of the United States, the first African American to serve in that position. In 1967 President Johnson appointed Marshall to the Supreme Court.

On the Court, Marshall became a staunch member of the liberal civil liberties and civil rights–oriented bloc of justices. In addition to his advocacy of racial justice, Marshall was a strong advocate of expanding the First Amendment protection of freedom of expression and of guaranteeing the right to privacy. In *Stanley v. Georgia* (1969) he held that individuals have a right to possess obscene materials in their own homes. And in *Police Department of Chicago v. Mosley* (1972) he held that the government may not favor some kinds of speech over others. He was one of only two justices to argue that the death penalty was unconstitutional per se as a violation of the Eighth Amendment prohibition on cruel and unusual punishment *(Furman v. Georgia,*

1972). For most of Marshall's last decade on the Court, as the liberal bloc dwindled in size, he was almost always in dissent on civil rights, civil liberties, and criminal justice decisions. Marshall retired from the Supreme Court in 1991, and he died in 1993.

George Mason (1725–1792)

George Mason is one of the nearly forgotten figures of the American Revolution. He is most important as the principal author of Virginia's 1776 Declaration of Rights (see Chapter 5 for the text), which served as a model for part of the Declaration of Independence and later the Bill of Rights.

Mason was born in 1725 and eventually became one of the richest landholders in Virginia. In the years before the revolution he was active in politics, serving as a judge, as an official of the city of Alexandria, and in the Virginia House of Burgesses. He continued his political activity after the revolution but retired in 1780 after becoming disgusted with politics. Mason returned to public life in 1787 and attended the Constitutional Convention in Philadelphia, where he was an active and influential participant. In the end, however, he did not sign the convention's final document, strenuously objecting to the lack of a bill of rights.

Although James Madison is widely regarded as the "father" of the Bill of Rights, in terms of securing its adoption in 1791, many historians regard George Mason as the real inspiration for the idea of a bill of rights and for the formulation of its specific terms. Mason died in 1792.

Eleanor Holmes Norton (1938–)

Eleanor Holmes Norton is an African American attorney who currently serves as a member of the House of Representatives representing the District of Columbia. Her contributions to civil liberties include a lifelong career devoted to civil rights, women's rights, freedom of speech, and other civil liberties issues.

Norton was born on April 8, 1938, in Washington, D.C. Her father was trained as a lawyer but worked for the federal government and did not practice law. She graduated from Antioch College in 1960 and earned both a graduate degree in American Studies and a law degree (1964) from Yale University. After clerking for a federal judge in Philadelphia, she moved to New York City in 1965 and became the assistant legal director of the

American Civil Liberties Union (ACLU), where she worked for five years. In perhaps her most celebrated case, in 1968 she represented George Wallace, former governor of Alabama and a leading opponent of civil rights, who was denied permission to hold a political rally at Shea Stadium. She also won a Supreme Court case on behalf of the white racist National States' Rights Party.

In 1970 Norton became the first woman to head the New York City Commission on Human Rights. In that capacity she directed the commission's report *Women's Role in Contemporary Society* (1972). She helped found the National Black Feminist Organization. In 1974 she was cited by *Time* magazine as one of the top 200 American leaders under the age of forty-five. In 1975 she was a coauthor of *Sex Discrimination and the Law: Causes and Remedies.* In 1977 President Jimmy Carter appointed Norton chair of the U.S. Equal Employment Opportunity Commission (EEOC), a position she held until 1981.

In 1990, while a tenured professor at Georgetown University Law Center, Norton was elected to represent the District of Columbia as nonvoting delegate to the U.S. House of Representatives. At the time, she was one of only three African American women in Congress. In 1993 she successfully lobbied for the right to vote on the House floor as a representative of the District of Columbia, a first in the history of the District. In 1995, however, her vote was taken away.

Scopes "Monkey" Trial (1925)

In 1925 the state of Tennessee passed a law forbidding the teaching of evolution in the state's public schools. John Scopes, a young biology teacher in Dayton, Tennessee, decided to challenge the law and sought help from the American Civil Liberties Union (ACLU), which had offered its assistance to anyone willing to challenge the law. The resulting trial immediately became a national cause célèbre and one of the most famous trials in U.S. history. The case is frequently referred to as the *Scopes* "Monkey" Trial because the media defined it as a contest between the Bible's account of human origins and Charles Darwin's theory of evolution, which in the popular imagination was associated with the idea that human beings are descended from monkeys.

Scopes was represented at trial by Clarence Darrow, perhaps the most famous criminal defense lawyer of the period, and

Arthur Garfield Hays of the ACLU. Representing the state of Tennessee was Williams Jennings Bryan, a three-time candidate for the U.S. presidency who at that time was one of the most prominent spokespersons for fundamentalist Protestant religious views.

The case raised two important constitutional questions. The first involved academic freedom. Could the state of Tennessee outlaw the teaching of certain ideas in the public schools (in this case evolution) because they were offensive to a majority of the people of Tennessee, or was the teaching of unpopular views protected by the First Amendment? The second was whether the ban on teaching evolution represented an establishment of religion in violation of the First Amendment. The first issue dramatized a basic question regarding the role of civil liberties in a democracy. In a democratic society, does the majority have an unrestricted right to control its government agencies, in this case the public schools? Or does the Constitution place certain limits on what the majority can do? The second issue involves the complex question of what constitutes an establishment of religion.

In the end, the constitutional issues raised by the *Scopes* case were never resolved in court. Scopes was convicted of violating the law, but his conviction was reversed by the Tennessee Supreme Court on the grounds that the judge had made a procedural error in imposing the sentence. The state of Tennessee, apparently embarrassed by the unflattering publicity surrounding the case, did not bring any additional prosecutions.

The *Scopes* case quickly became one of the most famous and widely cited controversies in American history. Public understanding of the case has been heavily influenced by the play (1955) and film (1960) *Inherit the Wind.* Heavily critical of the Tennessee law and the role of William Jennings Bryan in particular, both the play and the movie presented an oversimplified view of the case that glossed over some of the most important constitutional questions.

The issues raised by the *Scopes* case did not die, however; they continue to agitate U.S. society through to the present day. Subsequent cases did address the constitutional questions that were not resolved in the original *Scopes* case. In 1968 the U.S. Supreme Court declared unconstitutional an Arkansas law that prohibited the teaching of evolution *(Epperson v. Arkansas).* Then in 1987 the Supreme Court declared unconstitutional a Louisiana law that, under the rationale of "balanced treatment," required the teaching of "scientific creationism," an interpretation of creation favored by religious groups that opposed evolution *(Edwards v. Aguillard)*. The Court held that requiring the teaching of this view represented an establishment of religion.

Skokie and the Free Speech Rights of Nazis (1977–1978)

In 1977 a small American Nazi group requested a permit to hold a brief demonstration in the Village of Skokie, Illinois. The request provoked a national controversy over the scope of the First Amendment. The Village of Skokie is a suburb of Chicago, and in 1977 it was heavily Jewish (an estimated 30,000 out of a total population of 70,000) and included several thousand survivors of the Nazi persecution of Jews in the Holocaust. Many residents of Skokie were deeply and understandably offended by the idea of a Nazi demonstration in their community.

The Skokie case quickly erupted into a national controversy focusing on the issue of whether the First Amendment protected hate speech. In this particular case, it was not simply a matter of hateful speech but the views of a group that advocated the extermination of a group of people.

In response to community feelings, village authorities attempted to prevent the demonstration by several means. Contrary to legend, there was never a plan to "march" through the town. The village initially required the Nazi group to post a bond of $350,000, a sum that was clearly beyond its reach. Then the village enacted three ordinances directed at the proposed Nazi demonstration. The first clarified the bond requirement and authorized the village manager to deny permits where there was a possibility of a breach of the peace. The second ordinance made it a crime to disseminate material inciting group hatred. The third outlawed demonstrations by groups wearing military-style uniforms.

In the face of these legal obstacles, the group turned to the American Civil Liberties Union, which regarded the issue as a routine First Amendment case. ACLU offices were quickly deluged with hate mail, however, including resignations from many Jewish members. At that time, the ACLU was already in the midst of a membership decline—and the resulting financial crisis—that had begun in 1974. Although the ACLU did lose a number of members, when it issued an appeal for financial support it regained most of its membership losses.

Eventually, there were three separate court cases involving the proposed Nazi demonstration in Skokie. One involved a challenge to an injunction banning the demonstration. Another, the most important one, involved the constitutionality of the three Skokie ordinances. In the third case an individual plaintiff, Sol Goldstein, sought to ban the demonstration on the grounds that it would inflict psychological harm (or what was called "menticide").

Subsequently, the Seventh Circuit Court of Appeals declared the three Skokie ordinances unconstitutional violations of the First Amendment (*Collin v. Smith*, 1978). The Supreme Court refused to hear an appeal, and the circuit court's decision stood.

Although the Nazi group won a clear First Amendment victory in the courts, it never demonstrated in Skokie, Illinois. Under an agreement negotiated by the U.S. Community Relations Service, it held a brief demonstration in downtown Chicago on Saturday, June 24, 1978. The Nazi demonstrators were far outnumbered by counterdemonstrators and members of the news media.

Because the Skokie case raised fundamental issues about the scope of the First Amendment and the place of hate speech in the United States, it provoked the publication of many articles, a large number of books, and a television movie.

Stonewall Incident (1969)

The birth of the modern lesbian and gay rights movement was an incident at The Stonewall, a gay bar in New York City. On the night of June 21, 1969, the police raided the bar, for no apparent reason other than the fact that it was known as a gay bar. Several people were beaten by the police, and a riot erupted that spilled out onto the surrounding streets. The active resistance of gay and lesbian people to repressive police actions immediately became a powerful symbol of strength and autonomy for other homosexuals. For this reason, the incident is widely regarded as the inspiration for the modern, militant, public lesbian and gay rights movement. Virtually all of the existing lesbian and gay rights organizations were founded after the Stonewall incident.

The event's significance was acknowledged in the National Park Service's adding the building—at 53 Christopher Street in

Greenwich Village—and a nearby park to the National Register of Historic Places in 1999.

Nadine Strossen (1950–)

Nadine Strossen, a professor of law at New York Law School, is president of the American Civil Liberties Union (ACLU). Elected to that post in 1991, she is the first woman to head the nation's oldest and largest civil liberties organization.

Strossen was born in 1950, graduated Phi Beta Kappa from Harvard College in 1972 and magna cum laude from Harvard Law School in 1975. She was an editor of the *Harvard Law Review.* She practiced law for nine years in Minneapolis and New York City while at the same time assisting the ACLU as a member of its board of directors and as a volunteer attorney in several important cases. She became general counsel of the ACLU in 1986 and president in 1991. She has taught at New York University Law School and has been a professor at New York Law School since 1986.

Professor Strossen has received many awards for her writings and advocacy of civil liberties. In 1986 Strossen was one of the first three women to receive the U.S. Jaycees' "Ten Outstanding Young Americans" Award. The *National Law Journal* has twice named her one of "The 100 Most Influential Lawyers in America." In 1996 *Working Woman* magazine listed her among the "350 Women Who Changed the World 1976–1996." In December 1997 *Upside* magazine included her in the "Elite 100: 100 Executives Leading the Digital Revolution." In November 1998 *Vanity Fair* included Strossen among "America's 200 Most Influential Women." In November 1999 *Ladies Home Journal* included Strossen among "America's 100 Most Important Women."

As ACLU president, Strossen makes numerous public presentations (as many as 200 a year) and is frequently quoted in the news media on civil liberties issues. A prolific author, she has written more than 200 articles, including both scholarly law review articles and works addressed to the general public on civil liberties issues. Her book *Defending Pornography: Free Speech, Sex, and the Fight for Women's Rights* (1995) is a feminist and civil libertarian defense of freedom of expression for sexually oriented materials. It is a reply to feminists who seek to censor pornography or other sexually explicit material in the name of women's rights. The book was named a "notable book" of 1995 by the *New*

York Times. She is also coauthor of *Speaking of Race, Speaking of Sex: Hate Speech, Civil Rights, and Civil Liberties* (1995). The book was named an "outstanding book" by the Gustavus Myers Center for the Study of Human Rights.

Earl Warren (1891–1974)

Earl Warren was chief justice of the U.S. Supreme Court from 1953 to 1969. During that period he presided over the greatest expansion of civil liberties in the history of the Court. As a result, the term "the Warren Court" is synonymous with the activist, pro–civil libertarian period of the Court's history.

Warren was born in 1891 and died in 1974. He received both his undergraduate education and his law degree from the University of California at Berkeley. After working for five years in private practice, Warren began his public service career as a district attorney in Alameda County, California, and was named the best district attorney in the country in 1931. He was elected attorney general for the state of California in 1938, and in 1942 he was elected governor. Immensely popular, he was reelected in 1946 and 1950 and considered a possible Republican Party candidate for president of the United States during these years. In 1948 he was the party's vice presidential candidate. Although a Republican, he always received strong support from Democrats and independents. Considered for the Republican presidential nomination in 1952, he lost to Dwight Eisenhower, who appointed him chief justice of the Supreme Court in 1953.

Warren's early career was marked by several civil liberties controversies that are particularly surprising in light of his subsequent record on the Supreme Court. As a prosecutor he took a strong "law and order" stance and received great support from California police officers. In a few highly publicized cases, Warren was accused of using improper tactics to obtain convictions. As California attorney general in 1942 he supported the evacuation and internment of the Japanese Americans on the West Coast. Many of his statements in support of the evacuation expressed anti-Japanese stereotypes. In later years, Warren indicated his regret over the evacuation and internment but never discussed his role in detail.

As chief justice of the Supreme Court, Warren played a particularly important role in managing the Court's decision-making process. His political skills served him well; when he joined the

Court, it was deeply divided between judicial activists and advocates of judicial restraint. The legal challenge to racially segregated public schools (*Brown v. Board of Education*, 1954) immediately presented him with one of the greatest challenges of his career. He quickly took charge of the Court's deliberations and worked hard to achieve a unanimous opinion in the case.

Warren was a philosophical civil libertarian who developed a strong commitment to justice and equality for the powerless that was not readily apparent in his earlier career. Many legal scholars, for example, have criticized the legal reasoning in *Brown*, including some who agree with the result. As the Warren Court became more actively civil libertarian, Warren relied heavily on Justice William Brennan to develop the constitutional theory underlying many of the Court's important decisions.

Several of the decisions of the Warren Court are among the most controversial in the history of the Supreme Court. These include the *Brown* (1954) decision outlawing racially segregated schools; *Engel v. Vitale* (1962), outlawing religious prayer in public schools; *Griswold v. Connecticut* (1965), establishing a constitutional right of privacy; and a number of free speech cases, particularly those establishing First Amendment protection for sexually explicit materials. The activism of the Warren Court— and Warren's own philosophy—is perhaps best exemplified by *Miranda v. Arizona* (1966). The majority opinion, which Warren wrote, requires that police advise criminal suspects of their constitutional right to remain silent and to have the services of an attorney. This advisement procedure became famous as the "Miranda warning." The decision epitomized the vigorous judicial activism of the Warren Court and, like many other decisions, provoked a bitter controversy. Warren's opinion in *Miranda* discussed in detail the context of police interrogations and expressed great concern for the plight of persons in the coercive atmosphere of police custody.

In 1963, after the assassination of President Kennedy, President Lyndon Johnson appointed Warren to head the U.S. Commission to Report upon the Assassination of President John F. Kennedy (better known as the Warren Commission) to investigate the crime. Many people felt that it was inappropriate for a sitting Supreme Court justice to become involved in an extrajudicial government effort. The experience was not a happy one for Warren, and the Warren Commission report has been heavily criticized since its initial publication.

Warren planned to retire from the Court in the spring of 1968, allowing President Johnson to appoint a successor. Johnson's candidate was Associate Justice Abe Fortas. However, Fortas became embroiled in controversy over some of his extrajudicial activities, and he withdrew his nomination and eventually resigned from the Court. As a result, President Richard Nixon appointed Warren's successor as chief justice, Warren Burger, in 1969. Earl Warren died in 1974.

References

Cold War

Caute, David. 1978. *The Great Fear: The Anti-Communist Purge Under Truman and Eisenhower.* New York: Simon and Schuster.

Gentry, Curt. 1991. *J. Edgar Hoover: The Man and the Secrets.* New York: W. W. Norton.

Goodman, Walter. 1968. *The Committee: The Extraordinary Career of the House Committee on Un-American Activities.* New York: Farrar, Straus and Giroux.

Oshinsky, David M. 1983. *A Conspiracy So Immense: The World of Joe McCarthy.* New York: Free Press.

Navasky, Victor S. 1980. *Naming Names.* New York: Viking.

Schrecker, Ellen W. 1986. *No Ivory Tower: McCarthyism and the Universities.* New York: Oxford University Press.

Roger Baldwin

Cottrell, Robert C. 2000. *Roger Baldwin and the American Civil Liberties Union.* New York: Columbia University Press.

Lamson, Peggy. 1976. *Roger Baldwin: Founder of the American Civil Liberties Union.* Boston: Houghton Mifflin.

Walker, Samuel. 1990. *In Defense of American Liberties: A History of the ACLU.* New York: Oxford University Press.

"Banned in Boston"

Chesler, Ellen. 1992. *Woman of Valor: Margaret Sanger and the Birth Control Movement in America.* New York: Simon and Schuster.

Bode, Carl, ed. 1998. *The Editor, the Bluenose, and the Prostitute: H. L. Mencken's History of the "Hatrack" Censorship Case.* Boulder, CO: Roberts Rinehart.

Walker, Samuel. 1999. *In Defense of American Liberties: A History of the ACLU, 2nd* ed. Carbondale: Southern Illinois University Press.

Ruth Bader Ginsburg

"Ruth Joan Bader Ginsburg," *New York Times Biographical Service* (June 1993).

www.ussupremecourt.gov [Biographies of current justices]

Ginsburg, Ruth Bader. 2001. "The Supreme Court," *Vital Speeches of the Day* 67 (May 1): 420.

"Ginsburg, Ruth Bader." *Current Biography* 55 (February 1994): 28.

Japanese American Internment

Inada, Lawson Fusao. 2000. *Only What We Could Carry: The Japanese American Internment Experience.* San Francisco: California Historical Society.

Irons, Peter. 1983. *Justice at War: The Story of the Japanese American Internment Cases.* New York: Oxford University Press.

Irons, Peter, ed. 1989. *Justice Delayed: The Record of the Japanese American Internment Cases.* Middletown, CT: Wesleyan University Press.

Shimabukuro, Robert Sadamu. 2001. *Born in Seattle: The Campaign for Japanese American Redress.* Seattle: University of Washington Press.

Mildred and Richard Loving

Wallenstein, Peter. 2002. *Tell the Court I Love My Wife: Race, Marriage, and Law: An American History.* New York: Palgrave.

Mr. and Mrs. Loving. 1996. Artisan Entertainment. VHS, 96 minutes.

Thurgood Marshall

Ball, Howard. 1998. *A Defiant Life: Thurgood Marshall and the Persistence of Racism in America.* New York: Crown Publishers.

Kluger, Richard. 1977. *Simple Justice.* New York: Vintage Books.

Rowan, Carl T. 1993. *Dream Makers, Dream Breakers: The World of Justice Thurgood Marshall.* Boston: Little, Brown.

Thurgood Marshall. 1992. Arts and Entertainment Network. VHS, 50 minutes.

Tushnet, Mark V. 1994. *Making Civil Rights Law: Thurgood Marshall and the Supreme Court, 1936–1961.* New York: Oxford University Press.

www.ussupremecourt.gov [Biographies of Supreme Court justices]

George Mason

Pacheco, Josephine F., ed. 1983. *The Legacy of George Mason.* Fairfax, VA: George Mason University Press.

Shumate, T. Daniel. 1985. *The First Amendment: The Legacy of George Mason.* Fairfax, VA: George Mason University Press.

Eleanor Holmes Norton

Babcock, Barbara Allen, Ann E. Freedman, Eleanor Holmes Norton, and Susan C. Ross. 1975. *Sex Discrimination and the Law: Causes and Remedies.* Boston: Little, Brown.

Lester, Joan Steinau. 2003. *Eleanor Holmes Norton: Fire in My Soul.* New York: Atria Books.

Marcovitz, Hal. 2003. *Eleanor Holmes Norton.* Philadelphia: Chelsea House Publishers.

The *Scopes* Case

Ginger, Ray. 1974. *Six Days or Forever? Tennessee v. John Thomas Scopes.* New York: Oxford University Press.

Inherit the Wind. 1960. MGM. Director: Stanley Kramer. VHS, DVD, 127 minutes.

Larson, Edward J. 1997. *Summer for the Gods: The Scopes Trial and America's Continuing Debate over Science and Religion.* New York: Basic Books.

———. 1985. *Trial and Error: The American Controversy over Creation and Evolution.* New York: Oxford University Press.

Lawrence, Jerome, and Robert E. Lee. 1955. *Inherit the Wind.* New York: Random House.

Moran, Jeffrey P. 2002. *The Scopes Trial: A Brief History with Documents.* Boston: Bedford/St. Martin's.

Scopes, John T. 1967. *Center of the Storm: Memoirs of John T. Scopes.* New York: Holt, Rinehart and Winston.

The Skokie Case

Downs, Donald Alexander. 1985. *Nazis in Skokie: Freedom, Community, and the First Amendment.* Notre Dame, IN: University of Notre Dame Press.

Neier, Aryeh. 1979. *Defending My Enemy: American Nazis, the Skokie Case, and the Risks of Freedom.* New York: E. P. Dutton.

Skokie. 1990. ABC Television. VHS, 125 minutes.

Strum, Philippa. 1999. *When the Nazis Came to Skokie: Freedom for Speech We Hate.* Lawrence: University Press of Kansas.

Stonewall

Adam, Barry D. 1995. *The Rise of a Gay and Lesbian Movement.* New York: Twayne Publishers.

After Stonewall. 1999. First Run Features. VHS, 88 minutes.

Before Stonewall. 1986. First Run Features. VHS, 87 minutes.

Duberman, Martin. 1993. *Stonewall.* New York: Dutton.

Nadine Strossen

Strossen, Nadine. 1991. "The American Civil Liberties Union and Women's Rights." *New York University Law Review* 66: 1940–1961.

———. 1995. *Defending Pornography: Free Speech, Sex, and the Fight for Women's Rights.* New York: Scribner's.

———. 1996. "Due Process Rights of Public School Students," *Michigan Law and Policy Review:* 315–323.

———. 1990. "Regulating Campus Hate Speech: A Modest Proposal?" *Duke Law Journal:* 483–572.

Earl Warren

Cray, Ed. 1997. *Chief Justice: A Biography of Earl Warren.* New York: Simon and Schuster.

Schwartz, Bernard. 1983. *Super Chief: Earl Warren and His Supreme Court: A Judicial Biography.* New York: New York University Press.

Super Chief: The Life and Legacy of Earl Warren. 1990. California Newsreel. VHS, 88 minutes.

Urofsky, Melvin I. 2001. *The Warren Court: Justices, Rulings, and Legacy.* Santa Barbara, CA: ABC-CLIO.

White, G. Edward. 1982. *Earl Warren: A Public Life.* New York: Oxford University Press.

www.ussupremecourt.gov [biographies of Justices of the Supreme Court].

5

Documents

Origins of the Bill of Rights

*The first ten amendments to the U.S. Constitution, referred to as the Bill of
Rights, were the product of a long struggle over individual rights in English
and American history. This section presents excerpts from some of the most
important documents in that history, beginning with the Magna Carta in 1215
(Brant, 1965).*

The Magna Carta, 1215

*The Magna Carta, signed in 1215, is regarded as the foundation of the English
legal tradition of individual rights and limited government. Much of the Magna
Carta relates to specific issues of the time that are not relevant to the issue of
civil liberties. The most important provision with respect to civil liberties is
paragraph 39, which is reproduced here. This is the first statement of the concept of due process of law. In the context of 1215 it meant that even the king was
subject to the rule of law and could not impose arbitrary punishments.*

No free man shall be arrested or imprisoned or disseised or outlawed or exiled or in any way victimised, neither will we attack him or
send anyone to attack him, except by the lawful judgment of his peers
or by the law of the land.

Massachusetts Body of Liberties, 1641

*The Massachusetts Body of Liberties represents a major step forward toward the
development of the Bill of Rights. Provisions include early statements of due
process of law (section 1), the right to bail (sections 18 and 41), protection
against double jeopardy (section 42) and cruel and unusual punishment (sections 43 and 46), and protection against self-incrimination (section 45). It is*

interesting to note that the Massachusetts Body of Liberties contains no provi-
sion related to freedom of speech, the free exercise of religion, or the establish-
ment of religion. In fact, Section 94 states that a person can be executed for
incorrect religious belief or for the crime of blasphemy.

We do, therefore, this day religiously and unanimously decree
and confirm these following rights, liberties, and privileges concerning
our churches and civil state to be respectively, impartially, and invio-
lably enjoyed and observed throughout our jurisdiction forever.

1. No man's life shall be taken away, no man's honor or good
name shall be stained, no man's person shall be arrested, restrained,
banished, dismembered, nor any ways punished, no man shall be
deprived of his wife or children, no man's goods or estate shall be
taken away from him, nor any way indamaged under color of law or
countenance of authority, unless it be by virtue or equity of some
express law of the country warranting the same, established by a general court and sufficiently published, or in case of the defect of a law in
any particular case by the word of God. And in capital cases, or in
cases concerning dismembring or banishment, according to that word
to be judged by the General Court.

. . .

18. No man's person shall be restrained or imprisoned by any
authority whatsoever, before the law hath sentenced him thereto, if he
can put in sufficient security, bail, or mainprise, for his appearance,
and good behavior in the meantime, unless it be in crimes capital, and
contempts in open court, and in such cases where some express act of
court cloth allow it.

. . .

41. Every man that is to answer for any criminal cause, whether
he be in prison or under bail, his cause shall be heard and determined
at the next court that hath proper cognizance thereof and may be done
without prejudice of justice.

42. No man shall be twice sentenced by civil justice for one and
the same crime, offense, or trespass.

43. No man shall be beaten with above forty stripes, nor shall any
true gentleman, nor any man equal to a gentleman be punished with
whipping, unless his crime be very shameful, and his course of life
vicious and profligate.

. . .

45. No man shall be forced by torture to confess any crime against
himself nor any other, unless it be in some capital case where he is first
fully convicted by clear and sufficient evidence to be guilty, after which
if the cause be of that nature, that it is very apparent there be other
conspirators, or confederates with him, then he may be tortured, yet
not with such tortures as be barbarous and inhumane.

46. For bodily punishments we allow amongst us none that are inhumane, barbarous, or cruel.

. . .

94. Capital Laws

1   If any man after legal conviction shall have or worship any other god, but the Lord God, he shall be put to death.
2   If any man or woman be a witch (that is, hath or consulteth with a familiar spirit), they shall be put to death.
3   If any man shall blaspheme the name of God, the Father, Son, or Holy Ghost, with direct, express, presumptuous, or high-handed blasphemy, or shall curse God in the like manner, he shall be put to death.

. . .

95. A Declaration of the Liberties the Lord Jesus Hath Given to the Churches

1   All the people of God within this jurisdiction who are not in a church way, and be orthodox in judgment, and not scandalous in life, shall have full liberty to gather themselves into a church estate. Provided they do it in a Christian way, with due observation of the rules of Christ revealed in his Word.

Habeas Corpus Act, 1679

The right of habeas corpus is considered to be one of the most fundamental individual rights in Anglo-American law. It guarantees any citizen who is imprisoned or deprived of his or her liberty the right to petition a court to inquire into the reason for the detention. The petition is referred to as a writ of habeas corpus. The right of habeas corpus is designed to limit the power of the government to punish citizens unfairly. The English Habeas Corpus Act of 1679 formalized the right in English law. The right of habeas corpus is incorporated into the U.S. Constitution in Article I, Section 9(2). One of the greatest civil liberties crises in nineteenth-century U.S. history was President Abraham Lincoln's suspension of the right of habeas corpus during the Civil War (see below).

An act for the better securing the liberty of the subject, and for prevention of imprisonments beyond the seas.

WHEREAS great delays have been used by sheriffs, gaolers and other officers, to whose custody, any of the King's subjects have been committed for criminal or supposed criminal matters, in making returns of writs of habeas corpus to them directed, by standing out an alias and pluries habeas corpus, and sometimes more, and by other shifts to avoid their yielding obedience to such writs, contrary to their duty and the known laws of the land, whereby many of the King's subjects have been and hereafter may be long detained in prison, in such cases where by law they are bailable, to their great charges and vexation.

II. For the prevention whereof, and the more speedy relief of all persons imprisoned for any such criminal or supposed criminal matters;

(2) be it enacted by the King's most excellent majesty, by and with the advice and consent of the lords spiritual and temporal, and commons, in this present parliament assembled, and by the authority thereof. That whensoever any person or persons shall bring any *habeas corpus* directed unto any sheriff or sheriffs, gaoler, minister or other person whatsoever, for any person in his or their custody, and the said writ shall be served upon the said officer, . . .

(3) and bring or cause to be brought the body of the party so committed or restrained, unto or before the lord chancellor, or lord keeper of the great seal of *England* for the time being, or the judges or barons of the said court from which the said writ shall issue, or unto and before such other person or persons before whom the said writ is made returnable, according to the command thereof;

(4) and shall then likewise certify the true causes of his detainer or imprisonment, unless the commitment of the said party be in any place beyond the distance of twenty miles from the place or places where such court or person is or shall be residing. . . .

English Bill of Rights, 1689

The 1689 English Bill of Rights is the direct forerunner of the U.S. Bill of Rights. One paragraph mentions freedom of speech but limits it to debates in Parliament. There is no general freedom of speech for citizens outside of Parliament, although there is a right to petition the government. Other protections include the suspension of habeas corpus, a prohibition of excessive bail and cruel and unusual punishments, and the right to petition the government (Brant, 1965; Schwartz, 1980).

An Act Declaring the Rights and Liberties of the Subject and Settling the Succession of the Crown
. . .

That the pretended power of suspending the laws or the execution of laws by regal authority without consent of Parliament is illegal;

That the pretended power of dispensing with laws or the execution of laws by regal authority, as it hath been assumed and exercised of late, is illegal;

That it is the right of the subjects to petition the king, and all commitments and prosecutions for such petitioning are illegal;

That election of members of Parliament ought to be free;

That the freedom of speech and debates or proceedings in Parliament ought not to be impeached or questioned in any court or place out of Parliament;

That excessive bail ought not to be required, nor excessive fines imposed, nor cruel and unusual punishments inflicted;

That jurors ought to be duly impanelled and returned, and jurors which pass upon men in trials for high treason ought to be freeholders;

And that for redress of all grievances, and for the amending, strengthening and preserving of the laws, Parliaments ought to be held frequently.

Virginia Declaration of Rights, June 12, 1776

The Virginia Declaration of Rights contains many of the rights later embodied in the Bill of Rights. The principal author of the Declaration was George Mason, one of the most important but largely forgotten figures in U.S. history (see Chapter 4). It is interesting to note that the Virginia Declaration contains a guarantee of freedom of the press but not of freedom of speech.

VIII – That in all capital or criminal prosecutions a man hath a right to demand the cause and nature of his accusation to be confronted with the accusers and witnesses, to call for evidence in his favor, and to a speedy trial by an impartial jury of his vicinage, without whose unanimous consent he cannot be found guilty, nor can he be compelled to give evidence against himself; that no man be deprived of his liberty except by the law of the land or the judgement of his peers.

IX – That excessive bail ought not to be required, nor excessive fines imposed; nor cruel and unusual punishments inflicted.

X – That general warrants, whereby any officer or messenger may be commanded to search suspected places without evidence of a fact committed, or to seize any person or persons not named, or whose offense is not particularly described and supported by evidence, are grievous and oppressive and ought not to be granted.

XI – That in controversies respecting property and in suits between man and man, the ancient trial by jury is preferable to any other and ought to be held sacred.

XII – That the freedom of the press is one of the greatest bulwarks of liberty and can never be restrained but by despotic governments.

XIII – That a well regulated militia, composed of the body of the people, trained to arms, is the proper, natural, and safe defense of a free state; that standing armies, in time of peace, should be avoided as dangerous to liberty; and that, in all cases, the military should be under strict subordination to, and be governed by, the civil power.

XVI – That religion, or the duty which we owe to our Creator and the manner of discharging it, can be directed by reason and conviction, not by force or violence; and therefore, all men are equally entitled to the free exercise of religion, according to the dictates of conscience; and that it is the mutual duty of all to practice Christian forbearance, love, and charity towards each other.

Declaration of the Rights of Man, 1789

The Declaration of the Rights of Man, adopted by the French National Assembly in 1789 during the French Revolution, was heavily influenced by the U.S. Declaration of Independence. In addition, it contains many principles of law that were incorporated into the Bill of Rights in 1791.

Approved by the National Assembly of France, August 26, 1789

The representatives of the French people, organized as a National Assembly, believing that the ignorance, neglect, or contempt of the rights of man are the sole cause of public calamities and of the corruption of governments, have determined to set forth in a solemn declaration the natural, unalienable, and sacred rights of man, in order that this declaration, being constantly before all the members of the Social body, shall remind them continually of their rights and duties; . . . Therefore the National Assembly recognizes and proclaims, in the presence and under the auspices of the Supreme Being, the following rights of man and of the citizen:

Articles:

1. Men are born and remain free and equal in rights. Social distinctions may be founded only upon the general good.

2. The aim of all political association is the preservation of the natural and imprescriptible rights of man. These rights are liberty, property, security, and resistance to oppression.

3. The principle of all sovereignty resides essentially in the nation. No body nor individual may exercise any authority which does not proceed directly from the nation.

4. Liberty consists in the freedom to do everything which injures no one else; hence the exercise of the natural rights of each man has no limits except those which assure to the other members of the society the enjoyment of the same rights. These limits can only be determined by law.

5. Law can only prohibit such actions as are hurtful to society. Nothing may be prevented which is not forbidden by law, and no one may be forced to do anything not provided for by law.

6. Law is the expression of the general will. Every citizen has a right to participate personally, or through his representative, in its foundation. It must be the same for all, whether it protects or punishes. All

citizens, being equal in the eyes of the law, are equally eligible to all dignities and to all public positions and occupations, according to their abilities, and without distinction except that of their virtues and talents.

7. No person shall be accused, arrested, or imprisoned except in the cases and according to the forms prescribed by law. Any one soliciting, transmitting, executing, or causing to be executed, any arbitrary order, shall be punished. But any citizen summoned or arrested in virtue of the law shall submit without delay, as resistance constitutes an offense.

8. The law shall provide for such punishments only as are strictly and obviously necessary, and no one shall suffer punishment except it be legally inflicted in virtue of a law passed and promulgated before the commission of the offense.

9. As all persons are held innocent until they shall have been declared guilty, if arrest shall be deemed indispensable, all harshness not essential to the securing of the prisoner's person shall be severely repressed by law.

10. No one shall be disquieted on account of his opinions, including his religious views, provided their manifestation does not disturb the public order established by law.

11. The free communication of ideas and opinions is one of the most precious of the rights of man. Every citizen may, accordingly, speak, write, and print with freedom, but shall be responsible for such abuses of this freedom as shall be defined by law.

Civil Liberties in U.S. History

This section includes excerpts from some of the most important civil liberties–related documents in U.S. history that were issued between the time of adoption of the Constitution (1787) and the Bill of Rights (1791) and the contemporary United States. For the Bill of Rights, see Chapter 1.

The Sedition Act, 1798

The Sedition Act of 1789 represented the first great free speech controversy in the history of the United States and virtually the only major one until the crisis during World War I. Section 2 of the act in effect makes it a crime to criticize the government of the United States. A number of critics of President John Adams and his administration were prosecuted and convicted under the law. President Thomas Jefferson subsequently pardoned all of those convicted (Smith, 1956).

SEC. 2. That if any person shall write, print, utter, or publish, or shall cause or procure to be written, printed, uttered or published, or shall knowingly and willingly assist or aid in writing, printing, uttering or publishing any false, scandalous and malicious writing or writings against the government of the United States, or either house of the Congress of the United States, or the President of the United States, with intent to defame the said government, or either house of the said Congress, or the said President, or to bring them, or either of them, into contempt or disrepute; or to excite against them, or either or any of them, the hatred of the good people of the United States, or to excite any unlawful combinations therein, for opposing or resisting any law of the United States, or any act of the President of the United States, done in pursuance of any such law, or of the powers in him vested by the constitution of the United States, or to resist, oppose, or defeat any such law or act, or to aid, encourage or abet any hostile designs of any foreign nation against the United States, their people or government, then such person, being thereof convicted before any court of the United States having jurisdiction thereof, shall be punished by a fine not exceeding two thousand dollars, and by imprisonment not exceeding two years.

SEC. 3. That if any person shall be prosecuted under this act, for the writing or publishing any libel aforesaid, it shall be lawful for the defendant, upon the trial of the cause, to give in evidence in his defence, the truth of the matter contained in the publication charged as a libel. And the jury who shall try the cause, shall have a right to determine the law and the fact, under the direction of the court, as in other cases.

President Lincoln Suspends the Right of Habeas Corpus, 1861

In response to the emergency caused by the Civil War, President Abraham Lincoln suspended the right of habeas corpus (Neely, 1991). The right of habeas corpus is considered to be perhaps the most fundamental right in a free society. It grants the right of citizen who is being held against his or her will to petition a court for an inquiry into the reason for the detention. The U.S. Constitution explicitly states that the Judiciary Act of 1789 grants courts the right to issue writs. John Merryman was arrested in his house in Baltimore by Union military troops at 2:00 A.M. on May 26, 1861, and confined at Fort McHenry. He sought a writ of habeas corpus, which was granted by the circuit court. The commanding officer, however, denied the writ, acting on the orders of the president of the United States. In Ex parte Merryman (1861), the U.S. Supreme Court held Lincoln's action unconstitutional.

1. The guarantee of the right of habeas corpus is provided in the U.S. Constitution in Article I, Sec. 9(2).

The privilege of the Writ of Habeas Corpus shall not be suspended, unless when in Cases of Rebellion or invasion the public safety may require it. [Because the provision is in Article I, which refers to the legislature, only Congress has the power to suspend this right.]

2. Lincoln suspends habeas corpus:

A Proclamation

Whereas, it has become necessary to call into service not only volunteers but also portions of the militia of the States by draft in order to suppress the insurrection existing in the United States, and disloyal persons are not adequately restrained by the ordinary processes of law from hindering this measure and from giving aid and comfort in various ways to the insurrection;

Now, therefore, be it ordered, first, that during the existing insurrection and as a necessary measure for suppressing the same, all Rebels and Insurgents, their aiders and abettors within the United States, and all persons discouraging volunteer enlistments, resisting militia drafts, or guilty of any disloyal practice, affording aid and comfort to Rebels against the authority of the United States, shall be subject to martial law and liable to trial and punishment by Court Martial or Military Commission.

Second. That the Writ of Habeas Corpus is suspended in respect to all persons arrested, or who are now, or hereafter during the rebellion shall be, imprisoned in any fort, camp, arsenal, military prison, or other place of confinement by any military authority or by the sentence of any Court Martial or Military Commission.

In witness whereof, I have hereunto set my hand, and caused the seal of the United States to be affixed.

Done at the City of Washington this twenty-fourth day of September, in the year of our Lord one thousand eight hundred and sixty-two, and of the Independence of the United States the 87th.

Abraham Lincoln
By the President:
William H. Seward, Secretary of State

3. The Supreme Court overrules President Lincoln in
Ex Parte Merryman (1861)

On the 25th May 1861, the petitioner, a citizen of Baltimore County, in the state of Maryland, was arrested by a military force, acting under orders of a major general of the United States army, commanding in the state of Pennsylvania, and committed to the custody of the general commanding Fort McHenry, within the district of Maryland; on the 26th May 1861, a writ of habeas corpus was issued by the chief justice of the United States, sitting at chambers, directed to the commandant of the fort, commanding him to produce the body of the petitioner before the chief justice, in Baltimore City, on the 27th day of May, 1861.

. . .

The case, then, is simply this: a military officer, residing in Pennsylvania, issues an order to arrest a citizen of Maryland, upon vague and indefinite charges, without any proof, so far as appears; under this order, his house is entered in the night, he is seized as a prisoner, and conveyed to Fort McHenry, and there kept in close confinement; and when a habeas corpus is served on the commanding officer, requiring him to produce the prisoner before a justice of the Supreme Court, in order that he may examine into the legality of the imprisonment, the answer of the officer, is that he is authorized by the president to suspend the writ of habeas corpus at his discretion, and in the exercise of that discretion, suspends it in this case, and on that ground refuses obedience to the writ.

. . .

The great importance which the framers of the Constitution attached to the privilege of the writ of habeas corpus, to protect the liberty of the citizen, is proved by the fact that its suspension, except in cases of invasion or rebellion, is first in the list of prohibited powers; and even in these cases the power is denied, and its exercise prohibited, unless the public safety shall require it.

. . .

The only power, therefore, which the president possesses, where the "life, liberty, or property" of a private citizen is concerned, is the power and duty prescribed in the third section of the second article, which requires "that he shall take care that the laws shall be faithfully executed." He is not authorized to execute them himself, or through agents or officers, civil or military, appointed by himself, but he is to take care that they be faithfully carried into execution, as they are expounded and adjudged by the coordinate branch of the government to which that duty is assigned by the Constitution.

. . .

With such provisions in the constitution, expressed in language too clear to be misunderstood by anyone, I can see no ground whatever for supposing that the president, in any emergency, or in any state of things, can authorize the suspension of the privileges of the writ of habeas corpus, or the arrest of a citizen, except in aid of the judicial power. He certainly does not faithfully execute the laws, if he takes upon himself legislative power, by suspending the writ of habeas corpus, and the judicial power also, by arresting and imprisoning a person without due process of law.

. . .

These great and fundamental laws, which Congress itself could not suspend, have been disregarded and suspended, like the writ of habeas corpus, by a military order, supported by force of arms. Such is the case now before me, and I can only say that if the authority which the Constitution has confided to the judiciary department and judicial officers, may thus, upon any pretext or under any circumstances, be usurped by the military power, at its discretion, the people of the United States are no longer living under a government of laws, but every citizen holds life, liberty, and property at the will and pleasure of the army officer in whose military district he may happen to be found.

The Constitutionality of Racial Segregation, 1896, 1954

After the Civil War and the abolition of slavery in the southern states, a certain degree of racial equality existed. A number of African Americans, for example, were elected to public office. After the withdrawal of federal troops in the 1870s, however, racist forces began to gain the upper hand. In the 1890s this movement led to the imposition of de jure racial segregation in public accommodations and public schools and disenfranchisement of African Americans.

In one of the most infamous cases in the history of the U.S. Supreme Court, the Court upheld the constitutionality of racial segregation. Below are excerpts from the majority opinion in Plessy v. Ferguson *(1896), followed by an excerpt from the historic dissent by Justice John Marshall Harlan (Thomas, 1997).*

Plessy v. Ferguson, 1896

Opinion of the Court   The object of the amendment was undoubtedly to enforce the absolute equality of the two races before the law, but in the nature of things it could not have been intended to abolish distinctions based upon color, or to enforce social, as distinguished from political equality, or a commingling of the two races upon terms unsatisfactory to either. Laws permitting, and even requiring, their separation in places where they are liable to be brought into contact do not necessarily imply the inferiority of either race to the other, and have been generally, if not universally, recognized as within the competency of the state legislatures in the exercise of their police power. The most common instance of this is connected with the establishment of separate schools for white and colored children, which has been held to be a valid exercise of the legislative power even by courts of States where the political rights of the colored race have been longest and most earnestly enforced. . . .

The argument also assumes that social prejudices may be overcome by legislation, and that equal rights cannot be secured to the Negro except by an enforced commingling of the two races. We cannot accept this proposition. If the two races are to meet upon terms of social equality, it must be the result of natural affinities, a mutual appreciation of each other's merits and a voluntary consent of individuals . . . Legislation is powerless to eradicate racial instincts or to abolish distinctions based upon physical differences, and the attempt to do so can only result in accentuating the difficulties of the present situation. If the civil and political rights of both races be equal one cannot be inferior to the other civilly or politically. If one race be inferior to the other socially, the Constitution of the United States cannot put them upon the same plane.

Dissent by Justice John Marshall Harlan   In my opinion, the judgment this day rendered will, in time, prove to be quite as pernicious as the decision made by this tribunal in the Dred Scott case. . . . The present decision, it may well be apprehended, will not only stimulate aggressions, more or less brutal and irritating, upon the admitted rights of colored citizens, but will encourage the belief that it is possible, by means of state enactments, to defeat the beneficent purposes which the people of the United States had in view when they adopted the recent amendments of the Constitution, by one of which the blacks of this country were made citizens of the United States and of the States in which they respectively reside, and whose privileges and immunities, as citizens, the States are forbidden to abridge. Sixty millions of whites are in no danger from the presence here of eight millions of blacks. The destinies of the two races, in this country, are indissolubly linked together, and the interests of both require that the common government of all shall not permit the seeds of race hate to be planted under the sanction of law. What can more certainly arouse race hate, what more certainly create and perpetuate a feeling of distrust between these races, than state enactments, which, in fact, proceed on the ground that colored citizens are so inferior and degraded that they cannot be allowed to sit in public coaches occupied by white citizens? That, as all will admit, is the real meaning of such legislation as was enacted in Louisiana. . . .

I am of opinion that the statute of Louisiana is inconsistent with the personal liberty of citizens, white and black, in that State, and hostile to both the spirit and letter of the Constitution of the United States. If laws of like character should be enacted in the several States of the Union, the effect would be in the highest degree mischievous. Slavery, as an institution tolerated by law would, it is true, have disappeared from our country, but there would remain a power in the States, by sinister legislation, to interfere with the full enjoyment of the blessings of freedom; to regulate civil rights, common to all citizens, upon the basis of race; and to place in a condition of legal inferiority a large body of American citizens, now constituting a part of the political community called the People of the United States, for whom, and by whom through representatives, our government is administered.

Brown v. Board of Education, 1954

In the late 1930s, the National Association for the Advancement of Colored People (NAACP) began a legal assault on de jure segregation. That campaign reached its high point in Brown v. Board of Education, *where, in one of the most important decisions in the history of the Supreme Court, the justices unanimously overturned* Plessy *and held that racially segregating public schools was unconstitutional. The* Brown *decision inspired the civil rights movement to broader challenges to race discrimination and set the stage for gains in racial equality over the next fifteen years (Greenberg, 1994; Kluger, 1975; Martin, 1998).*

Opinion of the Court [Quoting the finding of a lower court:] "Segregation of white and colored children in public schools has a detrimental effect upon the colored children. The impact is greater when it has the sanction of the law, for the policy of separating the races is usually interpreted as denoting the inferiority of the Negro group. A sense of inferiority affects the motivation of a child to learn. Segregation with the sanction of law, therefore, has a tendency to [retard] the educational and mental development of Negro children and to deprive them of some of the benefits they would receive in a racial[ly] integrated school system." . . .

We conclude that, in the field of public education, the doctrine of "separate but equal" has no place. Separate educational facilities are inherently unequal. Therefore, we hold that the plaintiffs and others similarly situated for whom the actions have been brought are, by reason of the segregation complained of, deprived of the equal protection of the laws guaranteed by the Fourteenth Amendment. This disposition makes unnecessary any discussion whether such segregation also violates the Due Process Clause of the Fourteenth Amendment.

Motion Pictures and the First Amendment, 1915, 1952

Mutual Film Corp. v. Industrial Commission, 1915

In 1915 the Supreme Court considered the question of censorship of motion pictures, which at that time were a new form of expression. As the excerpt from the Mutual *decision below indicates, the Court concluded that the movies were a form of commerce and not a form of expression protected by the First Amendment (de Grazia and Newman, 1982).*

It cannot be put out of view that the exhibition of moving pictures is a business pure and simple, originated and conducted for profit, like other spectacles, not to be regarded, nor intended to be regarded by the

Ohio constitution, we think, as part of the press of the country or as organs of public opinion.

Joseph Burstyn, Inc. v. Wilson, 1952

In 1952 the Supreme Court reconsidered the question of motion picture censor-ship. At that time a number of states and cities, acting under the authority of the earlier Mutual *decision, licensed movies and often denied permits to or cen-sored movies they believed to be offensive. In the excerpts below, the Court reversed the earlier* Mutual *decision and ruled that movies were protected by the First Amendment. Having decided that, the Court then addressed the state of New York's claim that the movie in question was "sacrilegious." The Court held both that New York authorities had unrestrained power to decide what was acceptable and what was not, and that the inevitable result would be to favor certain religious views over others—a result that would violate the separation of church and state (de Grazia and Newman, 1982).*

We conclude that expression by means of motion pictures is included within the free speech and free press guaranty of the First and Fourteenth Amendments. To the extent that language in the opin-ion in *Mutual Film Corp. v. Industrial Comm'n* . . . is out of harmony with the views here set forth, we no longer adhere to it. . . .

In seeking to apply the broad and all-inclusive definition of "sacri-legious" given by the New York courts, the censor is set adrift upon a boundless sea amid a myriad of conflicting currents of religious views, with no . . . charts but those provided by the most vocal and powerful orthodoxies. New York cannot vest such unlimited restraining control over motion pictures in a censor. . . . Under such a standard the most careful and tolerant censor would find it virtually impossible to avoid favoring one religion over another, and he would be subject to an inevitable tendency to ban the expression of unpopular sentiments sacred to a religious minority. Application of the "sacrilegious" test, in these or other respects, might raise substantial questions under the First Amendment's guaranty of separate church and state with freedom of worship for all. However, from the standpoint of freedom of speech and the press, it is enough to point out that the state has no legitimate inter-est in protecting any or all religions from views distasteful to them which is sufficient to justify prior restraints upon the expression of those views. It is not the business of government in our nation to sup-press real or imagined attacks upon a particular religious doctrine, whether they appear in publications, speeches, or motion pictures.

Espionage Act, 1917

World War I marked a massive suppression of freedom of speech. There was very strong opposition among many Americans to U.S. involvement in the war, and the government responded by prosecuting opposition leaders and banning anti-war material from the mail. The government also prosecuted people who gave advice to young men thinking about applying for conscientious objector status on the grounds that it undermined the war effort. The Espionage Act was the legal basis for much of the suppression of free speech (Chafee, 1941; Murphy, 1979; Polenberg, 1987).

SEC. 3. Whoever, when the United States is at war, shall willfully make or convey false reports or false statements with intent to interfere with the operation or success of the military or naval forces of the United States, or to promote the success of its enemies, or shall willfully make or convey false reports, or false statements, or say or do anything except by way of bona fide and not disloyal advice to an investor . . . with intent to obstruct the sale by the United States of bonds . . . or the making of loans by or to the United States, or whoever, when the United States is at war, shall willfully cause . . . or incite . . . insubordination, disloyalty, mutiny, or refusal of duty in the military or naval forces of the United States, or shall willfully obstruct . . . the recruiting or enlistment service of the United States, and whoever, when the United States is at war, shall willfully utter, print, write, or publish any disloyal, profane, scurrilous, or abusive language about the form of government of the United States, or the Constitution of the United States, or the military or naval forces of the United States, or the flag . . . or the uniform of the Army or Navy of the United States, or any language intended to bring the form of government . . . or the Constitution . . . or the military or naval forces . . . or the flag . . . of the United States into contempt, scorn, contumely, or disrepute . . . or shall willfully display the flag of any foreign enemy, or shall willfully . . . urge, incite, or advocate any curtailment of production in this country of any thing or things . . . necessary or essential to the prosecution of the war . . . and whoever shall willfully advocate, teach, defend, or suggest the doing of any of the acts or things in this section enumerated and whoever shall by word or act support or favor the cause of any country with which the United States is at war or by word or act oppose the cause of the United States therein, shall be punished by a fine of not more than $10,000 or imprisonment for not more than twenty years, or both . . .

Gitlow v. New York, 1925

Before 1925, the specific protections of the Bill of Rights were understood to apply to the federal government but not the states. The decision in Gitlow v. New York *was a major landmark in the development of the law of civil liberties. Although the Court ruled against Gitlow, who had been convicted for his radical political ideas, the Court held that the Due Process Clause of the Fourteenth*

Amendment "incorporated" the guarantee of freedom of speech in the First Amendment and made it applicable to the states. In subsequent years, the Court incorporated other parts of the Bill of Rights in a process that has been described as "selective incorporation" (Curtis, 1986).

For present purposes we may and do assume that freedom of speech and of the press—which are protected by the First Amendment from abridgment by Congress—are among the fundamental personal rights and "liberties" protected by the due process clause of the Fourteenth Amendment from impairment by the States.

Tennessee Anti-Evolution Law, 1925

In 1925 the state of Tennessee passed a law prohibiting the teaching of evolution in the public schools. John T. Scopes, a Biology teacher in the town of Dayton, Tennessee, was prosecuted for violating the law. The trial in the summer of 1925 (see Chapter 4) is one of the most famous episodes in the history of civil liberties (Ginger, 1974; Larson, 1985, 1997; Moran, 2002).

[Tennessee] House Bill No. 185

AN ACT prohibiting the teaching of the Evolution Theory in all the Universities, Normals and all other public schools of Tennessee, which are supported in whole or in part by the public school funds of the State, and to provide penalties for the violations thereof.

Section 1. *Be it enacted by the General Assembly of the State of Tennessee,* That it shall be unlawful for any teacher in any of the Universities, Normals and all other public schools of the State which are supported in whole or in part by the public school funds of the State, to teach any theory that denies the story of the Divine Creation of man as taught in the Bible, and to teach instead that man has descended from a lower order of animals.

Section 2. *Be it further enacted,* That any teacher found guilty of the violation of this Act, shall be guilty of a misdemeanor and upon conviction, shall be fined not less than One Hundred $ (100.00) Dollars nor more than Five Hundred ($ 500.00) Dollars for each offense.

Section 3. *Be it further enacted,* That this Act take effect from and after its passage, the public welfare requiring it.

Passed March 13, 1925

The Smith Act, 1940

The Smith Act was adopted as an attempt to outlaw the Communist Party in the United States. It was the first attempt in U.S. history to outlaw the advocacy of specific political ideas. The law was the basis for the prosecution of the leaders of the American Communist Party in 1949 (Kalven, 1988; Smolla, 1992).

(a) It shall be unlawful for any person—

(1) to knowingly or willfully advocate, abet, advise, or teach the duty, necessity, desirability, or propriety of overthrowing or destroying any government in the United States by force or violence, or by the assassination of any officer of any such government;

(2) with intent to cause the overthrow or destruction of any government in the United States, to print, publish, edit, issue, circulate, sell, distribute, or publicly display any written or printed matter advocating, advising, or teaching the duty, necessity, desirability, or propriety of overthrowing or destroying any government in the United States by force or violence;

(3) to organize or help to organize any society, group, or assembly of persons who teach, advocate, or encourage the overthrow or destruction of any government in the United States by force or violence; or to be or become a member of, or affiliate with, any such society, group, or assembly of persons, knowing the purposes thereof.

The Four Freedoms, 1941

In his State of the Union address on January 6, 1941, President Franklin D. Roosevelt described his commitment to "the four essential human freedoms," which have become known as The Four Freedoms. Only two are specifically mentioned in the Bill of Rights: freedom of speech and freedom of religion. The other two—freedom from fear and freedom from want—are general human rights values.

In the future days which we seek to make secure, we look forward to a world founded upon four essential human freedoms.

The first is freedom of speech and expression—everywhere in the world.

The second is freedom of every person to worship God in his own way—everywhere in the world.

The third is freedom from want, which, translated into world terms, means economic understandings which will secure to every nation a healthy peacetime life for its inhabitants—everywhere in the world.

The fourth is freedom from fear, which, translated into world terms, means a world-wide reduction of armaments to such a point and in such a thorough fashion that no nation will be in a position to commit an act of physical aggression against any neighbor—anywhere in the world.

Executive Order 9066, The Japanese American Internment, 1942

One of the greatest single episodes of the violation of civil liberties in U.S. history was the evacuation and internment of Japanese Americans during World War II (1942–1945). This action was authorized by President Franklin D. Roosevelt under his powers as commander in chief of the armed forces. It is important to note that Executive Order 9066 does not specifically refer to Japanese Americans, nor does it mention confining people in what later became known as relocation centers and are more commonly referred to as concentration camps.

Executive Order 9066
Authorizing the Secretary of War to Prescribe Military Areas
WHEREAS the successful prosecution of the war requires every possible protection against espionage and against sabotage to national-defense material, national-defense premises, and national-defense utilities as defined in section 4, Act of April 20, 1918, 40 Stat. 533, as amended by the act of November 30, 1940, 54 Stat. 1220, and the Act of August 21, 1941, 55 Stat. 655 (U. S. C., Title 50, Sec. 104):

NOW, THEREFORE, by virtue of the authority vested in me as President of the United States, and Commander in Chief of the Army and Navy, I hereby authorize and direct the Secretary of War, and the Military Commanders whom he may from time to time designate, whenever he or any designated Commander deems such actions necessary or desirable, to prescribe military areas in such places and of such extent as he or the appropriate Military Commanders may determine, from which any or all persons may be excluded, and with such respect to which, the right of any person to enter, remain in, or leave shall be subject to whatever restrictions the Secretary of War or the appropriate Military Commander may impose in his discretion. The Secretary of War is hereby authorized to provide for residents of any such area who are excluded therefrom, such transportation, food, shelter, and other accommodations as may be necessary, in the judgement of the Secretary of War or the said Military Commander, and until other arrangements are made, to accomplish the purpose of this order. The designation of military areas in any region or locality shall supersede designations of prohibited and restricted areas by the Attorney General under the Proclamations of December 7 and 8, 1941, and shall supersede the responsibility and authority of the Attorney General under the said Proclamations in respect of such prohibited and restricted areas.

I hereby further authorize and direct the Secretary of War and the said Military Commanders to take such other steps as he or the appropriate Military Commander may deem advisable to enforce compliance with the restrictions applicable to each Military area hereinabove authorized to be designated, including the use of Federal troops and other Federal Agencies, with authority to accept assistance of state and local agencies.

Franklin D. Roosevelt, February 19, 1942

The Cold War and the Federal Loyalty Program, 1947

The Cold War resulted in some of the greatest violations of civil liberties in U.S. history. One of the first measures was the Federal Loyalty Program, designed to remove disloyal employees from the federal government. The Federal Loyalty Program was instituted by President Harry Truman in 1947 through Executive Order 9835. A person found to be disloyal could be denied employment with the federal government or fired if already employed. The program resulted in serious abuses of civil liberties. It penalized people on the basis of the associations and membership in organizations. Many people were accused of disloyalty on the basis of information from secret informants whom they had no opportunity to confront (Caute, 1978).

Executive Order 9835

Part I—Investigation of Applicants

There shall be a loyalty investigation of every person entering the civilian employment of any department or agency of the executive branch of the Federal Government. . . .

Part V—Standards

The standard for the refusal of employment or the removal from employment in an executive department or agency on grounds relating to loyalty shall be that, on all the evidence, reasonable grounds exist for belief that the person involved is disloyal to the Government of the United States.

Activities and associations of an applicant or employee which may be considered in connection with the determination of disloyalty may include one or more of the following:

. . .

8. Membership in, affiliation with or sympathetic association with any foreign or domestic organization, association, movement, group or combination of persons, designated by the Attorney General as totalitarian, fascist, communist, or subversive, or as having adopted a policy of advocating or approving the commission of acts of force or violence to deny other persons their rights under the Constitution of the United States, or as seeking to alter the form of government of the United States by unconstitutional means.

President Harry S. Truman Desegregates the Armed Forces, 1948

In 1947 President Harry S. Truman appointed a presidential commission on civil rights, the first such commission in U.S. history. The commission's report, To Secure These Rights, *made many recommendations, including an end to racial segregation of U.S. military forces. Until that time, the military had been segregated. African American soldiers served in separate units in both World Wars I and II. In 1948 President Truman implemented the commission's recommendation through Executive Order 9981 (Nieman, 1991).*

Executive Order 9981

Establishing the President's Committee on Equality of Treatment and Opportunity in the Armed Forces.

WHEREAS it is essential that there be maintained in the armed services of the United States the highest standards of democracy, with equality of treatment and opportunity for all those who serve in our country's defense:

NOW THEREFORE, by virtue of the authority vested in me as President of the United States, by the Constitution and the statutes of the United States, and as Commander in Chief of the armed services, it is hereby ordered as follows:

1. It is hereby declared to be the policy of the President that there shall be equality of treatment and opportunity for all persons in the armed services without regard to race, color, religion or national origin. This policy shall be put into effect as rapidly as possible, having due regard to the time required to effectuate any necessary changes without impairing efficiency or morale.

July 26, 1948

Title VII of the Civil Rights Act, 1964

The 1964 Civil Rights Act is one of the most important laws in U.S. history. It clearly establishes equal opportunity as a matter of social policy, providing for specific application of the general commitment to equal protection of the law expressed in the Fourteenth Amendment. The law contains several different provisions, covering a number of different areas. Title II, for example, outlawed discrimination in public accommodations—restaurants, buses, rest rooms, and so on. Title VII, excerpted here, prohibits discrimination in employment on the basis of race, color, religion, sex, or national origin (Urofsky, 1997).

(a) It shall be an unlawful employment practice for an employer—

(1) to fail or refuse to hire or to discharge any individual, or otherwise to discriminate against any individual with respect to his com-

pensation, terms, conditions, or privileges of employment, because of such individual's race, color, religion, sex, or national origin; or

(2) to limit, segregate, or classify his employees or applicants for employment in any way which would deprive or tend to deprive any individual of employment opportunities or otherwise adversely affect his status as an employee, because of such individual's race, color, religion, sex, or national origin.

(b) It shall be an unlawful employment practice for an employment agency to fail or refuse to refer for employment, or otherwise to discriminate against, any individual because of his race, color, religion, sex, or national origin, or to classify or refer for employment any individual on the basis of his race, color, religion, sex, or national origin.

Voting Rights Act, 1965

Until the 1965 Voting Rights Act, southern states used a variety of means to prevent African Americans from voting. Many had literacy tests that were used in a blatantly discriminatory manner. Most required a poll tax—a fee for registering to vote—that discriminated against poor people. The Voting Rights Act outlawed these and other methods and established a procedure for oversight of voting procedures by the U.S. Justice Department (Keyssar, 2000).

AN ACT To enforce the fifteenth amendment to the Constitution of the United States, and for other purposes.
. . .

SEC. 2. No voting qualification or prerequisite to voting, or standard, practice, or procedure shall be imposed or applied by any State or political subdivision to deny or abridge the right of any citizen of the United States to vote on account of race or color.

SEC. 3. (a) To assure that the right of citizens of the United States to vote is not denied or abridged on account of race or color, no citizen shall be denied the right to vote in any Federal, State, or local election because of his failure to comply with any test or device in any State with respect to which the determinations have been made under subsection (b) or in any political subdivision with respect to which such determinations have been made as a separate unit, unless the United States District Court for the District of Columbia in an action for a declaratory judgment brought by such State or subdivision against the United States has determined that no such test or device has been used during the five years preceding the filing of the action for the purpose or with the effect of denying or abridging the right to vote on account of race or color:

(c) The phrase "test or device" shall mean any requirement that a person as a prerequisite for voting or registration for voting (1) demonstrate the ability to read, write, understand, or interpret any matter,

(2) demonstrate any educational achievement or his knowledge of any particular subject, (3) possess good moral character, or (4) prove his qualifications by the voucher of registered voters or members of any other class.

Indian Bill of Rights, 1968

Native American tribes are semisovereign nations with a great deal of legal autonomy in terms of governing their own affairs. Many tribes have their own criminal justice systems, for example, with tribal police and courts. As a result, the legal status of individual Native Americans is complex and ambiguous. It is often difficult to determine whether federal or tribal law applies in a particular case. The application of the Bill of Rights is equally ambiguous. In an attempt to clarify the situation, Congress passed the Indian Bill of Rights Act in 1968. The law has not clarified all of the issues, however (Pevar, 2002).

Sec. 1302. Constitutional rights

No Indian tribe in exercising powers of self-government shall:

(1) make or enforce any law prohibiting the free exercise of religion, or abridging the freedom of speech, or of the press, or the right of the people peaceably to assemble and to petition for a redress of grievances;

(2) violate the right of the people to be secure in their persons, houses, papers, and effects against unreasonable search and seizures, nor issue warrants, but upon probable cause, supported by oath or affirmation, and particularly describing the place to be searched and the person or thing to be seized;

(3) subject any person for the same offense to be twice put in jeopardy;

(4) compel any person in any criminal case to be a witness against himself;

(5) take any private property for a public use without just compensation;

(6) deny to any person in a criminal proceeding the right to a speedy and public trial, to be informed of the nature and cause of the accusation, to be confronted with the witnesses against him, to have compulsory process for obtaining witnesses in his favor, and at his own expense to have the assistance of counsel for his defense;

(7) require excessive bail, impose excessive fines, inflict cruel and unusual punishments, and in no event impose for conviction of any one offense any penalty or punishment greater than imprisonment for a term of one year and . . . a fine of $5,000, or both;

(8) deny to any person within its jurisdiction the equal protection of its laws or deprive any person of liberty or property without due process of law;

(9) pass any bill of attainder or ex post facto law; or

(10) deny to any person accused of an offense punishable by imprisonment the right, upon request, to a trial by jury of not less than six persons.

The War Powers Resolution, 1973

The Vietnam War raised the issue of who has the power to commit the United States to military combat. The Constitution clearly states that only Congress has that power. Nonetheless, the United States has often engaged in military combat without a congressional declaration of war. Opponents of the Vietnam War tried to strengthen the meaning of the war powers clause of the Constitution with the War Powers Resolution. Most observers, however, believe that this measure has not been effective in limiting the power of the president to engage U.S. military forces (Fisher, 1995).

. . .

(b) Under article I, section 8, of the Constitution, it is specifically provided that the Congress shall have the power to make all laws necessary and proper for carrying into execution, not only its own powers but also all other powers vested by the Constitution in the Government of the United States, or in any department or officer thereof.

(c) The constitutional powers of the President as Commander-in-Chief to introduce United States Armed Forces into hostilities, or into situations where imminent involvement in hostilities is clearly indicated by the circumstances, are exercised only pursuant to (1) a declaration of war, (2) specific statutory authorization, or (3) a national emergency created by attack upon the United States, its territories or possessions, or its armed forces.

Contemporary Civil Liberties Issues

This section includes documents related to contemporary civil liberties issues. Each issue is discussed in detail in Chapter 2.

Freedom of Speech

Hate Speech

In the 1980s there was a rash of racist incidents on college and university campuses, including some campuses that are generally regarded as the best educational institutions in the country. In response, some campus groups representing African Americans, women, and lesbian and gay students advocated the adoption of codes of conduct that would punish students who committed hate speech. The first selection below is an excerpt from the speech code adopted by the University of Wisconsin. The code was declared an unconstitutional violation of the First Amendment in UWM Post v. University of Wisconsin (1991). The second selection below is the ACLU statement opposing campus speech codes on free speech grounds (Walker, 1994).

University of Wisconsin Speech Code   UWS 17.06 Offenses defined. The university may discipline a student in non-academic matters in the following situations.

(2)(a) For racist or discriminatory comments, epithets or other expressive behavior directed at an individual or on separate occasions at different individuals, or for physical conduct, if such comments, epithets or other expressive behavior or physical conduct intentionally:

1. Demean the race, sex, religion, color, creed, disability, sexual orientation, national origin, ancestry or age of the individual or individuals; and

2. Create an intimidating, hostile or demeaning environment for education, university-related work, or other university-authorized activity.

(b) Whether the intent required under par. (a) is present shall be determined by consideration of all relevant circumstances.

(c) In order to illustrate the types of conduct which this subsection is designed to cover, the following examples are set forth. These examples are not meant to illustrate the only situations or types of conduct intended to be covered.

1. A student would be in violation if: a. He or she intentionally made demeaning remarks to an individual based on that person's ethnicity, such as name calling, racial slurs, or "jokes"; and b. His or her purpose in uttering the remarks was to make the educational environment hostile for the person to whom the demeaning remark was addressed.

2. A student would be in violation if: a. He or she intentionally placed visual or written material demeaning the race or sex of an individual in that person's university living quarters or work area; and b. His or her purpose was to make the educational environment hostile for the person in whose quarters or work area the material was placed.

3. A student would be in violation if he or she seriously damaged or destroyed private property of any member of the university community or guest because of that person's race, sex, religion, color, creed, disability, sexual orientation, national origin, ancestry or age.

4. A student would not be in violation if, during a class discussion, he or she expressed a derogatory opinion concerning a racial or ethnic group. There is no violation, since the student's remark was addressed to the class as a whole, not to a specific individual. More-

over, on the facts as stated, there seems no evidence that the student's purpose was to create a hostile environment.

ACLU Position on Hate Speech on Campus *The American Civil Liberties Union has been the leading defender of freedom of speech. It is also a vigorous advocate of equality for racial minorities, women, and all other victims of discrimination. When confronted with the hate speech issue, the ACLU had to reconcile these two competing civil liberties principles. The following ACLU statement expresses its opposition to campus hate speech codes on the grounds that they violate free speech and are not effective remedies for discrimination (Walker, 1994).*

In recent years, a rise in verbal abuse and violence directed at people of color, lesbians and gay men, and other historically persecuted groups has plagued the United States. Among the settings of these expressions of intolerance are college and university campuses, where bias incidents have occurred sporadically since the mid-1980s. Outrage, indignation and demands for change have greeted such incidents—understandably, given the lack of racial and social diversity among students, faculty and administrators on most campuses.

Many universities, under pressure to respond to the concerns of those who are the objects of hate, have adopted codes or policies prohibiting speech that offends any group based on race, gender, ethnicity, religion or sexual orientation.

That's the wrong response, well-meaning or not. The First Amendment to the United States Constitution protects speech no matter how offensive its content. Speech codes adopted by government-financed state colleges and universities amount to government censorship, in violation of the Constitution. And the ACLU believes that all campuses should adhere to First Amendment principles because academic freedom is a bedrock of education in a free society.

How much we value the right of free speech is put to its severest test when the speaker is someone we disagree with most. Speech that deeply offends our morality or is hostile to our way of life warrants the same constitutional protection as other speech because the right of free speech is indivisible: When one of us is denied this right, all of us are denied. Since its founding in 1920, the ACLU has fought for the free expression of all ideas, popular or unpopular. That's the constitutional mandate.

Where racist, sexist and homophobic speech is concerned, the ACLU believes that more speech—not less—is the best revenge. This is particularly true at universities, whose mission is to facilitate learning through open debate and study, and to enlighten. Speech codes are not the way to go on campuses, where all views are entitled to be heard, explored, supported or refuted. Besides, when hate is out in the open, people can see the problem. Then they can organize effectively to counter bad attitudes, possibly change them, and forge solidarity against the forces of intolerance.

College administrators may find speech codes attractive as a quick fix, but as one critic put it: "Verbal purity is not social change." Codes that punish bigoted speech treat only the symptom: The problem itself is bigotry. The ACLU believes that instead of opting for gestures that only appear to cure the disease, universities have to do the hard work of recruitment to increase faculty and student diversity; counseling to raise awareness about bigotry and its history, and changing curricula to institutionalize more inclusive approaches to all subject matter.

Burning the American Flag

The issue of whether the First Amendment protects the burning of the American flag erupted as a national controversy in the late 1980s and early 1990s. In a case involving a Texas law making it a crime to burn the flag, the Supreme Court held that it was an expressive act protected by the First Amendment. The majority of Americans opposed the decision. A movement to amend the First Amendment to make flag burning an exception to the free speech clause failed, but Congress did enact a federal law, the Flag Protection Act of 1989, that made it a crime to burn the flag. This law was declared unconstitutional by the Supreme Court in United States v. Eichman *(1990) (Goldstein, 2000).*

Flag Protection Act of 1989   (a)(1) Whoever knowingly mutilates, defaces, physically defiles, burns, maintains on the floor or ground, or tramples upon any flag of the United States shall be fined under this title or imprisoned for not more than one year, or both.

United States v. Eichman, 496 U.S. 310 (1990)   As we explained in Johnson . . . "[I]f we were to hold that a State may forbid flag burning wherever it is likely to endanger the flag's symbolic role, but allow it wherever burning a flag promotes that role—as where, for example, a person ceremoniously burns a dirty flag—we would be . . . permitting a State to 'prescribe what shall be orthodox' by saying that one may burn the flag to convey one's attitude toward it and its referents only if one does not endanger the flag's representation of nationhood and national unity." Although Congress cast the Flag Protection Act of 1989 in somewhat broader terms than the Texas statute at issue in *Johnson,* the Act still suffers from the same fundamental flaw: It suppresses expression out of concern for its likely communicative impact.

Regulation of Speech on the Radio

Although the Supreme Court has extended First Amendment protection to most forms of expression and ruled that even highly offensive expression is protected, it has approved of restrictions in certain contexts. One of those contests involves radio communication. In a famous case, the Court upheld the right of the Federal Communications Commission (FCC) to prohibit the broadcast of certain words—seven to be exact—used by the comedian George Carlin. The original 1972 comedy routine, "Seven Words You Can Never Say on Television," was released in 2000 on the CD "Class Clown."

Federal Communications Commission v. Pacifica Foundation (1978)   The question in this case is whether a broadcast of patently offensive words dealing with sex and excretion may be regulated because of its content. Obscene materials have been denied the protection of the First Amendment because their content is so offensive to contemporary moral standards. But the fact that society may find speech offensive is not a sufficient reason for suppressing it. Indeed, if it is the speaker's opinion that gives offense, that consequence is a reason for according it constitutional protection. For it is a central tenet of the First Amendment that the government must remain neutral in the marketplace of ideas. If there were any reason to believe that the Commission's characterization of the Carlin monologue as offensive could be traced to its political content or even to the fact that it satirized contemporary attitudes about four-letter words, First Amendment protection might be required. But that is simply not this case. These words offend for the same reasons that obscenity offends. Their place in the hierarchy of First Amendment values was aptly sketched by Mr. Justice Murphy when he said: "[S]uch utterances are no essential part of any exposition of ideas, and are of such slight social value as a step to truth that any benefit that may be derived from them is clearly outweighed by the social interest in order and morality." Chaplinsky v. New Hampshire, 315 U.S., at 572.

Although these words ordinarily lack literary, political, or scientific value, they are not entirely outside the protection of the First Amendment. Some uses of even the most offensive words are unquestionably protected. Indeed, we may assume, arguendo, that this monologue would be protected in other contexts. Nonetheless, the constitutional protection accorded to a communication containing such patently offensive sexual and excretory language need not be the same in every context. It is a characteristic of speech such as this that both its capacity to offend and its "social value," to use Mr. Justice Murphy's term, vary with the circumstances. Words that are commonplace in one setting are shocking in another. To paraphrase Mr. Justice Harlan, one occasion's lyric is another's vulgarity.

In this case it is undisputed that the content of Pacifica's broadcast was "vulgar," "offensive," and "shocking." Because content of that character is not entitled to absolute constitutional protection under all circumstances, we must consider its context in order to determine whether the Commission's action was constitutionally permissible.

Freedom to Read

The American Library Association adopted a Library Bill of Rights in the late 1930s, affirming the right of libraries and library users to be free from censorship (Walker, 1999). The ALA has revised the Library Bill of Rights several times over the years. The current version appears here. Additional information may be found on the American Library Association Web site at www.ala.org.

American Library Association, Library Bill of Rights (January 1996 edition)

The American Library Association affirms that all libraries are forums for information and ideas, and that the following basic policies should guide their services.

Books and other library resources should be provided for the interest, information, and enlightenment of all people of the community the library serves. Materials should not be excluded because of the origin, background, or views of those contributing to their creation.

Libraries should provide materials and information presenting all points of view on current and historical issues. Materials should not be proscribed or removed because of partisan or doctrinal disapproval.

Libraries should challenge censorship in the fulfillment of their responsibility to provide information and enlightenment.

Libraries should cooperate with all persons and groups concerned with resisting abridgment of free expression and free access to ideas.

A person's right to use a library should not be denied or abridged because of origin, age, background, or views.

Libraries which make exhibit spaces and meeting rooms available to the public they serve should make such facilities available on an equitable basis, regardless of the beliefs or affiliations of individuals or groups requesting their use.

Separation of Church and State

The U.S. Supreme Court has ruled that officially sponsored religious activities in public schools are a violation of the separation of church and state (Frankel, 1994). Such activities include in-school prayers and instruction that advances religious doctrine. The Supreme Court's rulings, however, do not forbid all forms of religious activity by students in school. The 1998 Guidelines developed by the U.S. Department of Education describe the kinds of religious activities that are permissible under the First Amendment.

U.S. Department of Education Guidelines on Religious Activity in Public Schools (1998 rev.)

After many decades of controversy and litigation over religious activity in public schools, the U.S. Department of Education adopted formal guidelines specifying what kinds of activity are permitted within under the Establishment Clause of the First Amendment and what kinds of activity are not. The Guidelines were adopted after consultation with a broad range of religious and civil liberties groups. As the Guidelines indicate, private religious activities, initiated by individual students, are permitted. Thus, a student is free to say a prayer or read the Bible during lunch period. What is not permitted are activities that are sponsored by the school and as a result may be or be perceived to be officially sponsored religious activities.

Student Prayer and Religious Discussion   The Establishment Clause of the First Amendment does not prohibit purely private religious speech by students. Students therefore have the same right to engage in individual or group prayer and religious discussion during the school day as they do to engage in other comparable activity. For example, students may read their Bibles or other scriptures, say grace before meals, and pray before tests to the same extent they may engage in comparable nondisruptive activities. Local school authorities possess substantial discretion to impose rules of order and other pedagogical restrictions on student activities, but they may not structure or administer such rules to discriminate against religious activity or speech.

Generally, students may pray in a nondisruptive manner when not engaged in school activities or instruction, and subject to the rules that normally pertain in the applicable setting. Specifically, students in informal settings, such as cafeterias and hallways, may pray and discuss their religious views with each other, subject to the same rules of order as apply to other student activities and speech. Students may also speak to, and attempt to persuade, their peers about religious topics just as they do with regard to political topics. School officials, however, should intercede to stop student speech that constitutes harassment aimed at a student or a group of students.

Teaching about Religion   Public schools may not provide religious instruction, but they may teach *about* religion, including the Bible or other scripture: the history of religion, comparative religion, the Bible (or other scripture) as literature, and the role of religion in the history of the United States and other countries all are permissible public school subjects. Similarly, it is permissible to consider religious influences on art, music, literature, and social studies. Although public schools may teach about religious holidays, including their religious aspects, and may celebrate the secular aspects of holidays, schools may not observe holidays as religious events or promote such observance by students.

Faith-Based Initiatives

President George W. Bush proposed addressing social problems such as hunger, homelessness, and literacy by channeling federal funds through religious organizations. He labeled this approach the Faith-Based Initiative. Information about the Bush administration's position and activities regarding the faith-based initiative can be found at www.whitehouse.gov/government/fbci/.

 Civil libertarians oppose the program on the grounds that it would violate the separation of church and state. The first document below is President Bush's statement explaining the program. The second document is a statement by Americans United for Separation of Church and State (www.au.org) opposing the Faith-Based Initiative.

President George W. Bush, Statement Supporting Faith-Based Initiatives

America is rich materially, but there remains too much poverty and despair amidst abundance. Government can rally a military, but it cannot put hope in our hearts or a sense of purpose in our lives.

 Government has a solemn responsibility to help meet the needs of poor Americans and distressed neighborhoods, but it does not have a monopoly on compassion. America is richly blessed by the diversity and vigor of neighborhood healers: civic, social, charitable, and religious groups. These quiet heroes lift people's lives in ways that are beyond government's know-how, usually on shoestring budgets, and they heal our nation's ills one heart and one act of kindness at a time.

 The indispensable and transforming work of faith-based and other charitable service groups must be encouraged. Government cannot be replaced by charities, but it can and should welcome them as partners. We must heed the growing consensus across America that successful government social programs work in fruitful partnership with community-serving and faith-based organizations—whether run by Methodists, Muslims, Mormons, or good people of no faith at all.

 The paramount goal must be compassionate results, not compassionate intentions. Federal policy should reject the failed formula of towering, distant bureaucracies that too often prize process over performance. We must be outcome-based, insisting on success and steering resources to the effective and to the inspired. Also, we must always value the bedrock principles of pluralism, nondiscrimination, evenhandedness and neutrality. Private and charitable groups, including religious ones, should have the fullest opportunity permitted by law to compete on a level playing field, so long as they achieve valid public purposes, like curbing crime, conquering addiction, strengthening families, and overcoming poverty.

 In this blueprint, I outline my agenda to enlist, equip, enable, empower and expand the heroic works of faith-based and community groups across America. The building blocks are two Executive Orders, signed yesterday, that call for the creation of a high-level White House Office of Faith-Based and Community Initiatives, and instruct five Cabinet departments to establish Centers for Faith-Based and Community Initiatives.

As President, I will lead the federal government to take bold steps to rally America's armies of compassion. I look forward to working with Congress on these issues and am open to additional ideas to meet our shared goals. I invite all Americans to join this effort to unleash the best of America.

Statement by Americans United for Separation of Church and State   The Bush "Faith-Based" Initiative: Why It's Wrong

President George W. Bush has launched a major national drive to give broad-based public funding to churches and other religious groups to provide social services. As part of the administration's crusade, Bush has created a new federal agency, the Office of Faith-Based and Community Initiatives which formally begins operations today, that will work from the White House to expand government aid to religious ministries and create church-state "partnerships."

Americans United for Separation of Church and State has taken the lead nationally in opposing Bush's faith-based efforts. Here are 10 reasons why the president's campaign should be rejected.

1. Bush's plan violates the separation of church and state.

Under the First Amendment, American citizens are free to decide on their own whether or not to support religious ministries, and the government must stay out of it. Bush's faith-based plan turns the time-tested constitutional principle of church-state separation on its ear.

At its core, Bush's plan throws the massive weight of the federal government behind religious groups and religious conversions to solve social problems. While houses of worship have played an important role in this country since its founding, these institutions have thrived on *voluntary* contributions. Forcing taxpayers to subsidize religious institutions they may or not believe in is no different from forcing them to put money in the collection plates of churches, synagogues and mosques.

2. Federally funded employment discrimination is unfair.

Under the president's proposal, churches will be legally permitted to discriminate on the basis of religion when hiring, despite receiving public dollars. A Bob Jones–style religious group, for example, will be able to receive tax aid to pay for a social service job, but still be free to hang up a sign that says "Jews And Catholics Need Not Apply."

In other words, an American could help pay for a job but be declared ineligible for the position because of his or her religious beliefs. That's not compassionate conservatism, that's outrageous. And under Bush's plan, it's perfectly legal.

3. Religion could be forced on those in need of assistance.

Under Bush's approach, religious institutions would receive taxpayer support to finance social services and would still be free to proselytize people seeking assistance. The religious freedom of beneficiaries would therefore be seriously threatened. Those in need may face religious indoctrination when they are sent to a religious organization to obtain their government benefits.

The president has promised "secular alternatives" for those who don't want to be forced to go to a house of worship for help. But in some instances, particularly in rural and less populated areas, the closest "alternative" can be a great distance away.

Imagine, for example, a Jewish family looking for food and shelter in Texas. The government tells the family they can visit the Southern Baptist church nearby or travel 100 miles for help from a "secular alternative."

4. Bush's plan opens the door to federal regulation of religion.

Government always regulates what it finances. This occurs because public officials are obliged to make certain that taxpayer funds are properly spent. Once churches, temples, mosques and synagogues are being financed by the public, some of their freedom will be placed in jeopardy by the almost certain regulation to follow.

5. The vitality of our faith communities will be hurt.

For years, millions of Americans have become active with their local houses of worship, making special contributions as a way to strengthen their ties to their faith traditions and increase personal piety. Once religious institutions are working in tandem with the federal government and receiving tax dollars to provide services, members may be less inclined to "dig a little deeper" to help with expenses.

Once these contributions drop off, the attendant spirit of volunteerism may also wither away. Making religious institutions dependent on the government for money will only harm these institutions and their vitality in the long run.

6. Bush's plan pits faith groups against each other.

Since the founding of the nation, all religious groups have stood equal in the eyes of the law. With a separation between church and state, government has been neutral on religious issues and no specific faith tradition received favoritism or support.

The Bush plan, however, calls for competition between religious groups. For the first time in American history, religious groups will be asked, indeed encouraged, to battle it out for a piece of the government pie. Pitting houses of worship against each other in this fashion is a recipe for divisive conflict.

7. Some religions will be favored over others.

While on the campaign trail, Bush promised that he would "not discriminate for or against Methodist or Mormons or Muslims or good people with no faith at all."

Then he announced he would not allow funding of the Nation of Islam, because, as he sees it, the group "preaches hate." The president has not, however, explained how the government will decide which groups preach "hate," and which preach "love." Stephen Goldsmith, who will be chiefly responsible for implementing the president's plan, has indicated the administration may also discriminate against groups affiliated with the Wiccan faith.

8. There's no proof that religious groups will offer better care than secular providers.

Many supporters of Bush's proposal have insisted that faith-based institutions are better, and far more successful, than secular service providers. However, little empirical research supports these claims. Few studies have examined whether religious ministries are more successful than secular groups in providing aid or producing better results, and it is unwise to launch a major federal initiative with so little research in the area.

School Vouchers

One of the main educational reforms of conservatives is the idea of government-funded vouchers to help parents send their children to private schools, including religious institutions. Civil libertarians oppose vouchers programs on the grounds that they represent direct support for religion in violation of the separation of church and state. The Supreme Court upheld the constitutionality of vouchers in 2002. Below is a statement by the American Center for Law and Justice (www.aclj.org) in support of vouchers (Weil, 2002).

In Favor of Vouchers: American Center for Law and Justice, Memorandum of Law on the Constitutionality of School Vouchers   The ACLJ is committed to the principle that parents are responsible for the education of their children and that parents have the right to choose schools that best serve their educational needs. Maximizing educational choices for parents is therefore essential, especially for those families who are otherwise unable to afford private school tuition. School vouchers represent a permissible means of leveling the playing field so that all parents can choose the education that suits their values, and their children's needs. A state's efforts to provide funds to parents so that parents can more effectively choose the education they think best suits their children's needs is not an establishment of religion.

Religious Symbols in Public Places

Many religious groups and individuals want to have religious displays on public property. This includes, for example, placing Nativity scenes in front of courthouses or other public buildings. A recent controversy involves displays of the Ten Commandments in schools, courthouses, and public parks. Below is a statement by the Anti-Defamation League (www.adl.org) opposing the placement of the Ten Commandments in public areas (Hester, 2003).

Anti-Defamation League (ADL) on Placing the Ten Commandments in public areas The Anti-Defamation League believes that the increasing call for the government to post the Ten Commandments in schools, government buildings, courts and other public places—while often well-intentioned—is both unconstitutional and bad policy. Governmental posting of the Ten Commandments flies in the face of the Constitution's guarantee of separation of church and state and leads to the kind of religious quarreling that can draw sharp divides in otherwise harmonious communities. Before embracing this easy fix for some of society's most intractable problems, communities should consider its consequences for one of America's most precious traditions: religious tolerance. . . .

Even if posting the Ten Commandments in public schools and other public facilities were constitutional, it would still do great damage to religious tolerance in America. Advocates of such proposals assert that these Biblical injunctions are values universally accepted by all Americans. They fail, though, to take into account two crucial facts. First, not all Americans subscribe to religions that follow the Bible or the Ten Commandments. Millions of Muslims, Hindus and Buddhists (among others) in America adhere to religious, ethical and moral traditions that draw from a variety of texts other than the Bible. Second, those religions that do adhere to the Ten Commandments follow very different versions of the laws. The ancient Hebrew text followed by Jews is very different from the language found in the King James Bible version accepted by most Protestant churches in America today. Further, Catholics and Lutherans follow yet another text altogether. The assumption that the government-ordered posting of the Ten Commandments in public places would honor the beliefs of all Americans is itself an act of religious intolerance.

The Religious Freedom Restoration Act (RFRA)

In 1990 the Supreme Court held that a state could punish a Native American person for using peyote, a hallucinogenic drug, even though the use of that substance was a traditional religious practice for some Native American tribes. A broad coalition of civil rights groups regarded the decision as a threat to the First Amendment guarantee of free exercise of religion. Congress enacted the Religious Freedom Restoration Act (RFRA) in 1993 to override the Court's decision. In 1997, however, the Court ruled the RFRA unconstitutional. Below is an excerpt from the RFRA (Long, 2000).

Sec. 3. Free Exercise of Religion Protected

(a) In General: Government shall not substantially burden a person's exercise of religion even if the burden results from a rule of general applicability, except as provided in subsection (b).

(b) Exception: Government may substantially burden a person's exercise of religion only if it demonstrates that application of the burden to the person—(1) is in furtherance of a compelling governmental interest; and (2) is the least restrictive means of furthering that compelling governmental interest.

Due Process of Law

Miranda: The Right to Remain Silent

In the 1966 case of Miranda v. Arizona, *the Supreme Court held that a criminal suspect has the right to remain silent and that the police must advise a suspect of his or her rights before any questioning. There is much misunderstanding about what the Court actually said in* Miranda. *The following excerpt from the decision contains the Court's ruling on the "Miranda warning" (Baker, 1983).*

Miranda v. Arizona   By custodial interrogation, we mean questioning initiated by law enforcement officers after a person has been taken into custody. . . . As for the procedural safeguards to be employed . . . the following measures are required. Prior to any questioning, the person must be warned that he has a right to remain silent, that any statement he does make may be used as evidence against him, and that he has a right to the presence of an attorney, either retained or appointed. The defendant may waive effectuation of these rights, provided the waiver is made voluntarily, knowingly and intelligently. If, however, he indicates in any manner and at any stage of the process that he wishes to consult with an attorney before speaking there can be no questioning. Likewise, if the individual is alone and indicates in any manner that he does not wish to be interrogated, the police may not question him. The mere fact that he may have answered some questions or volunteered some statements on his own does not deprive him of the right to refrain from answering any further inquiries until he has consulted with an attorney and thereafter consents to be questioned. . . .

The Fifth Amendment privilege is so fundamental to our system of constitutional rule and the expedient of giving an adequate warning as to the availability of the privilege so simple, we will not pause to inquire in individual cases whether the defendant was aware of his rights without a warning being given.

Death Penalty

In the first document below, the group Pro–Death Penalty.com (www. prodeathpenalty.com) challenges the major arguments offered by death penalty opponents regarding the death penalty. In the second document, the Death Penalty Information Center (www.deathpenaltyinfo.org) describes cases of individuals who have been executed despite doubts about their guilt.

Death Penalty and Sentencing Information in the United States by Dudley Sharp   The death penalty debate in the U.S. is dominated by the

fraudulent voice of the anti–death penalty movement. The culture of lies and deceit so dominates that movement that many of the false-hoods are now wrongly accepted as fact, by both advocates and oppo-nents of capital punishment. The following report presents the true facts of the death penalty in America. If you are even casually aware of this public debate, you will note that every category contradicts the well-worn frauds presented by the anti–death penalty movement. The anti–death penalty movement specializes in the abolition of truth.

1. Imposition of the death penalty is extraordinarily rare. Since 1967, there has been one execution for every 1600 murders, or 0.06%. There have been approximately 560,000 murders and 358 executions from 1967–1996 FBI's Uniform Crime Report (UCR) & Bureau of Justice Statistics (BJS).

2. Approximately 5900 persons have been sentenced to death and 358 executed (from 1973–96). An average of 0.2% of those were exe-cuted every year during that time. 56 murderers were executed in 1995, a record number for the modern death penalty. This represented 1.8% of those on death row. The average time on death row for those 56 exe-cuted—11 years, 2 months ("Capital Punishment 1995," BJS, 1996), an all time record of longevity, breaking the 1994 record of 10 years, 2 months.

3. Death penalty opponents ("opponents") state that "Those who support the death penalty see it as a solution to violent crime." Oppo-nents, hereby, present one of many fabrications. In reality, executions are seen as the appropriate punishment for certain criminals commit-ting specific crimes. So says the U.S. Supreme Court and so say most death penalty supporters ("advocates").

4. Opponents equate execution and murder, believing that if two acts have the same ending or result, then those two acts are morally equivalent. This is a morally untenable position. Is the legal taking of property to satisfy a debt the same as auto theft? Both result in loss of property. Are kidnapping and legal incarceration the same? Both involve imprisonment against one's will. Is killing in self defense the same as capital murder? Both end in taking human life. Are rape and making love the same? Both may result in sexual intercourse. How absurd. Opponents' flawed logic and moral confusion mirror their "factual" arguments—there is, often, an absence of reality. The moral confusion of some opponents is astounding. Some equate the American death penalty with the Nazi holocaust. Opponents see no moral distinction between the slaughter of 12 million totally innocent men, women and children and the just execution of society's worst human rights violators.

Executed despite Doubts about Guilt   There is no way to tell how many of the over 750 people executed since 1976 may also have been innocent. Courts do not generally entertain claims of innocence when the defendant is dead. Defense attorneys move on to other cases where clients' lives can still be saved. Some of those with strong claims include:

Roger Keith Coleman, Virginia Conviction, 1982; Executed 1992

Coleman was convicted of raping and murdering his sister-in-law in 1981, but both his trial and appeal were plagued by errors made by his attorneys. The U.S. Supreme Court refused to consider the merits of his petition because his state appeal had been filed one day late. Considerable evidence was developed after the trial to refute the state's evidence, and that evidence might well have produced a different result at a re-trial. Governor Wilder considered a commutation for Coleman, but allowed him to be executed when Coleman failed a lie detector test on the day of his execution.

Joseph O'Dell, Virginia Conviction, 1986; Executed 1997

New DNA blood evidence has thrown considerable doubt on the murder and rape conviction of O'Dell. In reviewing his case in 1991, three Supreme Court Justices said they had doubts about O'Dell's guilt and whether he should have been allowed to represent himself. Without the blood evidence, there is little linking O'Dell to the crime. In September 1996, the 4th Circuit of the U.S. Court of Appeals reinstated his death sentence and upheld his conviction. The U.S. Supreme Court refused to review O'Dell's claims of innocence and held that its decision regarding juries being told about the alternative sentence of life-without-parole was not retroactive to his case. O'Dell asked the state to conduct DNA tests on other pieces of evidence to demonstrate his innocence but was refused. He was executed on July 23.

David Spence, Texas Conviction, 1984; Executed 1997

Spence was charged with murdering three teenagers in 1982. He was allegedly hired by a convenience store owner to kill another girl, and killed these victims by mistake. The convenience store owner, Muneer Deeb, was originally convicted and sentenced to death, but then was acquitted at a re-trial. The police lieutenant who supervised the investigation of Spence, Marvin Horton, later concluded: "I do not think David Spence committed this crime." Ramon Salinas, the homicide detective who actually conducted the investigation, said: "My opinion is that David Spence was innocent. Nothing from the investigation ever led us to any evidence that he was involved." No physical evidence connected Spence to the crime. The case against Spence was pursued by a zealous narcotics cop who relied on testimony of prison inmates who were granted favors in return for testimony.

Equal Protection
Racial Profiling

In the late 1990s, racial profiling emerged as a major civil rights issue. Racial minorities charged that the police stopped African American and Hispanic drivers because of the color of their skin and not because of actual traffic law vio-lations (American Civil Liberties Union, 1999; Harris, 2002). After the terror-ist attacks on the World Trade Center and the Pentagon on September 11, 2001, many people feared that there would be an outbreak of discrimination against Arab Americans similar to the racial profiling of African Americans. The fol-lowing document is a statement by the Leadership Conference on Civil Rights (www.civilrights.org) warning of the dangers of discrimination as a result of the terrorist attacks on September 11, 2001.

Leadership Conference on Civil Rights (LCCR), Wrong Then, Wrong Now

(2003) In the months preceding September 11, a national consensus had emerged on the need to combat racial profiling. In the fearful aftermath of the terrorist attacks, some reevaluated their views. It is now time to dispel those doubts, reawaken the national consensus, and ban racial profiling in America. Racial profiling occurs when law enforcement agents impermissibly use race, religion, ethnicity or national origin in deciding who to investigate. Compelling anecdotal and statistical evidence demonstrates that minorities are disproportion-ately targeted by law enforcement. Pretextual traffic stops of Blacks and Hispanics are common across the United States—the police fre-quently use race as a basis to suspect that minorities violate the drug and immigration laws. . . .

On September 11, this consensus evaporated. The 19 men who hijacked airplanes to carry out the horrific attacks on the World Trade Center and the Pentagon were Arabs from Muslim countries. The fed-eral government immediately focused massive investigative resources and law enforcement attention on Arabs, Arab Americans, Muslims, and those perceived to be Arab or Muslim, such as Sikhs and other South Asians. Many of the practices employed in the name of fighting terrorism—from the singling out of young Arab or Muslim men in the United States for questioning and detention to the selective application of the immigration laws to nationals of Arab or Muslim countries—amount to racial profiling. But despite public hostility to street-level racial profiling, anti-terror profiling has flourished.

Nevertheless, selectively targeting Arabs, Muslims, South Asians, and Sikhs for increased law enforcement attention based on race, eth-nicity, or religion is flawed for three reasons. First, such profiling is based on the same kinds of myths about particular groups and their propensity for particular criminal activity that fuel traditional, street-level profiling. Second, like street-level profiling, terrorism profiling is simply not an effective tool against the illegal activity it is designed to stop. Third, like traditional profiling, terrorism profiling and the selec-tive enforcement of immigration laws that accompanies it are inconsis-tent with basic constitutional principles. . . .

1. "Driving While Arab"

As demonstrated by the account of the Indian American motorist set forth in Chapter I, "driving while Arab" has joined the profiling lexicon alongside "driving while Black" and "driving while brown" since September 11. Arabs, Muslims, South Asians, and Sikhs are now subjected to traffic stops and searches based in whole or in part on their race, ethnicity, or religion due to law enforcement perceptions that they are likely participants in terrorist activity. For example:

On October 4, 2001, in Gwinnett, Georgia, an Arab American motorist was pulled over by a patrol car following an illegal U-turn. The police officer approached the car with gun drawn. He ordered the motorist out of his car, searched him, threatened him, and called him a "bin Laden supporter."

On December 5, 2001, in Burbank, Illinois, a veiled Muslim woman was stopped by a police officer for driving with suspended plates. After she showed the officer her license and registration, as requested, the officer allegedly asked her when Ramadan would be over. She was arrested for driving with suspended plates, was pushed by the officer as she got in the patrol car, and was asked inappropriate questions about her hair by the officer. The woman was released later that day.

Women's Rights

Women's rights activists believe that the Equal Protection Clause of the Fourteenth Amendment has not been interpreted in a manner that adequately protects the rights of women. Consequently, they have proposed adding an Equal Rights Amendment (ERA) to the Constitution. The ERA was first introduced in 1923. The complete text of the 1970s version of the ERA is as follows (Feinberg, 1986).

The Equal Rights Amendment   Section 1. Equality of rights under the law shall not be denied or abridged by the United States or by any state on account of sex.

Section 2. The Congress shall have the power to enforce, by appropriate legislation, the provisions of this article.

Section 3. This amendment shall take effect two years after the date of ratification.

Title IX of the Educational Amendments of 1972   *Title IX of the 1972 Education Act is designed to ensure equal treatment for women's athletics programs in public schools and colleges and universities. Below are excerpts from the law.*

106.41 Athletics

(a) *General.* No person shall, on the basis of sex, be excluded from participation in, be denied the benefits of, be treated differently from another person or otherwise be discriminated against in any interscholastic, intercollegiate, club or intramural athletics offered by a recipient, and no recipient shall provide any such athletics separately on such basis.

(b) *Separate teams.* Notwithstanding the requirements of paragraph (a) of this section, a recipient may operate or sponsor separate teams for members of each sex where selection for such teams is based upon competitive skill or the activity involved is a contact sport. However, where a recipient operates or sponsors a team in a particular sport for members of one sex but operates or sponsors no such team for members of the other sex, and athletic opportunities for members of that sex have previously been limited, members of the excluded sex must be allowed to try-out for the team offered unless the sport involved is a contact sport. For the purposes of this part, contact sports include boxing, wrestling, rugby, ice hockey, football, basketball and other sports the purpose or major activity of which involves bodily contact.

(c) *Equal opportunity.* A recipient which operates or sponsors interscholastic, intercollegiate, club or intramural athletics shall provide equal athletic opportunity for members of both sexes. In determining whether equal opportunities are available the Director will consider, among other factors:

(1) Whether the selection of sports and levels of competition effectively accommodate the interests and abilities of members of both sexes; (2) The provision of equipment and supplies; (3) Scheduling of games and practice time; (4) Travel and per diem allowance; (5) Opportunity to receive coaching and academic tutoring; (6) Assignment and compensation of coaches and tutors; (7) Provision of locker rooms, practice and competitive facilities; (8) Provision of medical and training facilities and services; (9) Provision of housing and dining facilities and services; (10) Publicity.

Opposition to Title IX

Conservatives oppose the requirements of Title IX, along with all affirmative action programs. The following press release by the conservative women's group the Independent Women's Forum (www.iwf.org) states its reasons for opposing Title IX.

No More Quotas! IWF Urges Title IX Commission to End Proportionality

WASHINGTON, D.C. (January 29, 2003)—Recommendations expected to be made in the coming days by the Commission on Opportunity in Athletics to Education Secretary Rod Paige will improve the unfair environment created by Title IX but not go nearly far enough, the Independent Women's Forum said today.

"What is needed is an end to the current proportionality test," says Editor of *The Women's Quarterly* Charlotte Hays. "The recommendations we expect the Commission to make—varying the proportionality, excluding non-traditional students from computation, and measuring student interest in athletics by sex – are a step in the right direction but, unfortunately, will still leave fairness out of intercollegiate sports."

The original intent of Title IX was to prohibit sex discrimination in federally funded educational programs. It was never intended to function as a quota system. Instead, this policy of proportionality has been implemented by the U.S. Department of Education (DOE)—placing unrealistic demands on colleges and institutionalizing discrimination against men.

The proportionality test used by the DOE's Office for Civil Rights (OCR) requires colleges and universities to demonstrate that participation in collegiate sports is proportional by sex to their respective enrollments. It is therefore an arbitrary and unfair means of determining a school's compliance with Title IX.

IWF Senior Fellow Melana Zyla Vickers notes: "Because the test fails to account for differing levels of interest between men and women, many universities have been forced to drop men's sports teams, such as wrestling, baseball, or gymnastics, in order comply with Title IX. Also, the proportionality test excludes those women who participate in traditional female physical activities, such as dance, cheerleading, and drill team, making it even more difficult for schools to meet the strict quotas."

Adds Hays, "Women are the majority of college students today. But women simply aren't as interested as men in sports. In intramural sports, for example, which are driven entirely by student interest, only 22% of female students participate compared to 78% of men. And at all-women's colleges, only 16% of women participate in sports."

Vickers concludes, "Title IX was enacted to guarantee equal opportunity. It was never meant to ensure equal outcomes."

People with Disabilities
The 1990 Americans with Disabilities Act outlawed discrimination in employment and accommodations against persons with physical or mental disabilities. The excerpts from the law, below, provide both the rationale for the law and the definition of disability (Pelka, 1997).

Americans with Disabilities Act, 1990 (a) Findings. The Congress finds that—(1) some 43,000,000 Americans have one or more physical or mental disabilities, and this number is increasing as the population as a whole is growing older; (2) historically, society has tended to isolate and segregate individuals with disabilities, and, despite some improvements, such forms of discrimination against individuals with disabilities continue to be a serious and pervasive social problem; (3) discrimination against individuals with disabilities persists in such critical areas as employment, housing, public accommodations, education, transportation, communication, recreation, institutionalization, health services, voting, and access to public services; (4) unlike individuals who have experienced discrimination on the basis of race, color, sex, national origin, religion, or age, individuals who have experienced discrimination on the basis of disability have often had no legal recourse to redress such discrimination; . . .

(2) Disability. The term "disability" means, with respect to an individual—(A) a physical or mental impairment that substantially limits one or more of the major life activities of such individual; (B) a record of such an impairment; or (C) being regarded as having such an impairment.

Genetic Discrimination

Advances in medical technology, particularly with regard to DNA, make it possible to estimate whether a person has a likelihood of developing a particular disease or disability. Civil libertarians worry that this capability will be used to discriminate in employment against people with particular genetic profiles. In response to those concerns, President Bill Clinton issued Executive Order 13145 in 2000 forbidding genetic discrimination by federal agencies.

Executive Order 13145 To Prohibit Discrimination in Federal Employment Based on Genetic Information

By the authority vested in me as President of the United States by the Constitution and the laws of the United States of America, it is ordered as follows:

Section 1. Nondiscrimination in Federal Employment on the Basis of Protected Genetic Information.

1-101. It is the policy of the Government of the United States to provide equal employment opportunity in Federal employment for all qualified persons and to prohibit discrimination against employees based on protected genetic information, or information about a request for or the receipt of genetic services. This policy of equal opportunity applies to every aspect of Federal employment.

1-102. The head of each Executive department and agency shall extend the policy set forth in section 1-101 to all its employees covered by section 717 of Title VII of the Civil Rights Act of 1964, as amended (42 U.S.C. 2000e-16).

1-103. Executive departments and agencies shall carry out the provisions of this order to the extent permitted by law and consistent with their statutory and regulatory authorities, and their enforcement mechanisms. The Equal Employment Opportunity Commission shall be responsible for coordinating the policy of the Government of the United States to prohibit discrimination against employees in Federal employment based on protected genetic information, or information about a request for or the receipt of genetic services.

Sec. 2. Requirements Applicable to Employing Departments and Agencies.

1-201. Definitions. Genetic test means the analysis of human DNA, RNA, chromosomes, proteins, or certain metabolites in order to detect disease-related genotypes or mutations. Tests for metabolites fall within the definition of "genetic tests" when an excess or deficiency of the metabolites indicates the presence of a mutation or mutations. The conducting of metabolic tests by a department or agency that are not intended to reveal the presence of a mutation shall not be considered a violation of this order, regardless of the results of the tests. Test results revealing a mutation shall, however, be subject to the provisions of this order.

1. Protected genetic information.

In general, protected genetic information means: information about an individual's genetic tests; information about the genetic tests of an individual's family members; or information about the occurrence of a disease, or medical condition or disorder in family members of the individual.

Information about an individual's current health status (including information about sex, age, physical exams, and chemical, blood, or urine analyses) is not protected genetic information unless it is described in subparagraph (1).

1-202. In discharging their responsibilities under this order, departments and agencies shall implement the following nondiscrimination requirements. The employing department or agency shall not discharge, fail or refuse to hire, or otherwise discriminate against any employee with respect to the compensation, terms, conditions, or privileges of employment of that employee, because of protected genetic information with respect to the employee, or because of information about a request for or the receipt of genetic services by such employee.

The employing department or agency shall not limit, segregate, or classify employees in any way that would deprive or tend to deprive any employee of employment opportunities or otherwise adversely affect that employee's status, because of protected genetic information with respect to the employee or because of information about a request for or the receipt of genetic services by such employee.

The employing department or agency shall not request, require, collect, or purchase protected genetic information with respect to an employee, or information about a request for or the receipt of genetic services by such employee.

The employing department or agency shall not disclose protected genetic information with respect to an employee, or information about a request for or the receipt of genetic services by an employee except:

to the employee who is the subject of the information, at his or her request; to an occupational or other health researcher, if the research conducted complies with the regulations and protections provided for under part 46 of title 45, of the Code of Federal Regulations; if required by a Federal statute, congressional subpoena, or an order issued by a court of competent jurisdiction, except that if the subpoena or court order was secured without the knowledge of the individual to whom the information refers, the employer shall provide the individual with adequate notice to challenge the subpoena or court order, unless the subpoena or court order also imposes confidentiality requirements; or to executive branch officials investigating compliance with this order, if the information is relevant to the investigation. The employing department or agency shall not maintain protected genetic information or information about a request for or the receipt of genetic services in general personnel files; such information shall be treated as confidential medical records and kept separate from personnel files.

The White House, February 8, 2000

Lesbian and Gay People

In 1996 it became apparent that one or more states might soon grant people of the same sex the right to legally marry—either through a state statute or a state supreme court ruling. In response, opponents of such a right sponsored the federal Defense of Marriage Act (DOMA), which holds that no state is required to recognize a same-sex marriage from another state.

The first selection below is an excerpt from the Defense of Marriage Act. The second selection is a statement by the Human Rights Campaign in support of same-sex marriage.

Defense of Marriage Act, 1996   Sec. 1738C. Certain acts, records, and proceedings and the effect thereof

No State, territory, or possession of the United States, or Indian tribe, shall be required to give effect to any public act, record, or judicial proceeding of any other State, territory, possession, or tribe respecting a relationship between persons of the same sex that is treated as a marriage under the laws of such other State, territory, possession, or tribe, or a right or claim arising from such relationship.

Human Rights Campaign: The Marriage Resolution   Because marriage is a basic human right and an individual personal choice,

RESOLVED, the State should not interfere with same gender couples who choose to marry and share fully and equally in the rights, responsibilities and commitment of civil marriage.

Privacy

In order to protect the privacy rights of U.S. citizens, Congress passed the Privacy Act of 1974. The law forbids the disclosure of private information about an individual to a third party unless the individual provides consent.

Privacy Act, 1974

The "No Disclosure without Consent" Rule No agency shall disclose any record which is contained in a system of records by any means of communication to any person, or to another agency, except pursuant to a written request by, or with the prior written consent of, the individual to whom the record pertains [subject to 12 exceptions].

Freedom of Information Act, 1966

The Freedom of Information Act (FOIA) is designed to hold government accountable to U.S. citizens by allowing them to obtain information in government files (subject to certain limitations). The FOIA has been instrumental in exposing abuses of individual rights by government agencies such as the FBI. The document below is an excerpt from a government document explaining how to file a request for government documents under FOIA.

A Citizen's Guide on Using the Freedom of Information Act and the Privacy Act of 1974 to Request Government Records C. Making a FOIA Request

The first step in making a request under the FOIA is to identify the agency that has the records. A FOIA request must be addressed to a specific agency. There is no central government records office that services FOIA requests. Often, a requester knows beforehand which agency has the desired records. If not, a requester can consult a government directory such as the United States Government Manual. This manual has a complete list of all Federal agencies, a description of agency functions, and the address of each agency. A requester who is uncertain about which agency has the records that are needed can make FOIA requests at more than one agency. Agencies require that FOIA requests be in writing. Letters requesting records under the FOIA can be short and simple. No one needs a lawyer to make a FOIA request. . . . The request letter should be addressed to the agency's FOIA officer or to the head of the agency. The envelope containing the written request should be marked "Freedom of Information Act Request" in the lower left-hand corner.

There are three basic elements to a FOIA request letter. First, the letter should state that the request is being made under the Freedom of Information Act. Second, the request should identify the records that are being sought as specifically as possible. Third, the name and address of the requester must be included. . . .

A requester should keep a copy of the request letter and related correspondence until the request has been finally resolved.

Reproductive Rights

The idea of a constitutional right to abortion is one of the most controversial issues in the civil liberties field. The U.S. Supreme Court affirmed the right to abortion in the 1973 decision in Roe v. Wade. *The decision is widely misunderstood. In particular, many people do not understand the trimester framework that the Court adopted, which permits increasing government regulation of abortion through the course of the three trimesters. The relevant sections of* Roe v. Wade *are excerpted below (McCorvey, 1994; Garrow, 1994).*

Roe v. Wade, 1973   This right of privacy, whether it be founded in the Fourteenth Amendment's concept of personal liberty and restrictions upon state action, as we feel it is, or, as the District Court determined, in the Ninth Amendment's reservation of rights to the people, is broad enough to encompass a woman's decision whether or not to terminate her pregnancy. The detriment that the State would impose upon the pregnant woman by denying this choice altogether is apparent. Specific and direct harm medically diagnosable even in early pregnancy may be involved. Maternity, or additional offspring, may force upon the woman a distressful life and future. Psychological harm may be imminent. Mental and physical health may be taxed by child care. There is also the distress, for all concerned, associated with the unwanted child, and there is the problem of bringing a child into a family already unable, psychologically and otherwise, to care for it. In other cases, as in this one, the additional difficulties and continuing stigma of unwed motherhood may be involved. All these are factors the woman and her responsible physician necessarily will consider in consultation.

On the basis of elements such as these, appellant and some *amici* argue that the woman's right is absolute and that she is entitled to terminate her pregnancy at whatever time, in whatever way, and for whatever reason she alone chooses. With this we do not agree. Appellant's arguments that Texas either has no valid interest at all in regulating the abortion decision, or no interest strong enough to support any limitation upon the woman's sole determination, are unpersuasive. The Court's decisions recognizing a right of privacy also acknowledge that some state regulation in areas protected by that right is appropriate. As noted above, a State may properly assert important interests in safeguarding health, in maintaining medical standards, and in protecting potential life. At some point in pregnancy, these respective interests become sufficiently compelling to sustain regulation of the factors that govern the abortion decision. The privacy right involved, therefore, cannot be said to be absolute. In fact, it is not clear to us that the claim asserted by some *amici* that one has an unlimited right to do with one's body as one pleases bears a close relationship to the right of privacy previously articulated in the Court's decisions. The Court has refused to recognize an unlimited right of this kind in the past. *Jacobson v. Massachusetts*, 197 U. S. 11 (1905) (vaccination); *Buck v. Bell*, 274 U. S. 200 (1927) (sterilization).

We, therefore, conclude that the right of personal privacy includes the abortion decision, but that this right is not unqualified and must be considered against important state interests in regulation. . . .

With respect to the State's important and legitimate interest in the health of the mother, the "compelling" point, in the light of present medical knowledge, is at approximately the end of the first trimester. This is so because of the now-established medical fact, referred to above at 149, that until the end of the first trimester mortality in abortion may be less than mortality in normal childbirth. It follows that, from and after this point, a State may regulate the abortion procedure to the extent that the regulation reasonably relates to the preservation and protection of maternal health. Examples of permissible state regulation in this area are requirements as to the qualifications of the person who is to perform the abortion; as to the licensure of that person; as to the facility in which the procedure is to be performed, that is, whether it must be a hospital or may be a clinic or some other place of less-than-hospital status; as to the licensing of the facility; and the like.

This means, on the other hand, that, for the period of pregnancy prior to this "compelling" point, the attending physician, in consultation with his patient, is free to determine, without regulation by the State, that, in his medical judgment, the patient's pregnancy should be terminated. If that decision is reached, the judgment may be effectuated by an abortion free of interference by the State.

With respect to the State's important and legitimate interest in potential life, the "compelling" point is at viability. This is so because the fetus then presumably has the capability of meaningful life outside the mother's womb. State regulation protective of fetal life after viability thus has both logical and biological justifications. If the State is interested in protecting fetal life after viability, it may go so far as to proscribe abortion during that period, except when it is necessary to preserve the life or health of the mother.

Legalization of Drugs

Many civil libertarians advocate the legalization of drugs, and they advance a variety of arguments in support of this idea. With respect to civil liberties, they argue that people have a privacy right to do what they want with their own bodies. Also, they argue that the government's war on drugs has resulted in many abuses of civil liberties by law enforcement agencies. Below is an excerpt from the Libertarian Party (www.lp.org) position on legalizing drugs.

Should We Re-Legalize Drugs? Libertarians, like most Americans, demand to be safe at home and on the streets.

Libertarians would like all Americans to be healthy and free of drug dependence. But drug laws don't help, they make things worse.

The professional politicians scramble to make names for themselves as tough anti-drug warriors, while the experts agree that the "war on drugs" has been lost, and could never be won. The tragic victims of that war are your personal liberty and its companion, responsibility. It's time to consider the re-legalization of drugs.

The Lessons of Prohibition

In the 1920's, alcohol was made illegal by Prohibition. The result: Organized Crime. Criminals jumped at the chance to supply the demand for liquor. The streets became battlegrounds. The criminals bought off law enforcement and judges. Adulterated booze blinded and killed people. Civil rights were trampled in the hopeless attempt to keep people from drinking.

When the American people saw what Prohibition was doing to them, they supported its repeal. When they succeeded, most states legalized liquor and the criminal gangs were out of the liquor business.

Today's war on drugs is a re-run of Prohibition. Approximately 40 million Americans are occasional, peaceful users of some illegal drug who are no threat to anyone. They are not going to stop. The laws don't, and can't, stop drug use.

Organized Crime Profits

Whenever there is a great demand for a product and government makes it illegal, a black market always appears to supply the demand. The price of the product rises dramatically and the opportunity for huge profits is obvious. The criminal gangs love the situation, making millions. They kill other drug dealers, along with innocent people caught in the crossfire, to protect their territory. They corrupt police and courts. Pushers sell adulterated dope and experimental drugs, causing injury and death. And because drugs are illegal, their victims have no recourse.

Crime Increases

Half the cost of law enforcement and prisons is squandered on drug related crime. Of all drug users, a relative few are addicts who commit crimes daily to supply artificially expensive habits. They are the robbers, car thieves and burglars who make our homes and streets unsafe.

An American Police State

Civil liberties suffer. We are all "suspects," subject to random urine tests, highway check points and spying into our personal finances. Your property can be seized without trial, if the police merely claim you got it with drug profits. Doing business with cash makes you a suspect. America is becoming a police state because of the war on drugs.

America Can Handle Legal Drugs

Today's illegal drugs were legal before 1914. Cocaine was even found in the original Coca-Cola recipe. Americans had few problems with cocaine, opium, heroin or marijuana. Drugs were inexpensive; crime was low. Most users handled their drug of choice and lived normal, productive lives. Addicts out of control were a tiny minority.

The first laws prohibiting drugs were racist in origin—to prevent Chinese laborers from using opium and to prevent blacks and Hispanics from using cocaine and marijuana. That was unjust and unfair, just as it is unjust and unfair to make criminals of peaceful drug users today.

Some Americans will always use alcohol, tobacco, marijuana or other drugs. Most are not addicts, they are social drinkers or occasional users. Legal drugs would be inexpensive, so even addicts could support their habits with honest work, rather than by crime. Organized crime would be deprived of its profits. The police could return to protecting us from real criminals; and there would be room enough in existing prisons for them.

Try Personal Responsibility

It's time to re-legalize drugs and let people take responsibility for themselves. Drug abuse is a tragedy and a sickness. Criminal laws only drive the problem underground and put money in the pockets of the criminal class. With drugs legal, compassionate people could do more to educate and rehabilitate drug users who seek help. Drugs should be legal. Individuals have the right to decide for themselves what to put in their bodies, so long as they take responsibility for their actions.

From the Mayor of Baltimore, Kurt Schmoke, to conservative writer and TV personality, William F. Buckley, Jr., leading Americans are now calling for repeal of America's repressive and ineffective drug laws. The Libertarian Party urges you to join in this effort to make our streets safer and our liberties more secure.

The War on Terrorism

In response to the terrorist attacks on the World Trade Center and the Pentagon on September 11, 2001, the federal government launched a "war on terrorism" (Hentoff, 2003). One of the most important parts of this effort is the USA Patriot Act. Civil libertarians argue that the law expands the powers of the government too far and threatens individual rights. The first document below is a critique of the USA Patriot Act by the American Civil Liberties Union (www.aclu.org). The second document is a statement by Attorney General John Ashcroft defending how the Justice Department has used the law.

ACLU, How the USA PATRIOT Act redefines "Domestic Terrorism," December 6, 2002

Section 802 of the USA PATRIOT Act (Pub. L. No. 107–52) expanded the definition of terrorism to cover "domestic," as opposed to international, terrorism. A person engages in domestic terrorism if they do an act "dangerous to human life"'" that is a violation of the criminal laws of a state or the United States, if the act appears to be intended to: (i) intimidate or coerce a civilian population; (ii) influence the policy of a government by intimidation or coercion; or (iii) to affect the conduct of a government by mass destruction, assassination or kidnapping. Additionally, the acts have to occur primarily within the territorial jurisdiction of the United States and if they do not, may be regarded as international terrorism.

Section 802 does not create a new crime of domestic terrorism. However, it does expand the type of conduct that the government can investigate when it is investigating "terrorism." The USA PATRIOT Act expanded governmental powers to investigate terrorism, and some of these powers are applicable to domestic terrorism.

The definition of domestic terrorism is broad enough to encompass the activities of several prominent activist campaigns and organizations. Greenpeace, Operation Rescue, Vieques Island and WTO protesters and the Environmental Liberation Front have all recently engaged in activities that could subject them to being investigated as engaging in domestic terrorism.

Statement by Attorney General John Ashcroft, March 4, 2003

Finally, I would like to point out that throughout this process, the Department of Justice has acted thoughtfully, carefully and within the framework of American freedom—the Constitution of the United States. Time and again, the actions in the war on terrorism have been subjected to thorough judicial review. And time and again, the Department has successfully defended legal challenges including:

Detaining enemy combatants—SUSTAINED

Detaining the enemy at Guantanamo Bay—SUSTAINED

Sharing FISA information—SUSTAINED

Withholding names of sensitive immigration detainees—SUSTAINED

Freezing assets of purported charities that fund terrorists—SUSTAINED

The President's powers to protect the American people are rooted in the Constitution and sustained in Court. The actions we take against the terrorist threat will always be rooted in the Constitution while accounting for the adapting and changing methods of our terrorist enemies.

As the President stated in a recent visit to the FBI, "There is no such thing as perfect security against a hidden network of cold-blooded killers. Yet, abroad and at home, we're not going to wait until the worst dangers are upon us."

Our strategy and tactics are working. Listen to the recorded conversation between charged terrorist cell member, Jeffrey Battle, and an FBI informant on May 8, 2002. Battle is part of the alleged Portland, Oregon cell.

In his conversation unsealed in court, Battle explained why his enterprise was not as organized as he thought it should have been (quote):

> Because we don't have support. Everybody's scared to give up any money to help us. You know what I'm saying? Because that law that Bush wrote about, you know, supporting terrorism, whatever, the whole thing. . . . Everybody's scared. . . . He made a law that says for instance I left out of the country and I fought, right, but I wasn't able to afford a ticket but you bought my plane ticket, you gave me the money to do it. . . . By me going and me fighting and doing that they can, by this new law, they can come and take you and put you in jail.

They are getting the message: we are gathering and cultivating detailed intelligence on terrorism in the U.S.; we are arresting and detaining potential terrorist threats; we are dismantling the terrorist financial network; we are disrupting potential terrorist travel; and we are building our long-term counter-terrorism capacity. We are winning the war on terrorism.

Public Opinion about Civil Liberties

Knowledge of the Bill of Rights

Many surveys of public opinion over the years have found that Americans have a very weak understanding of the basic features of U.S. government, including the Constitution and the Bill of Rights (McClosky and Brill, 1983). The First Amendment Center at Vanderbilt University conducts periodic surveys of knowledge about the First Amendment. As the results below indicate, not even half of all people know that the First Amendment protects freedom of speech, and very few people can name the other guarantees in the amendment.

The ability of people to name the specific rights guaranteed by the First Amendment.

Section of the First Amendment	Percentage Able to Name the Section
Freedom of speech	44 percent
Freedom of religion	13 percent
Freedom of the press	12 percent
Right of assembly/association	8 percent
Right to petition	2 percent
Other	6 percent
Don't know/Refused	49 percent

Adapted from Freedom Forum First Amendment Center at Vanderbilt University, "State of the First Amendment Survey," 1999.

In 2000 the Gallup Poll surveyed teenagers about their knowledge of civil liberties. They were asked what document guarantees freedom of the press. A combined total of 26 percent named the Bill of Rights and the First Amendment, while another 16 percent named the Constitution. But almost half did not know.

Document	Percent Identifying
Bill of Rights	18 percent
Constitution	16 percent
First Amendment	8 percent
Declaration of Independence	11 percent
All other answers	4 percent
Don't know	42 percent

Adapted from Gallup Poll, "American Teens Need a History Lesson" (May 5, 2000) (www.gallup.com).

Freedom of Speech

The Supreme Court has ruled that the First Amendment protects the right to burn the U.S. flag (see Chapter 2). Congress has rejected efforts to amend the First Amendment to make it illegal to burn the flag. As the poll below indicates, public opinion strongly supports such an amendment.

1. Support for a constitutional amendment making it illegal to burn the U.S. flag.

Favor	63 percent
Oppose	35 percent
No opinion	2 percent

Adapted from Gallup/CNN/*USA Today* Poll, June 25–27, 1999.

2. A survey of public opinion in the mid-1950s asked whether an atheist should be given the right to speak.

Group	Percentage agreeing
Community leaders	64 percent
General population	37 percent

Adapted from Samuel Stouffer, *Communism, Conformity, and Civil Liberties*, p. 34.

During the Cold War (see Chapter 3) there was widespread public hysteria about communism. As a result, the free speech rights of communists and alleged communists were denied in many different ways. The following poll, conducted in the mid-1950s, indicates that community leaders were more supportive of the right of a communist to give a public speech than was the general public.

3. Support for the right of a communist to speak

Group	Percentage agreeing
Community leaders	51 percent
General population	27 percent

Adapted from Stouffer, *Communism, Conformity, and Civil Liberties*, p. 42.

Church and State

The Supreme Court has held that the Establishment Clause of the First Amendment prohibits the government from promoting or supporting religion. As the poll below indicates, however, only about one-third of the public agrees with this position.

Percentage of the population believing that the government should avoid promoting religion:

Should avoid	36 percent
Should not	54 percent
Don't know	10 percent

Adapted from *Newsweek* Poll, June 27–28, 2002.

Although the Supreme Court has ruled that teaching creationism violates the separation of church and state, a 2000 Gallup Poll found that a large majority of Americans believe that creationism should be taught along with evolution in high school biology classes, while 40 percent feel it should be taught instead of evolution.

Policy	Percent who favor
Teaching creationism together with evolution	68 percent
Teaching creationism instead of evolution	40 percent

Adapted from Gallup Poll, "Americans React to Supreme Court Decisions," June 28, 2000.

Due Process of Law

The Miranda *decision requiring the police to advise a criminal suspect that he or she has the right to remain silent has been highly controversial. Generally, the police have strongly opposed the decision. However, the poll below, conducted in 2000, indicates overwhelming public support for advising a suspect of his or her rights, but mixed support for the admissibility of a confession when a suspect is not properly advised.*

Changing the specific wording of questions in public opinion polling can often produce different results. The poll below, conducted in the 1980s, seems to indicate less support for the rights of criminal suspects than the poll above that asked specifically about the Miranda warning.

Should a criminal suspect be advised of his or her rights?

Yes	94 percent
No	6 percent

Should a suspect's confession be admissible in court when he or she was not advised of his or her rights?

Yes	45 percent
No	49 percent

Adapted from the Gallup Poll, June 27, 2000

Equality
Racial Equality

Although racism and discrimination persist in U.S. society, racial attitudes changed dramatically as a result of the civil rights movement. The following table indicates the changes in responses to the question of whether white and African American children should attend the same schools, between 1942 and 1985.

Year	Percent Agreeing
1942	30 percent
1956	49 percent
1965	68 percent
1976	83 percent
1985	92 percent

Adapted from Neimi, Mueller, Smith, *Trends in Public Opinion: A Compendium of Survey Data,* p. 180.

Lesbian and Gay Rights
Should homosexual relations be legal?

Year	Percent Agreeing
1986	32 percent
2002	52 percent

Adapted from Gallup Poll, "Gallup Glance," April 28, 2003.

The War on Terrorism
Willingness to Give Up Civil Liberties
Percent of Americans believing we need to give up some of our civil liberties to fight terrorism:

Date	Percentage Agreeing
April 1995	49 percent
April 1997	29 percent
October 2001	79 percent
January 2002	55 percent
June 2002	46 percent

Adapted from Communitarian Network, Amitai Etzioni and Dierdre Mead, *The State of Society: A Rush to Pre-9/11.*

Eavesdropping on Attorneys
To civil libertarians, one of the most disturbing aspects of the war on terror is the government's policy of eavesdropping on conversations between suspected terrorists and their attorneys. Yet a large majority of the public approves of this activity.

Policy	Percent Favoring
Eavesdropping on suspected terrorists and their attorneys	73 percent

Adapted from Public Agenda (2001), "America's Global Role: Major Proposals," online at www.publicagenda.org.

Privacy
General Concern about Privacy
Americans are very concerned about their privacy, and a large majority believe their privacy is being seriously threatened or is already lost.

View of Privacy	Percent Agreeing
Under serious threat	41 percent
Already lost	24 percent
Basically safe	34 percent
Don't know	2 percent

What do people see as the greatest threats to their privacy?

Threat	Percent Agreeing
Banks and credit card companies	57 percent
Federal government	29 percent

Adapted from Public Agenda (September 2002) online at www.publicagenda.com.

Abortion

The attitudes of Americans about whether abortion should be legal have not changed since the mid-1970s.

Percentage of Americans who think abortion should be legal, legal only under certain circumstances, or illegal:

	1975	2003
Legal	21 percent	24 percent
Legal under certain circumstances	54 percent	57 percent
Illegal	22 percent	18 percent
No opinion	3 percent	1 percent

Source: Adapted from www.publicagenda.com, based on Gallup/CNN polls, 1975, 2003

National Identification Card

Percentage of Americans willing to carry a national identification card containing personal information:

Willing	50 percent
Not willing	44 percent
Don't know	6 percent

Adapted from CBS News Poll, February 24–26, 2002.

References

American Civil Liberties Union. 1999. *Driving While Black.* New York: American Civil Liberties Union.

Baker, Liva. 1983. Miranda: *The Crime, the Law, the Politics.* New York: Atheneum.

Brant, Irving. 1965. *The Bill of Rights: Its Origin and Meaning.* Indianapolis: Bobbs-Merrill.

Caute, David. 1978. *The Great Fear.* New York: Simon and Schuster.

Chafee, Zechariah, Jr. 1941. *Free Speech in the United States.* Cambridge, MA: Harvard University Press.

Curtis, Michael Kent. 1986. *No State Shall Abridge: The 14th Amendment and the Bill of Rights.* Durham, NC: Duke University Press.

de Grazia, Edward, and Roger K. Newman. 1982. *Banned Films: Movies, Censors, and the First Amendment.* New York: Bowker.

Etzioni, Amitai, and Deirdre Mead. 2003. *The State of Society: A Rush to Pre-9/11.* Washington, DC: The Communitarian Network.

Feinberg, Renee, comp. 1986. *The Equal Rights Amendment: An Annotated Bibliography of the Issues, 1976–1985.* Westport, CT: Greenwood Press.

Fisher, Louis. 1995. *Presidential War Power.* Lawrence: University Press of Kansas.

Frankel, Marvin. 1994. *Faith and Freedom: Religious Liberty in America.* New York: Hill and Wang.

Garrow, David J. 1994. *Liberty and Sexuality: The Right to Privacy and the Making of* Roe v. Wade. New York: Macmillan.

Ginger, Ray. 1974. *Six Days or Forever?* Tennessee v. John Thomas Scopes. New York: Oxford University Press.

Goldstein, Robert Justin. 2000. *Flag Burning and Free Speech: The Case of* Texas v. Johnson. Lawrence: University Press of Kansas.

Greenberg, Jack. 1994. *Crusaders in the Courts: How a Dedicated Band of Lawyers Fought for the Civil Rights Revolution.* New York: Basic Books.

Harris, David. 2002. *Profiles in Injustice: Why Racial Profiling Won't Work.* New York: The New Press.

Hentoff, Nat. 2003. *The War on the Bill of Rights and the Gathering Resistance.* New York: Seven Stories Press.

Hester, Joseph P. 2003. *The Ten Commandments: A Handbook of Religious, Legal, and Social Issues.* Jefferson, NC: McFarland.

Kalven, Harry, Jr. 1988. *A Worthy Tradition: Freedom of Speech in America.* New York: Harper and Row.

Keyssar, Alexander. 2000. *The Right to Vote: The Contested History of Democracy in the United States.* New York: Basic Books.

Kluger, Richard. 1975. *Simple Justice: The History of* Brown v. Board of Education *and Black America's Struggle for Equality.* New York: Knopf.

Larson, Edward J. 1997. *Summer for the Gods: The* Scopes *Trial and America's Continuing Debate Over Science and Religion.* New York: Basic Books.

———. 1985. *Trial and Error: The American Controversy over Creation and Evolution.* New York: Oxford University Press.

Long, Carolyn N. 2000. *Religious Freedom and Indian Rights: The Case of* Oregon v. Smith. Lawrence: University Press of Kansas.

McClosky, Herbert, and Alida Brill. 1983. *Dimensions of Tolerance: What Americans Believe about Civil Liberties.* New York: Russell Sage Foundation.

McCorvey, Norma. 1994. *I Am Roe: My life,* Roe v. Wade, *and Freedom of Choice.* New York: HarperCollins.

Martin, Waldo E., ed. 1998. Brown v. Board of Education: *A Brief History with Documents.* Boston: Bedford/St. Martin's.

Moran, Jeffrey P. 2002. *The* Scopes *Trial: A Brief History with Documents.* Boston: Bedford/St. Martin's.

Murphy, Paul L. 1979. *World War I and the Origin of Civil Liberties in the United States.* New York: Norton, 1979.

Neely, Mark E. 1991. *The Fate of Liberty: Abraham Lincoln and Civil Liberties.* New York: Oxford University Press.

Nieman, Donald G. 1991. *Promises to Keep: African Americans and the Constitutional Order, 1776 to the Present.* New York: Oxford University Press.

Niemi, Richard G., John Mueller, and Tom W. Smith. 1989. *Trends in Pubic Opinion: A Compendium of Survey Data.* Westport, CT: Greenwood Press.

Pelka, Fred. 1997. *The ABC-CLIO Companion to the Disability Rights Movement.* Santa Barbara, CA: ABC-CLIO.

Pevar, Stephen. 2002. *The Rights of Indians and Tribes.* Carbondale: Southern Illinois University Press.

Polenberg, Richard. 1987. *Fighting Faiths: The Abrams Case, The Supreme Court, and Free Speech.* New York: Viking.

Schwartz, Bernard, ed. 1980. *The Roots of the Bill of Rights: An Illustrated Source Book of American Freedom.* 5 vols. New York: Chelsea House.

Smith, James Morton. 1956. *Freedom's Fetters: The Alien and Sedition Laws and American Civil Liberties.* Ithaca, NY: Cornell University Press.

Smolla, Rodney. 1992. *Free Speech in an Open Society.* New York: Knopf.

Stouffer, Samuel. 1955. *Communism, Conformity, and Civil Liberties.* Garden City: Doubleday.

Thomas, Brook. 1997. Plessy v. Ferguson: *A Brief History with Documents.* Boston: Bedford Books.

Urofsky, Melvin. 1997. *Affirmative Action on Trial.* Lawrence: University Press of Kansas.

Walker, Samuel. 1994. *Hate Speech: The History of an American Controversy.* Lincoln: University of Nebraska Press.

———. 1999. *In Defense of American Liberties: A History of the ACLU.* 2nd ed. Carbondale: Southern Illinois University Press.

Weil, Danny. 2002. *School Vouchers and Privatization: A Reference Handbook.* Santa Barbara, CA: ABC-CLIO.

6

Organizations

This chapter provides an introduction to civil liberties–related organizations. Listings include both organizations that are generally considered pro–civil liberties and those that oppose traditional civil libertarian positions. Hence, this directory lists organizations that strongly support the rights of criminal suspects *and* those that want to limit those rights; organizations that support the right to burn the American flag as an expression of free speech *and* those that want to make flag burning a crime.

The reason for including all sides on civil liberties issues—and many issues include more than just two sides—is to enable readers to obtain a balanced view of each issue. At the same time, it is important to recognize that many people and organizations that oppose the traditional civil liberties point of view see themselves as defending individual rights. For example, opponents of affirmative action believe they are defending the rights of individuals who might not get a job because of an affirmative action program. Many opponents of abortion believe they are defending the rights of the unborn, and they portray themselves as the heirs to the civil rights movement.

American Arab Antidiscrimination Committee
4201 Connecticut Avenue, NW, Suite 300
Washington, DC 20008
Phone: (202) 244-2990
Fax: (202) 244-3196
Web site: www.adc.org

The American Arab Anti-Discrimination Committee is a national public interest group that fights discrimination against Arab

Americans on the basis of their national origins. In addition, it promotes civic participation by Arab Americans, encourages a balanced U.S. foreign policy toward the Middle East, and supports freedom and development in the Arab World.

American Association for Affirmative Action
12100 Sunset Hills Road
Reston, VA 20190
Phone: (800) 252-8952
Fax: (703) 435-4390
Web site: www.affirmativeaction.org

The American Association for Affirmative Action (AAAA) is a national professional association of persons engaged in managing affirmative action and diversity in employment.

American Association of People with Disabilities
1629 K Street NW, Suite 503
Washington, DC 20006
Phone: (800) 840-8844
Web site: www.aapd-DC.org

The American Association of People with Disabilities is a national nonprofit organization devoted to protecting the interests of people with disabilities. It engages in lobbying and public education.

American Association of University Professors
1012 14th Street, NW, Suite 500
Washington, DC 20005
Phone: (202) 737-5900
Fax: (202) 737-5526
Web site: www.aaup.org

The American Association of University Professors is a professional association of college and university faculty members. The organization is devoted to promoting academic freedom and other issues important to higher education.

American Bar Association
750 N. Lake Shore Drive
Chicago, IL 60611
Phone: (312) 988-5000
Web site: www.abanet.org

The American Bar Association is the largest professional association of lawyers in the United States. With respect to civil liberties,
it publishes public information materials about the Constitution
and the Bill of Rights.

American Booksellers Foundation for Free Expression
139 Fulton Street, Suite 302
New York, NY 10038
Phone: (212) 587-4025
Fax: (212) 587-2436
Web site: www.abffe.com

The American Booksellers Foundation for Free Expression is an
affiliate of the American Booksellers Association devoted to
fighting censorship of books and other forms of expression.

American Center for Law and Justice
P.O. Box 64429
Virginia Beach, VA 23467
Phone: (757) 226-2489
Fax: (757) 226-2836
Web site: www.aclj.org

The American Center for Law and Justice (ACLJ) is a national
nonpartisan public interest law firm with a conservative view on
civil liberties issues. It supports prayer in school, for example,
arguing that it is protected by the Free Exercise Clause of the First
Amendment. It also opposes abortion rights, arguing that the
fetus is a person protected by the Constitution.

American Civil Liberties Union
125 Broad Street
New York, NY 10004
Phone: (212) 549-2500
Web site: www.aclu.org

The American Civil Liberties Union, founded in 1920, is the oldest and largest civil liberties organization in the United States. Its
program encompasses the full spectrum of civil liberties issues:
First Amendment issues, due process of law, equal protection,
and privacy. The ACLU has a national office in New York City, a
legislative office in Washington, D.C., and affiliate offices in
every state.

American Constitution Society
50 F Street NW, Suite 5200
Washington, DC 20001
Phone: (202) 393-6181
Web site: www.americanconstitutionsociety.org

The American Constitution Society is a private nonprofit organization devoted to defending constitutional principles related to human rights, civil liberties, equality, and access to justice. Its membership consists primarily of lawyers, law professors, and law students.

American Family Association
P.O. Box 2440
Tupelo, MS 38803
Phone: (662) 844-5036
Fax: (662) 842-7798
Web site: www.afa.net

The American Family Association is a private nonprofit organization that opposes most traditional civil liberties issues. It is opposed to legal abortion and supports student prayer in public schools, for example.

American Humanist Association
1777 T Street, NW
Washington, DC 20009-7125
Phone: (800) 837-3792
Fax: (202) 238-9003
Web site: www.americanhumanist.org

The American Humanist Association is a private nonprofit organization devoted to the principles of a secular, human-centered society. It is opposed to all forms of government-supported religious activity, such as prayer in public schools.

American Immigration Lawyers Association
918 F Street, NW
Washington, DC 20004-1400
Phone: (202) 216-2400
Fax: (202) 783-7853
Web site: www.aila.org

The American Immigration Lawyers Association is a professional association of attorneys engaged in the practice of immigration law. It supports full legal protection for persons who are in the United States on immigrant status.

American Jewish Congress
165 East 56th Street
New York, NY 10022
Phone: (212) 751-4000 or (212) 879-4500
Fax: (212) 861-7056
Web site: www.ajc.org

The American Jewish Congress is a national nonpartisan public interest organization devoted to the rights of Jewish Americans. One of the oldest civil rights organizations in the country, it has been particularly active on issues such as civil rights, separation of church and state, and reproductive rights. Its civil liberties–related activities are primarily undertaken through its Commission on Law and Social Action.

American Library Association, Office for Intellectual Freedom
50 E. Huron
Chicago, IL 60611
Phone: (800) 545-2433
Web site: www.ala.org

The Office for Intellectual Freedom is a unit of the American Library Association devoted to fighting censorship of library materials.

Americans for Effective Law Enforcement
841 W. Touhy Avenue
Park Ridge, IL 60068-3351
Phone: (847) 685-0700
Fax: (847) 685-9700
Web site: www.aele.org

Americans for Effective Law Enforcement is a nonpartisan professional association devoted to advancing the interests of the police and other law enforcement professionals. With regard to civil liberties, it is primarily active in opposing expanded rights of criminal suspects, particularly on Fourth and Fifth Amendment issues. The AELE engages in research, training, and legal advocacy, often filing amicus briefs in police-related cases.

Americans United for Life
310 S. Peoria Street, Suite 310
Chicago IL 60607
Phone: (312) 492-7234
Web site: www.unitedforlife.org

Americans United for Life is a national nonprofit organization opposed to abortion. It is based on the principle that life begins at conception and that therefore the fetus is a person entitled to full legal protection.

Americans United for Separation of Church and State
518 C Street, NE
Washington, DC 20002
Phone: (202) 466-3234
Fax: (202) 466-2587
Web site: www.au.org

Americans United for Separation of Church and State is a nonpartisan public interest group devoted to advancing the separation of church and state. It is active in opposing organized prayer in public schools, the expenditure of tax dollars for religious schools, and government-funded vouchers for public schools.

Amnesty International USA
322 8th Avenue
New York, NY 10001
Phone: (212) 807-8400
Fax: (212) 463-9193
Web site: www.amnestyusa.org

Amnesty International USA is the U.S. affiliate of the international group, Amnesty International. Its civil liberties issues include opposition to the persecution of people because of their political beliefs, police misconduct, the abuse of prisoners, and the death penalty.

Anti-Defamation League
823 United Nations Plaza
New York, NY 10017

Phone: (212) 490-2525
Web site: www.adl.org

The Anti-Defamation League is a private nonprofit organization devoted to the rights of Jewish Americans. It is an arm of B'nai B'rith. It is also active in civil liberties issues related to all people in the areas of civil rights, hate crimes, and separation of church and state.

Arab American Institute

1600 K Street NW, Suite 601
Washington, DC 20006
Phone: (202) 429-9210
Fax: (202) 429-9214
Web site: www.aaiusa.org

The Arab American Institute is a private nonprofit organization representing the interests of Arab Americans. It serves as a clearinghouse for information, lobbies in Congress, and provides support for political candidates.

Asian American Legal Defense and Education Fund

99 Hudson Street, 12th Floor
New York, NY 10013
Phone: (212) 966-5932
Fax: (212) 966-4303
Web site: www.aaldef.org

The Asian American Legal Defense and Education Fund is a national nonprofit organization devoted to protecting the rights of Americans of Asian descent.

Bazelon Center for Mental Health Law

1101 15th Street, NW, Suite 1212
Washington, DC 20005-5002
Phone: (202) 467-5730
Fax: (202) 223-0409
Web site: www.bazelon.org

The Bazelon Center for Mental Health Law is a private nonprofit organization devoted to the rights of persons with mental health problems, including those who are incarcerated in mental health facilities. It was established in memory of the late Judge David

Bazelon, who was a pioneer in the area of the rights of the mentally ill.

Brennan Center for Justice
161 Avenue of the Americas, 12th Floor
New York, NY 10013
Phone: (212) 998-6730
Fax: (212) 995-4550
Web site: www.brennancenter.org

The Brennan Center is a nonprofit research center located at New York University Law School in New York City, established to honor the ideas and values of the late Supreme Court Justice William J. Brennan. The center engages in a program of scholarship, public education, and legal advocacy on issues related to criminal justice, poverty, and democracy.

Cato Institute
1000 Massachusetts Avenue, NW
Washington DC 20001-5403
Phone: (202) 842-0200
Fax: (202) 842-3490
Web site: www.cato.org

The Cato Institute is a nonprofit public interest group based in Washington, D.C., devoted to advocating a libertarian philosophy. Generally considered a conservative group, it supports traditional civil liberties issues such as opposition to government intrusion into individual privacy. It strongly opposes government regulation of gun ownership and regulation of contributions to political candidates.

Center for Campus Free Speech
29 Temple Place
Boston, MA 02111
Phone: (617) 747-4441
Fax: 617-292-8057
Web site: www.campusspeech.org

The Center for Campus Free Speech is a national nonprofit organization devoted to protecting freedom of speech on college and university campuses.

Center for Constitutional Rights
666 Broadway, 7th Floor
New York, NY 10012
Phone: (212) 614-6464
Fax: (212) 614-6499
Web site: www.ccr-ny.org

The Center for Constitutional Rights is a private nonprofit public interest law firm devoted to the defense of civil liberties. Unlike many other civil liberties organizations, the CCR generally does not defend individuals or groups with whom it disagrees politically.

Center for Democracy and Technology
1634 Eye Street NW, Suite 1100
Washington, DC 20006
Phone: (202) 637-9800
Fax: (202) 637-0968
Web site: www.cdt.org

The Center for Democracy and Technology is a private nonprofit organization dedicated to protecting the rights of free speech and privacy on issues related to digital technology.

Center for Individual Rights
1233 20th Street, NW, Suite 300
Washington, DC 20036
Phone: (202) 833-8400
Fax: (202) 833-8410
Web site: www.cir-usa.org

The Center for Individual Rights is a national nonprofit organization that defends individual rights. It is a generally conservative group that supports freedom of speech but opposes affirmative action on the grounds that it represents reverse discrimination.

Center for Reproductive Law and Policy
20 Wall Street
New York, NY 10005
Phone: (917) 637-3600
Fax: (917) 637-3666
Web site: www.crlp.org

The Center for Reproductive Law and Policy (CRLP) is a non-partisan group based in New York City that focuses on abortion rights and related issues of reproductive freedom. Its activities primarily involve litigation and public education.

Center for Voting and Democracy
6930 Carroll Avenue, Suite 610
Takoma Park, MD 20912
Phone: (301) 270-4616
Fax: (301) 270-4133
Web site: www.fairvote.org

The Center for Voting and Democracy is a nonprofit public interest group dedicated to ensuring open elections where all votes are counted and all voters equally represented.

Children's Defense Fund
25 E Street, NW
Washington, DC 20001
Phone: (202) 628-8787
Web site: www.childrensdefense.org

The Children's Defense Fund is a national nonprofit organization devoted to promoting the rights and welfare of children.

Communitarian Network
2130 H Street, NW, Suite 703
Washington, DC 20052
Phone: (202) 994-7997
Web site: www.gwu.edu/~ccps

The Communitarian Network is a private nonprofit organization devoted to the idea that individual rights need to be balanced with personal responsibility and the needs of the community.

Creationism.org
P.O. Box 13327
Berkeley, CA 94712
Web site: www.creationism.org

Creationism.org is a Web site devoted to the principle that the creation of the universe was an act of God, and that the theory of the religious origins of the universe should be taught in the public schools.

Death Penalty Information Center
1320 18th Street NW, 2nd Floor
Washington, DC 20036
Phone: (202) 293-6970
Fax: (202) 822-4787
Web site: www.deathpenaltyinfo.org

The Death Penalty Information Center is a resource center for information about capital punishment. It publishes data on executions along with arguments against capital punishment.

Disability Rights Education Defense Fund
2212 Sixth Street
Berkeley, CA 94710
Phone: (510) 644-2555
Fax: (510) 841-8645
Web site: www.dredf.org

The Disability Rights Education Defense Fund is a national nonprofit organization devoted to protecting the rights of persons with disabilities.

Electronic Frontier Foundation (EFF)
454 Shotwell Street
San Francisco, CA 94110-1914
Phone: (415) 436-9333
Fax: (415) 436-9993
Web site: www.eff.org

The Electronic Frontier Foundation is a national nonprofit organization devoted to protecting individual rights related to digital technology.

Electronic Privacy Information Center
1718 Connecticut Avenue, NW, Suite 200
Washington, DC 20009
Phone: (202) 483-1140
Fax: (202) 483-1248
Web site: www.epic.org

EPIC is a public interest organization in Washington, D.C., that focuses on emerging civil liberties issues related to digital technology, protection of privacy, and the First Amendment.

Equal Rights Advocates
1663 Mission Street, Suite 250
San Francisco, CA 94103
Phone: (415) 621-0672
Fax: (415) 621-6744
Web site: www.equalrights.org

Equal Rights Advocates is a national nonprofit organization devoted to advancing the rights of women on issues such as employment discrimination, sexual harassment, and reproductive rights.

Families Against Mandatory Minimums
1612 K Street, NW, Suite 700
Washington, DC 20006
Phone: (202) 822-6700
Fax: (202) 822-6704
Web site: www.famm.org

Families Against Mandatory Minimums is a national nonprofit organization representing family members of persons who have been sentenced to prison with long mandatory prison terms. It works to reform criminal sentencing laws.

Federalist Society
1015 18th Street, NW
Washington, DC 20036
Phone: (202) 822-8138
Web site: www.fed-soc.org

The Federalist Society is a nonpartisan professional association of lawyers and law students. It takes a conservative position on traditional civil liberties issues, opposing affirmative action, and the rights of criminal suspects.

Feminist Majority
1600 Wilson Boulevard, Suite 801
Arlington, VA 22209
Phone: (703) 522-2214
Fax: (703) 522-2219
or
433 S. Beverly Drive
Beverly Hills, CA 90212

Phone: (310) 556-2500
Fax: (310) 556-2509
Web site: www.feminist.org

The Feminist Majority is a national nonprofit organization devoted to advancing the rights of women on such issues as employment discrimination, reproductive rights, and sexual harassment.

First Amendment Center
Vanderbilt University
1207 18th Avenue S.
Nashville, TN 37212
Phone: (615) 727-1600
Fax: (615) 727-1319
E-mail: info@fac.org
or
1101 Wilson Boulevard
Arlington, VA 22209
Phone: (703) 528-0800
Fax: (703) 284-3519
Web site: www.firstamendmentcenter.org

The First Amendment Center is a private nonprofit organization devoted to the defense of free speech and freedom of the press.

Foundation for Individual Rights in Education
210 West Washington Square, Suite 303
Philadelphia, PA 19106
Phone: (215) 717-3473
Fax: (215) 717-3440
Web site: www.thefire.org

The Foundation for Individual Rights in Education (FIRE) is a private nonprofit organization devoted to supporting free speech for faculty and students on college and university campuses.

Gay and Lesbian Alliance Against Defamation
248 West 35th Street, 8th Floor
New York, NY 10001
Phone: (212) 629-3322
Fax: (212) 629-3225
Web site: www.glaad.org

The Gay and Lesbian Alliance Against Defamation is a national nonprofit organization devoted to protecting the rights of gay and lesbian people.

Human Rights Campaign
919 18th Street, NW
Washington, DC 20006
Phone: (202) 628-4160
Fax: (202) 347-5323
Web site: www.hrc.org

The Human Rights Campaign is a national gay and lesbian rights organization. It lobbies Congress regarding legislation and supports candidates for political office who support gay and lesbian rights.

Human Rights Watch
350 Fifth Avenue, 34th Floor
New York, NY 10118-3299
Phone: (212) 290-4700
Fax: (212) 736-1300
or
1630 Connecticut Avenue, NW, Suite 500
Washington, DC 20009
Phone: (202) 612-4321
Fax: (202) 612-4333
Web site: www.hrw.org

Human Rights Watch is a nonpartisan public interest group dedicated to protecting human rights around the world. With regard to civil liberties, it is involved in issues related to police misconduct, prisoners' rights, and the death penalty. It is active in issues in the United States and other countries.

Independent Women's Forum
P.O. Box 3058
Arlington, VA 22203-0058
Phone: (800) 224-6000 or (703) 558-4991
Fax: (703) 558-4994
Web site: www.iwf.org

The Independent Women's Forum is a nonpartisan organization

devoted to women's rights. It represents a conservative point of view and opposes the positions taken by the traditional women's rights organizations. The IWF, for example, opposes affirmative action programs for women.

The Innocence Project
Benjamin N. Cardozo School of Law
55 5th Avenue, 11th Floor
New York, NY 10003
Web site: www.innocenceproject.org

The Innocence Project is a private nonprofit law clinic that provides free legal services to persons who have been falsely convicted of a crime and for whom DNA evidence can provide evidence of their innocence.

Japanese American Citizens League
1765 Sutter Street
San Francisco, CA 94115
Phone: (415) 921-5225
Web site: www.jacl.org

The Japanese American Citizens League is the largest national organization representing the interests of Japanese Americans.

Lambda Legal Defense and Education Fund
120 Wall Street, Suite 1500
New York, NY 10005-3904
Phone: (212) 809-8585
Fax: (212) 809-0055
Web site: www.lambdalegal.org

The Lambda Legal Defense and Education Fund is a national nonprofit organization devoted to protecting the rights of gay and lesbian people.

Lawyers Committee for Civil Rights under Law
1401 New York Avenue, NW, Suite 400
Washington, DC 20005
Phone: (202) 662-8600
Fax: (202) 783-0857
Web site: www.lawyerscomm.org

The Lawyers Committee for Civil Rights under Law is a national nonprofit organization devoted to protecting the civil rights of all persons.

Lawyers Committee for Human Rights
333 Seventh Avenue, 13th Floor
New York, NY 10001-5004
Phone: (212) 845-5200
Fax: (212) 845-5299
Web site: www.lchr.org

The Lawyers Committee for Human Rights is a nonprofit organization devoted to protecting human rights around the world, including in the United States. It has a special interest in police misconduct and prison conditions.

Leadership Conference on Civil Rights
1629 K Street, NW, Suite 1010
Washington, DC 20006
Phone: (202) 466-3311
Fax: (202) 466-3435
Web site: www.civilrights.org

The Leadership Conference on Civil Rights is a coalition of more than 185 national civil rights organizations based in Washington, D.C. Its constituent members represent over 50 million Americans. It functions primarily as a lobbying group to advance civil rights issues in Congress and the White House. The LCCR Web site is a convenient link to its members' Web sites.

League of United Latin American Citizens
2000 L Street, NW, Suite 610
Washington, DC 20036
Phone: (202) 833-6130
Web site: www.lulac.org

The League of United Latin American Citizens is a national membership organization of Latino and Hispanic citizens that is active in political affairs to advance the interests of its members.

Libertarian Party
2600 Virginia Avenue, NW, Suite 100
Washington, DC 20037

Phone: (202) 333-0008
Fax: (202) 333-0072
Web site: www.lp.org

The Libertarian Party is a political party committed to individual liberty. On issues of individual rights, its positions are generally similar to those of traditional civil liberties organizations (e.g., opposition to government restraints on speech and association). On political and economic issues, however, its positions are usually closer to traditionally conservative political groups (e.g., a strong opposition to taxes and government spending). Unlike the nonpartisan civil liberties organizations, the Libertarian Party runs candidates for political office.

Mexican American Legal Defense and Education Fund
634 S. Spring Street
Los Angeles, CA 90014
Phone: (213) 629-2512
Web site: www.maldef.org

The Mexican American Legal Defense and Education Fund is a national nonprofit organization devoted to protecting the rights of Latino and Hispanic people.

NAACP Legal Defense and Education Fund
99 Hudson Street, Suite 1600
New York, NY 10013
Phone: (212) 965-2202
Web site: www.naacpldf.org

The NAACP Legal Defense and Education Fund is a national nonprofit organization devoted to protecting the civil rights of African Americans. Although originally affiliated with the NAACP, it is now a separate organization.

NARAL Pro-Choice America
1156 15th Street, Suite 700
Washington, DC 20005
Phone: (202) 973-3000
Fax: (202) 973-3096
Web site: www.naral.org

NARAL Pro-Choice America, formerly the National Abortion and Reproductive Rights Action League, is a national nonprofit organization representing abortion providers and devoted to protecting the right to legal abortions.

National Association for the Advancement of Colored People (NAACP)
4805 Mt. Hope Drive
Baltimore, MD 21215
Phone: (877) NAA-CP98
Web site: www.naacp.org

The NAACP, founded in 1909, is the nation's oldest and largest African American civil rights organization. The NAACP engages in litigation, lobbying, and public education.

National Association for Citizen Oversight of Law Enforcement
Box 19261
Denver, CO 80219
Phone: (866) 4NA-COLE
Fax: (303) 794-0264
Web site: www.nacole.org

The National Association for Citizen Oversight of Law Enforcement is a national professional association of persons involved in citizen oversight of the police, such as civilian review boards.

National Association of Criminal Defense Lawyers
1150 18th Street NW, Suite 950
Washington DC 20036
Phone: (202) 872-8600
Fax: (202) 872-8690
Web site: www.nacdl.org

The National Association of Criminal Defense Lawyers is a national professional association of private criminal defense attorneys. Its interests in civil liberties concern the constitutional rights of criminal defendants, including Fourth Amendment, Fifth Amendment, and Sixth Amendment issues.

National Center for Science Education
420 40th Street, Suite 2
Oakland, CA 94609-2509
Phone: (510) 601-7203

Fax: (510) 601-7204
Web site: www.natcenscied.org

The National Center for Science Education is a national nonprofit organization devoted to advancing the teaching of science. With respect to civil liberties, it is opposed to religious-based restrictions on the teaching of the theory of evolution and also to the teaching of creationism.

National Coalition against the Death Penalty
920 Pennsylvania Avenue, SE
Washington, DC 20003
Phone: (202) 543-9577
Fax: (202) 543-7798
Web site: www.ncadp.org

The National Coalition against the Death Penalty is a national nonprofit organization devoted to abolishing the death penalty.

National Coalition against Censorship
275 Seventh Avenue
New York, NY 10001
Phone: (212) 807-6222
Fax: (212) 807-6245
Web site: www.ncac.org

The National Coalition against Censorship is a national nonprofit organization representing a coalition of organizations opposed to all forms of censorship.

National Conference for Community and Justice
475 Park Avenue South, 19th Floor
New York, NY 10016
Phone: (212) 545-1300
Fax: (212) 545-8053
Web site: www.nccj.org

Formerly the National Conference of Christians and Jews, the NCCJ is a nonpartisan public interest group devoted to tolerance and equality for all racial, ethnic, and religious groups.

National Congress for Puerto Rican Rights
P.O. Box 1307

New York, NY 10159
Phone: (212) 631-4263

The National Congress for Puerto Rican Rights is a nonprofit organization devoted to ending discrimination against Puerto Ricans, both in the continental United States and in Puerto Rico.

National Congress of American Indians
1301 Connecticut Avenue, NW, Suite 200
Washington, DC 20036
Phone: (202) 466-7767
Fax: (202) 466-7797
Web site: www.ncai.org

The National Congress of American Indians represents the interests of more than 250 Native American Indian tribes.

National Council of La Raza
111 West Monroe, Suite 1610
Phoenix, AZ 85003
Phone: (602) 252-7101
Fax: (602) 252-0315
Web site: www.nclr.org

The National Council of La Raza is a national nonprofit organization that represents the interests of Latino and Hispanic people.

National Gay and Lesbian Task Force
1325 Massachusetts Avenue, NW, Suite 600
Washington, DC 20005
Phone: (202) 393-5177
Fax: (202) 393-2241
Web site: www.ngltf.org

The National Gay and Lesbian Task Force is a national nonprofit organization that defends the rights of gay and lesbian people.

National Law Center on Homelessness and Poverty
1411 K Street NW, Suite 1400
Washington, DC 20005
Phone: (202) 638-2535
Fax: (202) 628-2737
Web site: www.nlchp.org

The National Law Center on Homelessness and Poverty is a national nonprofit organization devoted to protecting the rights of homeless people and poor people.

National Lawyers Guild
143 Madison Ave, 4th Floor
New York, NY 10016
Phone: (212) 679-5100
Fax: (212) 679-2811
Web site: www.nlg.org

The National Lawyers Guild is a professional association of attorneys devoted to defending civil liberties on such issues as freedom of speech, police misconduct, and prisoners rights.

National Organization for Women (NOW)
733 15th Street, NW
Washington, DC 20005
Phone: (202) 628-8669
Fax: (202) 785-8576
Web site: www.now.org

The National Organization for Women (NOW) is the largest women's civil rights organization in the United States. It has 500,000 contributing members, with chapters in all fifty states and the District of Columbia. It is active on issues such as employment discrimination and reproductive rights.

National Organization on Disability
910 Sixteenth Street, NW, Suite 600
Washington, DC 20006
Phone: (202) 293-5960
Fax: (202) 293-7999
Web site: www.nod.org

The National Organization on Disability is a national nonprofit organization devoted to protecting the rights of disabled persons.

National Prison Project of the ACLU
733 15th Street, NW, Suite 620
Washington, DC 20005
Phone: (202) 393-4930
Fax: (202) 393-4931

The National Prison Project is a special project of the American Civil Liberties Union devoted to protecting the rights of prisoners and improving prison conditions. The National Prison Project engages in litigation, public education, and lobbying.

National Right to Life Committee
512 10th Street, NW
Washington, DC 20004
Phone: (202) 626-8800
Web site: www.nrlc.org

The National Right to Life Committee is a national nonprofit organization opposed to the right to abortion.

National Urban League
120 Wall Street
New York, NY 10005
Phone: (212) 558-5300
Fax: (212) 344-5332
Web site: www.nul.org

The National Urban League is a national African American civil rights organization. Its activities include many programs that do not involve civil liberties issues, such as economic and social welfare policy.

National Women's Law Center
11 Dupont Circle, NW, Suite 800
Washington, DC 20036
Phone: (202) 588-5180
Fax: (202) 588-5158
Web site: www.nwlc.org

The National Women's Law Center is a national nonprofit organization devoted to advancing the rights of women.

People for the American Way (PFAW)
2000 M Street, NW, Suite 400
Washington, DC 20036
Phone: (800) 326-PFAW
Fax: (202) 293-2672
Web site: www.pfaw.org

People for the American Way (PFAW) is a nonpartisan organization devoted to a broad range of civil liberties issues. It gives special attention to separation of church and state, civil rights, and freedom of speech.

Planned Parenthood Federation of America
810 Seventh Avenue
New York, NY 10019
Phone: (212) 541-7800
Fax: (212) 245-1845
Web site: www.ppfa.org

Planned Parenthood Federation of America is a national organization devoted to promoting family planning and reproductive rights. Planned Parenthood maintains 875 health centers in 49 states. In addition to public education and counseling about sexuality-related issues, some affiliates provide direct medical services.

Positive Atheism
P.O. Box 16811
Portland, OR 97292
Web site: www.positiveatheism.org

Positive Atheism is a private nonprofit organization devoted to atheism and, with respect to civil liberties, defending the separation of church and state.

Privacy Rights Clearinghouse
3100 5th Avenue, Suite B
San Diego, CA 92103
Phone: (619) 298-3396
Fax: (619) 298-5681
Web site: www.privacyrights.org

The Privacy Rights Clearinghouse is a national nonprofit organization devoted to research, consumer education, , and advocacy related to the privacy rights of consumers.

Pro–Death Penalty.com
www.prodeathpenalty.com

Pro–Death Penalty.com is a Web-based information resource center that supports the death penalty.

Reporters Committee for Freedom of the Press
1815 N. Fort Myer Drive, Suite 900
Arlington, VA 22209
Phone: (800) 336-4243
Web site: www.rcfp.org

The Reporters Committee for Freedom of the Press is a professional association of journalists devoted to defending freedom of the press and the rights of journalists.

Rutherford Institute
P.O. Box 7482
Charlottesville, VA 22906-7482
Phone: (434) 978-3888
Fax: (434) 978-1789
Web site: www.rutherford.org

The Rutherford Institute is a private nonpartisan public interest group that generally adopts conservative positions in opposition to traditional civil liberties issues such as prayer in public schools.

Second Amendment Foundation
12500 NE 10th Place
Bellevue, WA 98005
Phone: (425) 454-7012
Web site: www.saf.org

The Second Amendment Foundation is a national nonprofit organization devoted to the rights of gun owners.

Student Press Law Center
1815 N. Fort Myer Drive, Suite 900
Arlington, VA 22209
Phone: (703) 807-1904
Web site: www.splc.org

The Student Press Law Center is a national nonprofit organization devoted to protecting the First Amendment rights of school newspapers and other publications.

U.S. Commission on Civil Rights
624 9th Street, NW
Washington, DC 20425

Phone: (202) 376-8312
Web site: www.usccr.gov

The U.S. Commission on Civil Rights is an independent federal
agency whose mission is to promote the civil rights of all people
in the U.S. The Commission investigates allegations of discrimination, holds public hearings, and issues reports on specific civil
rights problems.

U.S. Department of Justice, Civil Rights Division
950 Pennsylvania Avenue, NW, Suite 3623
Washington, DC 20530
Phone: (202) 514-2151
Fax: (202) 514-0293
Web site: www.usdoj.gov/crt

The Civil Rights Division of the U.S. Department of Justice is
charged with the responsibility of enforcing federal civil rights
laws. The division investigates complaints of violations of civil
rights and in some cases files lawsuits against violators. The Special Litigation Section of the Division is responsible for civil
rights violations by police departments, prison systems, and
other institutions.

**U.S. Equal Employment Opportunity
Commission (EEOC)**
1801 L Street, NW
Washington, DC 20507
Phone: (202) 663-4900
Web site: www.eeoc.gov

The Equal Employment Opportunity Commission is a U.S. government agency charged with the responsibility of enforcing the
1964 Civil Rights Act. The EEOC investigates complaints of employment discrimination and in some cases brings lawsuits
against employers.

References

Atterberry, Tara, ed. 2001. *Encyclopedia of Associations: International Organizations*, 37th ed. Detroit, MI: Gale Research.

Barrett, Jacqueline K., ed. 1993. *Encyclopedia of Women's Associations Worldwide: A Guide to Over 3,400 National and Multinational Nonprofit Women's and Women-related Organizations.* Detroit, MI: Gale Research.

Encyclopedia of Associations, 34th ed. Detroit, MI: Gale Research, 2000.

Gall, Susan, ed. 1995. *Reference Library of Asian America.* Detroit, MI: Gale Research.

Leadership Conference on Civil Rights Web site: *www.civilrights.org.*

Lopez, Antoinette Sedillo, ed. 1995. *Latino Employment, Labor Organizations, and Immigration.* New York: Garland.

Mjagkij, Nina. 2001. *Organizing Black America: An Encyclopedia of African American Associations.* New York: Garland.

Ness, Immanuel. 2000. *Encyclopedia of Interest Groups and Lobbyists in the United States.* Armonk, NY: Sharpe Reference.

O'Connor, Karen, and Lee Epstein. 1989. *Public Interest Law Groups: Institutional Profiles.* Westport, CT: Greenwood Press.

Public Interest Profiles, 2001–2002. 2002. Washington, DC: Foundation for Public Affairs.

Slavin, Sarah, ed. 1995. *U.S. Women's Interest Groups: Institutional Profiles.* Westport, CT: Greenwood Press.

Tulloch, Paulette P., comp. 1992. *NWO: A Directory of National Women's Organizations.* New York: National Council for Research on Women.

Weber, Paul J., and W. Landis Jones. 1994. *U.S. Religious Interest Groups: Institutional Profiles.* Westport, CT: Greenwood Press.

7

Print and Nonprint Resources

As this chapter indicates, the subject of civil liberties is large and extremely complex. All of the issues are covered in a large number of books and other resources—and this bibliography by no means includes all available material on each topic. Many of the books listed here are written primarily for legal scholars and would not be useful for the person who is just learning about civil liberties or a particular civil liberties issue.

This chapter, designed to help people get started, first lists books that provide a good introduction to their subject. Each of these books has been selected because it is very readable and makes the topic come alive for those with no background in the subject. For most topics, two or three such books are listed, followed by a list of further reading suggestions.

Books

Civil Liberties in General

Alderman, Ellen, and Caroline Kennedy. 1991. *In Our Defense: The Bill of Rights in Action.* New York: William Morrow.

Ellen Alderman and Caroline Kennedy selected cases to illustrate each of the ten amendments in the Bill of Rights. Four cases involve First Amendment issues, and each of the other amendments is illustrated by a single case. One of the virtues of their book is that they cover the often-neglected Ninth and Tenth Amendments.

The controversies Alderman and Kennedy select are not the recognized landmark court cases (although several are celebrated cases), but the book succeeds in covering all of the amendments in the Bill of Rights. Brief and highly readable, the stories in this book are also an excellent introduction to how civil liberties affect the lives of Americans in many ways.

Burns, James MacGregor, and Stewart Burns. 1991. *A People's Charter: The Pursuit of Rights in America*. New York: Knopf.

A People's Charter is a broad narrative account of the history of rights in the United States, covering the full sweep of U.S. history. Although contemporary civil liberties did not emerge until the twentieth century, this book places that development in the context of the adoption of the Constitution in 1787 and the Bill of Rights in 1791 and subsequent struggles over slavery and other important issues. The principal author, James MacGregor Burns, is among the most eminent political scientists in the United States.

Glasser, Ira. 1991. *Visions of Liberty: The Bill of Rights for All Americans*. New York: Arcade Books.

Visions of Liberty is an excellent book on civil liberties, combining text and photographs to bring to life the history of the Bill of Rights and the major civil liberties issues. The text was written by Ira Glasser, who was executive director of the American Civil Liberties Union from 1978 to 2001. An initial chapter on the creation of the Bill of Rights is followed by chapters on the major civil liberties issues, including freedom of religion and freedom of expression. The book is illustrated with photographs by the noted documentary photographer Bob Adelman, who was on the scene capturing the drama of many of the confrontations that are part of the recent history of civil liberties. Adelman's photographs are supplemented by many historical photographs illustrating events related to civil rights and civil liberties issues.

Glendon, Mary Ann. 1991. *Rights Talk: The Impoverishment of Political Discourse*. New York: Free Press.

The communitarian movement that emerged in the 1990s is a particularly challenging critique of established civil liberties principles. Communitarians argue that U.S. law and culture places too much emphasis on individual rights and not enough on the needs of a healthy community. In fact, they argue that the pursuit of individual rights has undermined the communal bonds on which a free society rests. Communitarianism is a special kind of criticism of mainstream civil liberties; it is a liberal philosophy that places great emphasis on equality, tolerance, and individual freedom. This is very different from traditional conservative criticism of civil liberties.

Mary Ann Glendon's *Rights Talk* is an articulate critique of the dominant view of civil liberties in U.S. society. She argues that society has gone too far in protecting individual rights and, as a consequence, has neglected the needs of community. The rights of individuals, she argues, should be balanced with responsibilities to others and to the community as a whole. The author is a distinguished professor at Harvard Law School, but this book is written for a general audience.

Irons, Peter. 1988. *The Courage of Their Convictions.* New York: Free Press.

Peter Irons selects sixteen recognized major cases in the history of civil liberties and offers two perspectives on each. First, he describes the issue involved and the history of the case that reached the Supreme Court. The second section involves a first-hand account by the leading figure in the case. We get to read Mary Beth Tinker's own story about how she wore an armband to school in Des Moines one day in December 1965. We also hear Michael Hardwick's story of how the police entered his bedroom while he was with another man and was arrested and later convicted of sodomy under a Georgia law.

Rarely do we get to read such first-hand accounts by the individuals involved in what eventually become landmark Supreme Court cases. Discussions of cases often focus on the abstract legal issues involved, with the real people behind the story left out. Focusing on the human drama behind the grand principles of constitutional law, Peter Irons's *The Courage of Their Convictions* is an excellent introduction to the world of civil liberties.

Mill, John Stuart. 1975. *On Liberty.* New York: W. W. Norton.

Every student of civil liberties must read John Stuart Mill's classic work, *On Liberty.* It is essentially the founding statement of the principle of individual rights and one of the masterpieces of English literature. The arguments Mill sets forth are as relevant to contemporary debates over civil liberties—from freedom of speech to the rights of homosexuals—as they were when he wrote *On Liberty* in 1859.

Walker, Samuel. 1999. *In Defense of American Liberties: A History of the ACLU,* 2nd ed. Carbondale: Southern Illinois University Press.

A history of the American Civil Liberties Union (ACLU), this book offers the best single overview of the origins and development of civil liberties in twentieth-century America. It provides summaries of the major civil liberties crises of the past century— the suppression of free speech during World War I, the Cold War assault on civil liberties, and the eruption of the "rights revolution" in the 1960s, for example—and places them in the larger context of their times. The book highlights the critical role of the ACLU as an advocacy group in the development of civil liberties.

American Civil Liberties Union. 2002. *Insatiable Appetite: The Government's Demand for New and Unnecessary Powers after September 11.* New York: ACLU.

———. 2003. *Freedom under Fire: Dissent in Post-9/11 America.* New York: ACLU.

———. 2003. *Seeking Truth from Justice: The Justice Department's Campaign to Mislead the Public about the USA Patriot Act.* New York: ACLU.

Amnesty International. 1998. *United States of America: Rights for All.* New York: Amnesty International USA.

Banning, Lance. 1995. *The Sacred Fire of Liberty: James Madison and the Founding of the Federal Republic.* Ithaca, NY: Cornell University Press.

Brant, Irving. 1965. *The Bill of Rights: Its Origin and Meaning.* Indianapolis: Bobbs-Merrill.

Brownlie, Ian, and Guy S. Goodwin-Gill, eds. 2002. *Basic Documents on Human Rights,* 4th ed. Oxford, England: Clarendon Press.

Casper, Jonathan D. 1972. *The Politics of Civil Liberties.* New York: Harper and Row.

Chandler, Ralph C., Richard A. Enslen, and Peter G. Renstrom. 1985–1987. *The Constitutional Law Dictionary.* Santa Barbara, CA: ABC-CLIO.

Cole, David, and James X. Dempsey. 2002. *Terrorism and the Constitution:*

Sacrificing Civil Liberties in the Name of National Security. New York: New Press.

Cottrell, Robert C. 2000. *Roger Baldwin and the American Civil Liberties Union.* New York: Columbia University Press.

Curtis, Michael Kent. 1986. *No State Shall Abridge: The 14th Amendment and the Bill of Rights.* Durham, N.C.: Duke University Press.

Dorsen, Norman, ed. 1989. *The Evolving Constitution: Essays on the Bill of Rights and the U.S. Supreme Court.* Middletown, CT: Wesleyan University Press.

Epstein, Lee, and Thomas G. Walker. 2000. *Constitutional Law for a Changing America: A Short Course.* Washington, DC: Congressional Quarterly Press.

Etzioni, Amitai. 1993. *The Spirit of Community: Rights, Responsibilities, and the Communitarian Agenda.* New York: Crown.

First Amendment Center. 2003. *State of the First Amendment.* Available at www.freedomforum.org.

Fisher, Louis. 1995. *Presidential War Power.* Lawrence: University Press of Kansas.

Garey, Diane. 1998. *Defending Everybody: A History of the American Civil Liberties Union.* New York: TV Books.

Hall, Kermit L., ed. 1987. *Civil Liberties in American History: Major Historical Interpretations.* New York: Garland.

———. 1990. *The Historic Background of the Bill of Rights,* vol. 1. New York: Garland.

Handler, Jack G. 1994. *Ballentine's Law Dictionary.* Albany, NY: Lawyer's Cooperative Publishing.

Hays, Arthur Garfield. 1928. *Let Freedom Ring.* New York: Boni and Liveright.

Hentoff, Nat. 2003. *The War on the Bill of Rights, and the Gathering Resistance.* New York: Seven Stories Press.

Kennedy, Sheila Suess. 1997. *What's a Nice Republican Girl Like Me Doing in the ACLU?* Amherst, NY: Prometheus Books.

Keyssar, Alexander. 2000. *The Right to Vote: The Contested History of Democracy in the United States.* New York: Basic Books.

Kurland, Philip B., and Ralph Lerner. 1987. *The Founders' Constitution.* Chicago: University of Chicago Press.

Lacquer, Walter, and Barry Rubin, eds. 1989. *The Human Rights Reader,* rev. ed. New York: New American Library.

Lawyers' Committee for Human Rights. 2003. *Imbalance of Powers: How Changes to U.S. Law and Policy since 9/11 Erode Human Rights and Civil Liberties.* Washington, DC: Lawyers' Committee for Human Rights.

Leahy, James. 1991. *The First Amendment, 1791–1991: Two Hundred Years of Freedom.* Jefferson, N.C.: McFarland.

Levin, Michael. 2003. *Complete Idiot's Guide to Your Civil Liberties.* Indianapolis: Alpha.

Levy, Leonard W. 1963. *Jefferson and Civil Liberties: The Darker Side.* Cambridge, Mass.: Harvard University Press.

———. 1988. *Original Intent and the Framers' Constitution.* New York: Macmillan.

Levy, Leonard, and Kenneth L. Karst, eds. 2000. *Encyclopedia of the American Constitution.* 2nd ed. New York: Free Press.

Linfield, Michael. 1990. *Freedom under Fire: U.S. Civil Liberties in Times of War.* Boston: South End Press.

Maddex, Robert L. 1998. *State Constitutions of the United States.* Washington, DC: Congressional Quarterly Press.

Massaro, Tone Marie. 1993. *Constitutional Literacy: A Core Curriculum for a Multicultural Nation.* Durham, N.C.: Duke University Press.

McClosky, Herbert, and Alida Brill. 1983. *Dimensions of Tolerance: What Americans Believe about Civil Liberties.* New York: Russell Sage Foundation.

Melanson, Philip H. 2001. *Secrecy Wars: National Security, Privacy, and the Public's Right to Know.* Washington, DC: Brassey's.

Morgan, Charles, Jr. 1979. *One Man, One Voice.* New York: Holt, Reinhart, and Winston.

Murphy, Paul L. 1979. *World War I and the Origin of Civil Liberties in the United States.* New York: W. W. Norton.

Murphy, Paul L., ed. 1990. *Pre-1960 Developments in the Bill of Rights Area.* Vol. 2 of *The Bill of Rights and American Legal History.* New York: Garland.

———. 1990. *The Bill of Rights and the States.* Vol. 9 of *The Bill of Rights and American Legal History.* New York: Garland.

———. 1990. *Rights of Assembly, Petition, Arms, and Just Compensation.* Vol. 5 of *The Bill of Rights and American Legal History.* New York: Garland.

Neely, Mark E. 1991. *The Fate of Liberty: Abraham Lincoln and Civil Liberties.* New York: Oxford University Press.

Neier, Aryeh. 2003. *Taking Liberties: Four Decades in the Struggle for Rights.* New York: Random House.

Pacheco, Josephine F., ed. 1983. *The Legacy of George Mason*. Fairfax, Va.: George Mason University Press.

Rakove, Jack N. 1990. *James Madison and the Creation of the American Republic*. Glenview, Ill.: Scott, Foresman/Little, Brown Higher Education.

———. 1996. *Original Meanings: Politics and Ideas in the Making of the Constitution*. New York: Knopf.

Reitman, Alan, ed. 1975. *The Pulse of Freedom: American Liberties: 1920–1970s*. New York: W. W. Norton.

Rosenfeld, Richard N. 1997. *American Aurora: A Democratic-Republican Returns—The Suppressed History of Our Nation's Beginnings and the Heroic Newspaper That Tried to Report It*. New York: St. Martin's Press.

Scheiber, Harry. 1960. *The Wilson Administration and Civil Liberties, 1917–1921*. Ithaca, NY: Cornell University Press.

Schulhofer, Stephen J. 2002. *The Enemy Within: Intelligence Gathering, Law Enforcement, and Civil Liberties in the Wake of September 11*. New York: Century Foundation Press.

Schwartz, Bernard. 1977. *The Great Rights of Mankind: A History of the American Bill of Rights*. New York: Oxford University Press.

Schwartz, Bernard., ed. 1980. *The Roots of the Bill of Rights: An Illustrated Source Book of American Freedom*. 5 vols. New York: Chelsea House.

Shumate, T. Daniel. 1985. *The First Amendment: The Legacy of George Mason*. Fairfax, Va.: George Mason University Press.

Svonkin, Stuart. 1997. *Jews against Prejudice: American Jews and the Fight for Civil Liberties*. New York: Columbia University Press.

Tarr, G. Alan. 1998. *Understanding State Constitutions*. Princeton, N.J.: Princeton University Press.

Vile, John R. 1996. *Encyclopedia of Constitutional Amendments, Proposed Amendments, and Amending Issues, 1789–1995*. Santa Barbara, CA: ABC-CLIO.

Walker, Samuel. 1992. *The American Civil Liberties Union: An Annotated Bibliography*. New York: Garland.

Weinberg, Arthur, and Lila Weinberg. 1987. *Clarence Darrow: A Sentimental Rebel*. New York: Atheneum.

Wills, Garry. 2002. *James Madison*. New York: Times Books.

Zelden, Charles L. 2002. *Voting Rights on Trial: A Handbook with Cases, Laws, and Documents*. Santa Barbara, CA: ABC-CLIO.

Civil Liberties: The Supreme Court

Bork, Robert. 1980. *The Tempting of America.* New York: Free Press.

This book expresses the extreme conservative attack on the modern role of the Supreme Court in defending civil liberties. In 1987, Robert Bork was nominated for a position on the U.S. Supreme Court. Because of his views on abortion and other subjects, liberal groups organized a successful campaign to block his nomination. The controversy over his nomination was one of the major news stories of the year. After his nomination was rejected, Bork wrote *The Tempting of America* to explain his views in detail. One part of the book is his version of the nomination controversy. The other part sets forth his views on the role of the Supreme Court, arguing that Supreme Court justices have substituted their personal views for the true meaning of the Constitution. One particularly important part of Bork's argument is his interpretation of the landmark 1954 *Brown v. Board of Education* decision declaring racially segregated public schools unconstitutional. As he sees it, *Brown* set the stage for many pro–civil liberties decisions that followed.

O'Brien, David M. 2003. *Storm Center: The Supreme Court in American Politics,* 6th ed. New York: Norton.

Storm Center is a highly readable and scholarly account of the place of the Supreme Court in U.S. politics: the impact of landmark decisions on society and politics, and the process by which justices are appointed to the Court. Two other books, *Gideon's Trumpet* and *Minnesota Rag,* are excellent and highly readable accounts of individual cases, but O'Brien's book places those books in the larger context of U.S. politics and history. The Supreme Court has been the major instrument in advancing civil liberties in U.S. society. The ways of the Court can be mysterious and dramatic, and this book goes a long way toward explaining how this institution actually works in our society.

Schwartz, Bernard. 1996. *Decision: How the Supreme Court Decides Cases.* New York: Oxford University Press.

Based on the internal working papers of the Supreme Court, including memos by justices and early drafts of opinions, this book is the best inside view of how the Supreme Court actually works. It is especially good on the role of personalities and leadership. One chapter is devoted to Chief Justice Earl Warren's leadership in several landmark cases during the 1960s, including *Miranda v. Arizona.* Another chapter is devoted to justices switching their votes on important issues, illustrating the different factors that can influence a judge's position.

Abraham, Henry J., and Barbara A. Perry. 2003. *Freedom and the Court: Civil Rights and Liberties in the United States,* 8th ed. Lawrence: University Press of Kansas.

Ball, Howard, and Phillip J. Cooper. 1992. *Of Power and Right: Hugo Black, William O. Douglas, and America's Constitutional Revolution.* New York: Oxford University Press.

Biskupic, Joan, and Elder Witt. 1997. *Guide to the U.S. Supreme Court.* Washington, DC: Congressional Quarterly Press.

Brisbin, Richard A., Jr. 1997. *Justice Antonin Scalia and the Conservative Revival.* Baltimore: Johns Hopkins University Press.

Cray, Ed. 1997. *Chief Justice: A Biography of Earl Warren.* New York: Simon and Schuster.

Cushman, Clare, ed. 2001. *Supreme Court Decisions and Women's Rights: Milestones to Equality.* Washington, DC: Congressional Quarterly Press.

Epstein, Lee. 1985. *Conservatives in Court.* Knoxville: University of Tennessee Press.

Epstein, Lee, and Joseph F. Kobylka. 1992. *The Supreme Court and Legal Change: Abortion and the Death Penalty.* Chapel Hill: University of North Carolina Press.

Hall, Kermit L., ed. 1992. *The Oxford Companion to the Supreme Court of the United States.* New York: Oxford University Press.

Horwitz, Morton J. 1998. *The Warren Court and the Pursuit of Justice.* New York: Hill and Wang.

Irons, Peter. 1994. *Brennan versus Rehnquist: The Battle for the Constitution.* New York: Knopf.

———. 1999. *A People's History of the Supreme Court.* New York: Viking.

Jost, Kenneth, ed. 1998. *The Supreme Court, A to Z.* Washington, DC: Congressional Quarterly Press.

Lasser, William. 1988. *The Limits of Judicial Power: The Supreme Court in American Politics.* Chapel Hill: University of North Carolina Press.

Marshall, Thomas R. 1989. *Public Opinion and the Supreme Court.* Boston: Unwin Hyman.

Murphy, Bruce. 2003. *Wild Bill: The Life and Legend of William O. Douglas.* New York: Random House.

Newman, Roger K. 1994. *Hugo Black: A Biography.* New York: Pantheon.

Pertschuk, Michael, and Wendy Schaetzel. 1989. *The People Rising: The Campaign against the Bork Nomination.* New York: Thunder's Mouth Press.

Pritchett, C. Herman. 1954. *Civil Liberties and the Vinson Court.* Chicago: University of Chicago Press.

Raskin, Jamin B. 2000. *We the Students: Supreme Court Decisions for and about Students.* Washington, DC: Congressional Quarterly Press.

Rosenkranz, E. Joshua, and Bernard Schwartz, eds. 1997. *Reason and Passion: Justice Brennan's Enduring Influence.* New York: W. W. Norton.

Scalia, Antonin. 1998. *A Matter of Interpretation: Federal Courts and the Law.* Princeton, N.J.: Princeton University Press.

Sepinuck, Stephen L., and Mary Pat Treuhart, eds. 1999. *The Conscience of the Court: Selected Opinions of Justice William J. Brennan Jr. on Freedom and Equality.* Carbondale: Southern Illinois University Press.

Simon, James F. 2002. *What Kind of Nation: Thomas Jefferson, John Marshall, and the Epic Struggle to Create a United States.* New York: Simon and Schuster.

Stern, Robert L. 1993. *Supreme Court Practice: For Practice in the Supreme Court of the United States.* Washington, DC: Bureau of National Affairs.

Tushnet, Mark V. 1961. *Making Civil Rights Law: Thurgood Marshall and the Supreme Court, 1936–1961.* New York: Oxford University Press.

Urofsky, Melvin I. 1991. *Felix Frankfurter: Judicial Restraint and Individual Liberties.* Boston: Twayne.

———. 2001. *The Warren Court: Justices, Rulings, and Legacy.* Santa Barbara, CA: ABC-CLIO.

Urofsky, Melvin I., ed. 1994. *The Supreme Court Justices: A Biographical Dictionary.* New York: Garland.

Vestal, Theodore M. 2002. *The Eisenhower Court and Civil Liberties.* New York: Praeger.

Weizer, Paul I. 2000. *The Supreme Court and Sexual Harassment: Preventing Harassment While Preserving Free Speech.* Lanham, Md.: Lexington Books.

White, G. Edward. 1982. *Earl Warren: A Public Life.* New York: Oxford University Press.

Criminal Justice and Civil Liberties

Lewis, Anthony. 1964. *Gideon's Trumpet.* New York: Random House.

Anthony Lewis's short book is a genuine classic. Clarence Gideon was an impoverished drifter who was convicted of breaking and entering with the intent to commit larceny and sent to prison in the state of Florida. Gideon never had the benefit of a lawyer. His appeal led to the Supreme Court decision, *Gideon v. Wainwright* (1963), holding that all criminal defendants charged with a felony had a constitutional right to an attorney. It is probably the best book on a single landmark Supreme Court case, and it provides an excellent picture of how a case originates and eventually makes its way to the highest court in the land.

Meares, Tracey L., and Dan M. Kahan. 1999. *Urgent Times: Policing and Rights in Inner-City Communities.* Boston: Beacon Press.

The classic debate over police practices involves the conflict between crime control and individual rights. How much power should the police have in their efforts to control crime? Where do crime control practices begin to infringe on individual rights?

One area where this debate came to a head involved police efforts to control urban gangs. The City of Chicago passed an ordinance in the 1980s giving police officers great discretion to stop and question people they suspected of being gang members and to order them to disperse or arrest them. The ACLU challenged the law and eventually succeeded in having the Supreme Court declare it unconstitutional, in large part because of the adverse impact on young African Americans.

This book offers a valuable debate over the issues surrounding the Chicago gang ordinance. The principal authors played a major role in defending the ordinance. They argue that the gang ordinance protects the rights of the majority of the residents in crime-ridden African American neighborhoods. Their view is challenged by other contributors. This book is an excellent introduction to one of the basic civil liberties issues involving the police. All of the essays are short, clear, and to the point.

Wicker, Tom. 1975. *A Time to Die.* New York: Quadrangle.

Tom Wicker's book is an account of the riot at the New York state penitentiary at Attica in 1971. More than 1,300 prisoners revolted, took forty guards hostage, and occupied major parts of the prison for four days. The prisoners issued twenty-eight demands that included establishing minimum standards of decent treatment. The demands included "adequate food, water and shelter for all inmates"; an end to censorship of mail and reading material; "true religious freedom" (this primarily involved an end to restrictions on Muslim practices); a "modernized" education system, a Spanish-language library, and an "effective narcotics treatment program." The governor of New York sent in the state police in an assault that resulted in forty-three deaths, including ten hostages.

From the standpoint of civil liberties, the value of Wicker's book is in dramatizing the ghastly conditions that prevailed at Attica before the riot. By today's standards, the conditions that lay behind the prisoners' demands in 1971 seem almost unbelievable. In the years since the riot, the prisoners' rights movement has challenged these and other conditions in court and has succeeded in eliminating the worst abuses.

American Bar Association. 1983. Policy against Executing Juveniles. Available at *www.abanet.org.*

Amnesty International. 1999. *Killing with Prejudice: Race and the Death Penalty.* New York: Amnesty International USA.

———. 2001. *Abuse of Women in Custody: Sexual Misconduct and Shackling of Pregnant Women: A State-by-State Survey of Policies and Practices in the United States.* New York: Amnesty International.

Baker, Liva. 1983. *Miranda: The Crime, the Law, the Politics.* New York: Atheneum.

Banaszak, Ronald, ed. 2002. *Fair Trial Rights of the Accused: A Documentary History.* Westport, CT: Greenwood.

Banner, Stuart. 2002. *The Death Penalty: An American History.* Cambridge, Mass.: Harvard University Press.

Barkan, Steven E. 1985. *Protesters on Trial: Criminal Justice in the Southern Civil Rights and Vietnam Antiwar Movements.* New Brunswick, N.J.: Rutgers University Press.

Bedau, Hugo Adam. 1987. *Death Is Different: Studies in the Morality, Law, and Politics of Capital Punishment.* Boston: Northeastern University Press.

Bodenhamer, David J. 1992. *Fair Trial: Rights of the Accused in American History.* New York: Oxford University Press.

Champion, Dean J. 2001. *Police Misconduct in America: A Reference Handbook.* Santa Barbara, CA: ABC-CLIO.

Fliter, John A. 2001. *Prisoners' Rights: The Supreme Court and Evolving Standards of Decency.* Westport, CT: Greenwood Press.

Freedman, Warren. 1989. *The Constitutional Right to a Speedy and Fair Criminal Trial.* New York: Quorum Books.

Goldfarb, Ronald. 1965. *Ransom: A Critique of the American Bail System.* New York: Harper and Row.

Human Rights Watch. 1998. *Shielded from Justice: Police Brutality and Accountability in the United States.* New York: Human Rights Watch.

———. 1999. *No Minor Matter: Children in Maryland's Jails.* New York: Human Rights Watch.

———. 2001. *No Escape: Male Rape in U.S. Prisons.* New York: Human Rights Watch.

Husak, Douglas N. 2002. *Legalize This! The Case for Decriminalizing Drugs.* New York: Verso.

Inciardi, James A., ed. 1999. *The Drug Legalization Debate.* Thousand Oaks, CA: Sage Publications.

Knight, Barbara B., and Stephen T. Early, Jr. 1986. *Prisoners' Rights in America.* Chicago: Nelson-Hall.

Levy, Leonard W. 1968. *Origins of the Fifth Amendment: The Right against Self-Incrimination.* New York: Oxford University Press.

Lock, Shmuel. 1999. *Crime, Public Opinion, and Civil Liberties: The Tolerant Public.* New York: Praeger.

Manfredi, Christopher P. 2000. *The Supreme Court and Juvenile Justice.* Lawrence: University Press of Kansas.

Murphy, Paul L., ed. 1990. *Criminal Procedure.* Vol. 8 of *The Bill of Rights and American Legal History.* New York: Garland.

Palmer, Louis J., Jr. 2001. *Encyclopedia of Capital Punishment in the United States.* Jefferson, N.C.: McFarland.

Radelet, Michael L., and Margaret Vandiver. 1988. *Capital Punishment in America: An Annotated Bibliography.* New York: Garland.

Rudovsky, David, Alvin Bronstein, Ed Koren, and Julia Cade. 1992. *The Rights of Prisoners.* 4th ed. Carbondale: Southern Illinois University Press.

Sentencing Project. 1998. *Losing the Vote: The Impact of Felony Disenfranchisement Laws in the United States.* Washington, DC: Sentencing Project.

Streib, Victor L. 1987. *Death Penalty for Juveniles.* Bloomington: Indiana University Press.

Thomas, Wayne H., Jr. 1976. *Bail Reform in America.* Berkeley: University of California Press.

Vila, Bryan, and Cynthia Morris, eds. 1997. *Capital Punishment in the United States: A Documentary History.* Westport, CT: Greenwood.

Freedom for Unpopular Political Beliefs

Faulk, John Henry. 1964. *Fear on Trial.* New York: Simon and Schuster.

One of the worst violations of civil liberties was the practice of "blacklisting" movie, television, and radio figures because of their alleged Communist affiliations or "disloyal" ideas. John Henry Faulk was a popular radio entertainer who lost his job through blacklisting. This memoir is his first-hand account of the experience and how, after many years of struggle, he managed to regain his career.

Gentry, Curtis. 1991. *J. Edgar Hoover: The Man and the Secrets.* New York: W. W. Norton.

The Federal Bureau of Investigation, under the direction of J. Edgar Hoover from 1924 until his death in 1972, conducted a massive program of spying on Americans and using information to destroy people's lives.

Curtis Gentry's book is not only the best biography of Hoover but also the best account of the FBI's illegal spying program. One of the best parts of the book is the discussion of how Hoover maintained a system to separate files that preserved the secrecy of his illegal activities. This is a very long book, but it is never boring.

Miller, Arthur. 1954. *The Crucible: Drama in Two Acts.* New York: Dramatists Play Service.

The term "witch hunt" has entered the English language as a shorthand for the hysterical pursuit of imagined enemies in the community. The Cold War attack on alleged "subversives" and Communist Party members is often characterized as a witch hunt.

The original witch hunt in U.S. history occurred in Salem, Massachusetts, in 1692. In a story that is the subject of many scholarly historical interpretations, people were put to death as suspected witches.

At the height of the Cold War, the great American playwright Arthur Miller wrote a play about the Salem witch trials, *The Crucible.* Clearly, Miller was thinking about the assault on ideas that had engulfed U.S. society during the Cold War. *The Crucible* is a great play that raises important issues about two major periods in American history.

Navasky, Victor. 1980. *Naming Names.* New York: Viking Press.

The Cold War represented one of the greatest assaults on freedom of speech and association in U.S. history. People lost their jobs and had their lives ruined because of their ideas or organizations they belonged to. And in many cases, they were persecuted because they had joined—and soon quit—some group fifteen years earlier, when they were college students.

Victor Navasky's *Naming Names* tells only one small part of the story of the Cold War, but it tells it in a way that dramatizes the ethical dilemmas as well as the personal tragedies that pervaded the Cold War years. Persons accused of being Communists were often offered the chance to "clear" their names by naming other people as Communists. A small industry of informers, lawyers, and "fixers" arose to facilitate the process of "clearing" the accused.

Navasky's account focuses on a number of prominent motion picture and theater artists, some of whom were and still are regarded as the best in their fields. This book is gripping and very disturbing reading.

Norton, Mary Beth. 2002. *In the Devil's Snare: The Salem Witchcraft Crisis of 1692.* New York: Alfred A. Knopf.

The Salem witchcraft trials continue to fascinate Americans. At least twelve books on the subject have been published since 1990. Historians have offered a number of different interpretations, including economic conflicts, gender issues, and even medical explanations. The Salem tragedy touches on themes that are central to American history and the history of civil liberties in particular: intolerance, mass hysteria, and the capacity of otherwise decent people to perpetrate gross injustices on innocent people. Mary Beth Norton, a distinguished historian who has written widely on a number of subjects on early American history, offers her own interpretation of this episode, emphasizing the changing place of the colonies in the larger world. Presented in a clear chronological format, her account allows the reader to follow the unfolding events of this tragedy.

Bernstein, Walter. 1996. *Inside Out: A Memoir of the Blacklist.* New York: Knopf.

Boyer, Paul, and Stephen Nissenbaum. 1974. *Salem Possessed: The Social Origins of Witchcraft.* Cambridge, Mass.: Harvard University Press.

Caute, David. 1978. *The Great Fear: The Anti-Communist Purge under Truman and Eisenhower.* New York: Simon and Schuster.

Davis, James Kirkpatrick. 1997. *Assault on the Left: The FBI and the Sixties Antiwar Movement.* New York: Praeger.

Fariello, Griffin. 1995. *Red Scare: Memories of the American Inquisition: An Oral History.* New York: W. W. Norton.

Foster, Stuart J. 2000. *Red Alert! Educators Confront the Red Scare in American Public Schools, 1947–1954.* New York: Peter Lang.

Frankfurter, Felix. 1961 [1927]. *The Case of Sacco and Vanzetti.* New York: Grosset and Dunlap.

Gerdes, Louise, ed. 2003. *The Cold War.* Great Speeches in History Series. San Diego, CA: Greenhaven.

Goodman, Walter. 1968. *The Committee: The Extraordinary Career of the House Committee on Un-American Activities.* New York: Farrar, Straus, and Giroux.

Hoffer, Peter Charles. 1996. *The Devil's Disciples: Makers of the Salem Witchcraft Trials.* Baltimore: Johns Hopkins University Press.

Kutler, Stanley I. 1982. *The American Inquisition: Justice and Injustice in the Cold War.* New York: Hill and Wang.

O'Reilly, Kenneth. 1983. *Hoover and the Un-Americans: The FBI, HUAC, and the Red Menace.* Philadelphia: Temple University Press.

Reeves, Thomas C. 1982. *The Life and Times of Joe McCarthy: A Biography.* New York: Stein and Day.

Robins, Natalie. 1992. *Alien Ink: The FBI's War on Intellectual Freedom.* New York: William Morrow.

Schrecker, Ellen W. 1986. *No Ivory Tower: McCarthyism and the Universities.* New York: Oxford.

Stouffer, Samuel A. 1992. [1955]. *Communism, Conformity, and Civil Liberties.* New Brunswick, N.J.: Transaction Books.

Theoharis, Athan. 1978. *Spying on Americans: Political Surveillance from Hoover to the Huston Plan.* Philadelphia: Temple University Press.

————. 2002. *Chasing Spies: How the FBI Failed in Counterintelligence but Promoted the Politics of McCarthyism in the Cold War Years.* Chicago: Ivan R. Dee.

Freedom of Sexual Expression

Collins, Ronald K. L., and David M. Skover. 2002. *The Trials of Lenny Bruce: The Fall and Rise of an American Icon.* Naperville, Ill.: Sourcebooks MediaFusion.

Without Lenny Bruce, modern stand-up comedy would not exist. There would be no Richard Pryor, no Chris Rock, and almost none of today's irreverent, sexually explicit comedians. Lenny Bruce was the pioneer of this genre in the early 1960s who made it possible for the comedians who have followed. His comedy was wickedly irreverent and offensive, with a strong social and political edge. Most of all he hated hypocrisy, and especially the hypocrisy of racism in a society allegedly committed to equality. Organized religion was another favorite target.

Bruce's routines regularly got him in trouble with the law. He was arrested and prosecuted for obscenity and other charges in New York, Chicago, and other cities. His trials became major First Amendment cases. This book vividly recaptures the drama of this period in American life when the rules of strict censorship were first being challenged. In late 2003, the governor of New York granted Bruce a posthumous pardon for his 1965 conviction on obscenity charges.

The book is accompanied by a CD that includes many of Bruce's original comedy routines, allowing readers of the book to hear for themselves what all the controversy was about. The CD also includes interviews with other figures from the period, and it is narrated by the noted civil libertarian Nat Hentoff, who places particular events in their historical context.

Heins, Marjorie. 2001. *Not in Front of the Children: "Indecency," Censorship, and the Innocence of Youth.* New York: Hill and Wang.

Over the years many censorship efforts have been designed to protect children from alleged harm. There are continuing efforts to remove certain books from public schools because they are allegedly "indecent," and there is an ongoing struggle involving attempts to restrict sex education. The most important recent Supreme Court case in this area involved the federal Communications Decency Act (CDA), which prohibited indecent material from the Internet (*ACLU v. Reno*, 1997). A 2003 Supreme Court decision held that public libraries could place filters on their computers to block access to Web sites that allegedly contain indecent materials. Marjorie Heins's fine book provides a good overview of efforts to protect children through censorship.

Hunter, James Davison. 1991. *Culture Wars: The Struggle to Define America.* New York: Basic Books.

Many civil liberties controversies have arisen from conflicting cultural and moral standards: censorship of allegedly "indecent" books and movies; laws making private sexual behavior, including the use of contraceptives, illegal; efforts to instill morality in young people through compulsory public school prayers. Contrary to what many people believe, the "culture wars" are nothing new. They extend back through all of U.S. history. This book provides a very useful historical perspective on the underlying sources of so many contemporary civil liberties crises.

MacKinnon, Catharine A. 1993. *Only Words.* Cambridge, Mass.: Harvard University Press.

Catharine MacKinnon is a distinguished law professor who is widely credited with developing the concept of sexual harassment in the workplace as a form of sex discrimination. She is also one of the leading advocates of the view that pornography, and especially violent pornography, is a form of sex discrimination. She and Andrea Dworkin helped write the Indianapolis, Indiana, law that gave women the right to sue the producers and sellers of pornography. The law was declared unconstitutional by the Seventh Circuit Court of Appeals.

In this short book she explains her view that pornography (and other offensive forms of expression) represent discrimination and should not be protected by the First Amendment. This book is the most articulate statement advocating censorship in this area. Although MacKinnon's view has been rejected by the courts, it is one that even opponents of censorship should be familiar with. Nadine Strossen's book *Defending Pornography* (see below) is essentially a rebuttal of MacKinnon's view, and the two books should be read in conjunction with each other.

Strossen, Nadine. 1995. *Defending Pornography: Free Speech, Sex, and the Fight for Women's Rights.* New York: Scribners.

Censorship of sexually oriented materials has been one of the major themes in the history of the fight for freedom of speech. In recent years, this issue has become more complicated as some feminists have come to advocate censorship of pornography on the grounds that it violates the rights of women. Thus, the recent battles over censorship in this area have involved conflicts between different groups of rights advocates.

Nadine Strossen, president of the ACLU, has written a vigorous defense of freedom of expression with respect to sexually oriented materials. In clear and forcefully written prose, she argues that censorship has always been a weapon of those who would deny women full equality. The particular value of *Defending Pornography* is that it moves far beyond narrow legal issues to discuss the role of women, the complex meaning of sexuality in modern society, and the significance of the First Amendment.

Boyer, Paul S. 1968. *Purity in Print: The Vice-Society Movement and Book Censorship in America.* New York: Scribner's.

Bruce, Lenny. 1965. *How to Talk Dirty and Influence People.* Chicago: Playboy Press.

Downs, Donald Alexander. 1989. *The New Politics of Pornography.* Chicago: University of Chicago Press.

Harvey, Philip D. 2000. *The Government versus Erotica: The Siege of Adam and Eve.* Buffalo, NY: Prometheus Books.

Heins, Marjorie. 1993. *Sex, Sin, and Blasphemy: A Guide to America's Censorship Wars.* New York: New Press.

———. 2001. *Violence and the Media: An Exploration of Cause, Effect, and the First Amendment.* Arlington, Va.: First Amendment Center.

Mackey, Thomas C. 2002. *Pornography on Trial: A Handbook with Cases, Laws, and Documents.* Santa Barbara, CA: ABC-CLIO.

Moscato, Michael, and Leslie LeBlanc. 1984. *The United States of America v. One Book Entitled* Ulysses *by James Joyce: Documents and Commentary: A 50-year Retrospective.* Frederick, Md.: University Publications of America.

Freedom of Speech and Academic Freedom

Goines, David L. 1993. *The Free Speech Movement: Coming of Age in the 1960s.* Berkeley, CA: Ten Speed Press.

The free speech movement on the Berkeley campus of the University of California in the fall of 1964 was one of the pivotal events of the 1960s. It marked the beginning of mass student protest on college campuses and set the stage for protests against the Vietnam War just a few months later. In this book David Goines, one of the leaders of the movement, vividly recreates the passions of the moment with the cool distance of historical perspective. Many readers will be astonished to learn of the restrictions placed on college students—both in their personal and in their political lives—in the early 1960s, before the student revolt. Several of the free speech movement leaders had been active in the civil rights movement, and this book does an excellent job of establishing the influence of the African American struggle for rights on the thinking and actions of white college students.

Hentoff, Nat. 1980. *The First Freedom: The Tumultuous History of Free Speech in America.* New York: Delacorte.

In this book, Hentoff, a veteran journalist who writes a regular newspaper column on civil liberties issues, provides a very readable introduction to the history of free speech. He makes it clear that freedom of speech is something that people have had to fight to achieve and maintain. This is a good book for readers who feel they have no background on the history of free speech. It is written in a brisk, lively style. Readers who feel somewhat knowledgeable about the subject might want to choose one of the longer books cited below.

Leff, Leonard J., and Jerold L. Simmons. 2001. *The Dame in the Kimono: Hollywood, Censorship, and the Production Code.* Lexington: University Press of Kentucky.

Film lovers will find this an extremely entertaining book. The authors use the official records of the motion picture industry to examine in detail how Hollywood officials censored the movies between the 1930s and the early 1960s. Young readers who have grown up after the collapse of censorship will be particularly astonished to learn what could not be shown in the movies during these years. The book does an excellent job of showing how the threat of government censorship encouraged the film industry to engage in private self-censorship. *The Dame in the Kimono* brings back an almost forgotten period in American life and in the history of the movies.

Matsuda, Mari, Charles Lawrence, and Richard Delgado. 1993. *Words That Wound: Critical Race Theory, Assaultive Speech, and the First Amendment.* Boulder, CO: Westview.

The authors of the articles in this collection are among the most vigorous advocates of restricting hate speech that is offensive to racial and ethnic minorities, women, and other powerless groups. During the national debate over hate speech in the 1980s and 1990s these authors, and these articles in particular, were very influential. Charles Lawrence makes a strong argument that offensive speech inflicts actual harm in the same way that a physical attack does. Mari Matsuda contributes an important article arguing that First Amendment law has failed to take into account the experiences and voices of the historic victims of discrimination. Although the view advocated by these authors did not succeed in influencing public opinion and the position of the courts, it represents an important challenge to the prevailing view that the First Amendment does protect hate speech.

Neier, Aryeh. 1979. *Defending My Enemy: American Nazis, the Skokie Case, and the Risks of Freedom.* New York: E. P. Dutton.

The core principle of freedom of speech is that the First Amendment protects all forms of expression, including expression of ideas we find offensive. The issue of freedom for expression of thought or ideas we hate is dramatized by cases involving Nazi groups. Aryeh Neier's book is particularly compelling for two reasons. He was executive director of the ACLU in 1977, when a national controversy erupted over the attempt by a neo-Nazi group to hold a demonstration in the predominantly Jewish community of Skokie, Illinois. This book, part history, part memoir, provides a vivid first-hand account of that controversy. Neier is himself Jewish, and his parents fled Nazi Germany in the 1930s. In his book he relates his personal experience and feelings as a Jew to his principled defense of the free speech rights of Nazis. As the book's subtitle suggests, this account highlights the extent to which the defense of civil liberties often involves difficult and risky choices.

Smolla, Rodney A. 1992. *Free Speech in an Open Society.* New York: Knopf.

The question behind this book is, "What good are civil liberties?"—in this case, free speech. The function of the First Amendment is to promote and maintain a culture committed to the principles of openness, tolerance, and individual freedom. Along with many of the other books recommended in this chapter, *Free Speech in an Open Society* is written by a law professor but in a clear and forceful style that is accessible to a general audience. Chapter 2, "The Shortcomings of All Simple Answers," is particularly useful, especially for readers who are just beginning to explore freedom of speech and the First Amendment. Smolla does an excellent job of explaining why many popular but simple answers to questions about free speech are not adequate. Later chapters address specific issues such as political dissent, hate speech, and public funding of the arts.

Strum, Philippa. 1999. *When the Nazis Came to Skokie: Freedom for the Speech We Hate.* Lawrence: University Press of Kansas.

Neier's book is a first-hand account, written in the immediate aftermath of the Skokie crisis. Philippa Strum's book is a full history of the affair, with the benefit of perspective that comes with time. It has an excellent discussion of the First Amendment issues involved in the case and a good discussion of the aftermath of the controversy. Strum is a prominent ACLU leader, a distinguished political scientist, and a prolific writer who has written on a number of civil liberties issues, including privacy, women's rights, and Supreme Court Justice Louis Brandeis.

Sunstein, Cass. 1993. *Democracy and the Problem of Free Speech.* New York: Free Press.

Sunstein's book offers an excellent discussion of the meaning of free speech in a democratic society. Although Sunstein is among the most eminent law professors in the country, this book is written in a style that is quite accessible to the general reader. Sunstein believes in the classic Madisonian view of the First Amendment, which holds that the central role of free speech is to enhance democratic self-governance. Consequently, he does not take as "absolutist" position on some free speech issues as does the ACLU, for example. The most important forms of speech are those that contribute to political debate. Some forms of hate speech, however, contribute nothing to political debate. For a more absolutist view of free speech, you might want to read *Defending Pornography* (see above) by Nadine Strossen, president of the ACLU.

Aby, Stephen H., and James C. Kuhn IV, comp. 2000. *Academic Freedom: A Guide to the Literature.* Westport, CT: Greenwood.

American Library Association. 2002. *Intellectual Freedom Manual.* Chicago: American Library Association Office for Intellectual Freedom.

Bernstein, David E. 2003. *You Can't Say That: The Growing Threat to Civil Liberties from Antidiscrimination Laws.* Washington, DC: Cato Institute.

Bollinger, Lee C., and Geoffrey R. Stone, eds. 2001. *Eternally Vigilant: Free Speech in the Modern Era.* Chicago: University of Chicago.

Chafee, Zechariah, Jr. 1941. *Free Speech in the United States.* Cambridge, Mass.: Harvard University Press.

Cleary, Edward J. 1994. *Beyond the Burning Cross: The First Amendment and the Landmark* R.A.V. *Case.* New York: Random House.

Curtis, Michael Kent. 2000. *Free Speech, "The People's Darling Privilege": Struggles for Freedom of Expression in American History.* Durham, N.C.: Duke University Press.

Daly, James K., Rosemary W. Skeele, and Patricia L. Schall. 2001. *Protecting the Right to Teach and Learn: Power, Politics, and Public Schools.* New York: Teachers College Press.

DeGrazia, Edward, and Roger K. Newman. 1982. *Banned Films: Movies, Censors, and the First Amendment.* New York: Bowker.

Delgado, Richard, and Jean Stefancic. 1997. *Must We Defend Nazis? Hate Speech, Pornography, and the New First Amendment.* New York: New York University Press.

Downs, Donald Alexander. 1985. *Nazis in Skokie: Freedom, Community, and the First Amendment.* Notre Dame, Ind.: Notre Dame University Press.

Eldridge, Larry D. 1994. *A Distant Heritage: The Growth of Free Speech in Early America.* New York: New York University Press.

Emerson, Thomas I. 1970. *The System of Freedom of Expression.* New York: Vintage.

———. 1967. *Toward a General Theory of the First Amendment.* New York: Vintage.

Foerstel, Herbert N. 1994. *Banned in the U.S.A.: A Reference Guide to Book Censorship in Schools and Public Libraries.* Westport, CT: Greenwood.

Foerstel, Herbert N. 1997. *Free Expression and Censorship in America: An Encyclopedia.* Westport, CT: Greenwood.

Foley, Michael. 2003. *Confronting the War Machine: Draft Resistance during the Vietnam War.* Chapel Hill: University of North Carolina Press.

Fortas, Abe. 1970. *Concerning Dissent and Civil Disobedience.* New York: New American Library.

Freedman, Warren. 1988. *Freedom of Speech on Private Property.* New York: Quorum Books.

Freedom Forum. 2002. *Comedy and Freedom of Speech.* Available at www.freedomforum.com.

Friedman, Leon, and Burt Neuborne. 1972. *Unquestioning Obedience to the President: the ACLU Case against the Illegal War in Vietnam.* New York: W. W. Norton.

Godwin, Mike. 1998. *Cyber Rights: Defending Free Speech in the Digital Age.* New York: Times Books.

Goldstein, Robert Justin. 1995. *Saving Old Glory: The History of the American Flag Desecration Controversy.* Boulder, CO: Westview Press.

———. 1996. *Burning the Flag: The Great 1989–1990 American Flag Desecration Controversy.* Kent, Ohio: Kent State University Press.

———. 2000. *Flag Burning and Free Speech: The Case of* Texas v. Johnson. Lawrence: University Press of Kansas.

Goodale, James C., comp. 1971. The New York Times Company v. United States: *A Documentary History of the Pentagon Papers Litigation.* New York: Arno Press.

Gora, Joel M., David Goldberger, Gary Stern, and Morton H. Halperin. 1991. *The Right to Protest.* Carbondale: Southern Illinois University.

Graber, Mark A. 1991. *Transforming Free Speech: The Ambiguous Legacy of Civil Libertarianism.* Berkeley: University of California Press.

Greenawalt, Kent. 1995. *Fighting Words: Individuals, Communities, and Liberties of Speech.* Princeton, N.J.: Princeton University Press.

Haiman, Frank. 1993. *"Speech Acts" and the First Amendment.* Carbondale: Southern Illinois University Press.

Harer, John B. 1992. *Intellectual Freedom: A Reference Handbook.* Santa Barbara, CA: ABC-CLIO.

Hawke, Constance S. 2001. *Computer and Internet Use on Campus: A Legal Guide to Issues of Intellectual Property, Free Speech, and Privacy.* San Francisco: Jossey-Bass.

Hentoff, Nat. 1992. *Free Speech for Me—But Not for Thee*. New York: HarperCollins.

———. 1997. *Speaking Freely: A Memoir*. New York: Knopf.

Heumann, Milton, and Thomas W. Church, with David P. Redlawsk. 1997. *Hate Speech on Campus: Cases, Case Studies, and Commentary*. Boston: Northeastern University Press.

Hudson, David L. 2002. *Balancing Act: Public Employees and Free Speech*. Arlington, Va.: First Amendment Center.

Johnson, John W. 1997. *The Struggle for Student Rights:* Tinker v. Des Moines *and the 1960s*. Lawrence: University Press of Kansas.

Kalven, Harry, Jr. 1988. *A Worthy Tradition: Freedom of Speech in America*. New York: Harper and Row.

Kennedy, Sheila Suess, ed. 1999. *Free Expression in America: A Documentary History*. Westport, CT: Greenwood.

Kors, Alan Charles, and Harvey A. Silverglate. 1968. *The Shadow University: The Betrayal of Liberty on America's Campuses*. New York: Free Press.

Levy, Leonard W. 1993. *Blasphemy: Verbal Offense against the Sacred, from Moses to Salman Rushdie*. New York: Knopf.

Lewis, Anthony. 1991. *Make No Law: The Sullivan Case and the First Amendment*. New York: Random House.

Lewis, Jon. 2000. *Hollywood versus Hard Core: How the Struggle over Censorship Saved the Modern Film Industry*. New York: New York University Press.

Lipschultz, Jeremy Harris. 2000. *Free Expression in the Age of the Internet: Social and Legal Boundaries*. Boulder, CO: Westview Press.

Maggs, Peter B., John T. Soma, and James A. Sprowl. 2001. *Internet and Computer Law: Cases, Comments, Questions*. St. Paul, Minn.: West.

Meiklejohn, Alexander. 1948. *Free Speech and Its Relation to Self-Government*. New York: Harper and Brothers.

Mitford, Jessica. 1970. *The Trial of Dr. Spock*. New York: Vintage Books.

Mitgang, Herbert. 1988. *Dangerous Dossiers: Exposing the Secret War against America's Greatest Authors*. New York: D. I. Fine.

Murphy, Paul L. 1972. *The Meaning of Freedom of Speech: First Amendment Freedoms from Wilson to FDR*. Westport, CT: Greenwood.

Murphy, Paul L., ed. 1990. *Free Speech*. Vol. 3 of *The Bill of Rights and American Legal History*. New York: Garland.

Norwick, Kenneth P., and Jerry Simon Chasen. 1992. *The Rights of Authors, Artists, and Other Creative People*, 2nd ed. Carbondale: Southern Illinois University Press.

O'Neil, Robert M. 1997. *Free Speech in the College Community.* Bloomington: Indiana University Press.

Peck, Robert S. 2000. *Libraries, the First Amendment, and Cyberspace: What You Need to Know.* Chicago: American Library Association.

Polenberg, Richard. 1987. *Fighting Faiths: The Abrams Case, the Supreme Court, and Free Speech.* New York: Viking.

Rabban, David. 1997. *Free Speech in Its Forgotten Years.* New York: Cambridge University Press.

Riley, Gail Blasser. 1998. *Censorship.* New York: Facts-on-File.

Rorabaugh, William J. 1989. *Berkeley at War: The 1960s.* New York: Oxford University Press.

Rubin, David, and Steven Greenhouse. 1984. *The Rights of Teachers.* New York: Bantam Books.

Simmons, John S., and Eliza T. Dresang. 2001. *School Censorship in the 21st Century: A Guide for Teachers and School Library Media Specialists.* Newark, Del.: International Reading Association.

Spacks, Patricia Meyer. 1996. *Advocacy in the Classroom: Problems and Possibilities.* New York: St. Martin's Press.

Steele, Richard W. 1999. *Free Speech in the Good War.* New York: St. Martin's Press.

Symons, Ann K., and Sally Gardner Reed. 1999. *Speaking Out: Voices in Celebration of Intellectual Freedom.* Chicago: American Library Association.

Tollefson, James W. 1993. *The Strength Not to Fight: An Oral History of Conscientious Objectors of the Vietnam War.* Boston: Little, Brown.

Walker, Samuel. 1994. *Hate Speech: The History of an American Controversy.* Lincoln: University of Nebraska Press.

Weinstein, James. 1999. *Hate Speech, Pornography, and the Radical Attack on Free Speech Doctrine.* Boulder, CO: Westview Press.

Welch, Michael. 2000. *Flag Burning: Moral Panic and the Criminalization of Protest.* New York: de Gruyter.

Winfield, Betty Houchin, and Sandra Davidson, eds. 1999. *Bleep! Censoring Rock and Rap Music.* Westport, CT: Greenwood Press.

Freedom of the Press

Friendly, Fred W. 1982. **Minnesota Rag: The Dramatic Story of the Landmark Supreme Court Case That Gave New Meaning to Freedom of the Press.** New York: Vintage Books.

The title of this book tells it all. It is a dramatic story, told by a veteran journalist in a style that is a joy to read. The case of *Near v. Minnesota* in 1931 represented the beginning of modern law protecting freedom of the press. Jay Near published a tabloid newspaper that attacked local politicians. He was convicted under a local law for being a "public nuisance." Friendly's account is particularly valuable in illustrating how landmark court cases often begin with the actions of rather unsavory people. *Minnesota Rag* rivals *Gideon's Trumpet* (cited below) as an excellent account of how a case begins with a seemingly minor local dispute and eventually wends it way to the U.S. Supreme Court and results in a landmark decision.

Ungar, Sanford J. 1972. *The Papers and the Papers: An Account of the Legal and Political Battle over the Pentagon Papers.* New York: Dutton.

The *Pentagon Papers* case was one of the great confrontations of the Vietnam War era. The Pentagon had compiled a secret history of U.S. involvement in Vietnam, reaching back to the 1950s. Daniel Ellsberg, a former Defense Department employee who had become an opponent of the war, leaked a copy of the classified report to The *New York Times*, which began publishing excerpts in June 1971. The Justice Department obtained an injunction to stop the *Times*'s publication, setting up a dramatic confrontation over freedom of the press. In a swiftly decided decision, the U.S. Supreme Court overturned the injunction and ruled in favor of The *New York Times*. This book is a vivid account of a major civil liberties crisis. It recaptures the drama of the Vietnam War years, the personalities involved in the case, and the First Amendment issues that it raised.

Benjamin, Louise M. 2001. *Freedom of the Air and the Public Interest: First Amendment Rights in Broadcasting to 1935.* Carbondale: Southern Illinois University Press.

Campbell, Douglas S. 1994. *Free Press versus Fair Trial: Supreme Court Decisions since 1807.* New York: Praeger.

Cortner, Richard C. 1996. *The Kingfish and the Constitution: Huey Long, the First Amendment, and the Emergence of Modern Press Freedom in America.* Westport, CT: Greenwood.

Gora, Joel M. 1974. *The Rights of Reporters.* New York: Discus Books.

Ingelhart, Louis Edward. 1997. *Press and Speech Freedoms in America, 1619–1995: A Chronology.* Westport, CT: Greenwood.

Kane, Peter. 1986. *Murder, Courts, and the Press: Issues in Free Press/Fair Trial.* Carbondale: Southern Illinois University Press.

Levy, Leonard W. 1987. *Emergence of a Free Press.* New York: Oxford University Press.

Martin, Robert W. T. 2001. *The Free and Open Press: The Founding of American Democratic Press Liberty, 1640–1800.* New York: New York University Press.

McCoy, Ralph E. 1993. *Freedom of the Press: An Annotated Bibliography: Second Supplement, 1978–1992.* Carbondale: Southern Illinois University Press.

Murphy, Paul L., ed. 1990. *Free Press.* Vol. 4 of *The Bill of Rights and American Legal History.* New York: Garland.

Reporters Committee for Freedom of the Press. 2003. *First Amendment Handbook.* Available at www.rcfp.org.

Saunders, Kevin W. 1996. *Violence as Obscenity: Limiting the Media's First Amendment Protection.* Durham, N.C.: Duke University Press.

Smith, Jeffrey A. 1999. *War and Press Freedom: The Problem of Prerogative Power.* New York: Oxford University Press.

Yalof, David A., and Kenneth Dautrich. 2002. *The First Amendment and the Media in the Court of Public Opinion.* New York: Cambridge University Press.

Gay and Lesbian Rights

Duberman, Martin. 1993. ***Stonewall.*** New York: Dutton.

The police raid on the gay bar Stonewall in 1969 is generally regarded as the event that sparked the militant lesbian and gay rights movement (see Chapter 4). This book is a brilliant history of the event by a distinguished historian and gay activist. He tells the story through the lives of six individuals, examining their personal histories and the impact the Stonewall event had on them. As a historian, Duberman is able to present these personal stories in the context of an important historical event.

Adam, Barry D. 1995. *The Rise of a Gay and Lesbian Movement.* New York: Twayne.

Bourassa, Kevin, and Joe Varnell. *Just Married: Gay Marriage and the Expansion of Human Rights.* Madison: University of Wisconsin Press.

Casey, Charles. 2003. *The Sharon Kowalski Case: Lesbian and Gay Rights on Trial*. Lawrence: University Press of Kansas.

Clendinen, Dudley, and Adam Nagourney. 1999. *Out for Good: The Struggle to Build a Gay Rights Movement in America*. New York: Simon and Schuster.

Coles, Matthew. 1996. *Try This at Home! A Do-It-Yourself Guide for Instituting Lesbian/Gay Rights Policy*. New York: New Press.

Dupuis, Martin. 2002. *Same-Sex Marriage, Legal Mobilization, and the Politics of Rights*. New York: Peter Lang.

Eskridge, William N., Jr. 2002. *Equality Practice: Civil Unions and the Future of Gay Rights*. New York: Routledge.

Hunter, Nan D., Courtney G. Joslin, and Sharon M. McGowan. 2004. *The Rights of Lesbians, Gay Men, Bisexuals, and Transgender People*, 4th ed. Carbondale: Southern Illinois University Press.

Leonard, Arthur S. 1997. *Homosexuality and the Constitution*. New York: Garland.

Merin, Yuval. 2002. *Equality for Same-Sex Couples: The Legal Recognition of Gay Partnerships in Europe and the United States*. Chicago: University of Chicago Press.

Newton, David E. 1994. *Gay and Lesbian Rights: A Reference Handbook*. Santa Barbara, CA: ABC-CLIO.

Sherman, Suzanne, ed. 1997. *Lesbian and Gay Marriage: Private Commitments, Public Ceremonies*. Philadelphia: Temple University Press.

Shilts, Randy. 1993. *Conduct Unbecoming: Gays and Lesbians in the U.S. Military*. New York: St. Martin's.

Strasser, Mark. 1997. *Legally Wed: Same-Sex Marriage and the Constitution*. Ithaca, NY: Cornell University Press.

Thomas, Laurence M., and Michael E. Levin. 1999. *Sexual Orientation and Human Rights*. Lanham, Md.: Rowman and Littlefield.

Vaid, Urvashi. 1995. *Virtual Equality: The Mainstreaming of Gay and Lesbian Liberation*. New York: Anchor Books.

Walzer, Lee. 2002. *Gay Rights on Trial: A Reference Handbook*. Santa Barbara, CA: ABC-CLIO.

Privacy Rights

Alderman, Ellen, and Caroline Kennedy. 1995. ***The Right to Privacy***. New York: Knopf.

As they did in their earlier book, *In Our Defense,* Alderman and Kennedy examine an important area of civil liberties through actual case studies involving real people. The cases covered include strip searches of girls stopped for traffic offenses, school officials' search of a student's purse, and a dispute over who owns some frozen embryos. This is a particularly good introduction to an extremely complex area of the law.

American Civil Liberties Union. 1986. *Preserving the Right to Choose: How to Cope with Violence and Disruption at Abortion Clinics.* New York: American Civil Liberties Union.

Baer, Judith A., ed. 2002. *Historical and Multicultural Encyclopedia of Women's Reproductive Rights in the United States.* Westport, CT: Greenwood.

Bullough, Vern L. 2001. *Encyclopedia of Birth Control.* Santa Barbara, CA: ABC-CLIO.

Cate, Fred H. 2003. *The Privacy Problem: A Broader View of Information Privacy and the Costs and Consequences of Protecting It.* Arlington, Va.: First Amendment Center.

Chen, Constance M. 1996. *"The Sex Side of Life": Mary Ware Dennett's Pioneering Battle for Birth Control and Sex Education.* New York: New Press.

Chesler, Ellen. 1992. *Woman of Valor: Margaret Sanger and the Birth Control Movement in America.* New York: Simon and Schuster.

Critchlow, Donald T. 1999. *Intended Consequences: Birth Control, Abortion, and the Federal Government in Modern America.* New York: Oxford University Press.

Faux, Marian. 1988. *Roe v. Wade.* New York: New American Library.

Feldt, Gloria, with Carol Trickett Jennings. 2003. *Behind Every Choice Is a Story.* Denton: University of North Texas Press.

Foerstel, Herbert N. 1999. *Freedom of Information and the Right to Know: The Origins and Applications of the Freedom of Information Act.* Westport, CT: Greenwood.

Garrow, David J. 1994. *Liberty and Sexuality: The Right to Privacy and the Making of* Roe v. Wade. New York: Macmillan.

Givens, Beth. 1997. *The Privacy Rights Handbook: How to Take Control of Your Personal Information.* New York: Avon Books.

Hillyard, Daniel, and John Dombrink. 2001. *Dying Right: The Death with Dignity Movement.* New York: Routledge.

Hull, N. E. H., and Peter Charles Hoffer. 2001. Roe v. Wade: *The Abortion Rights Controversy in American History.* Lawrence: University Press of Kansas.

Humphry, Derek, and Mary Clement. 1998. *Freedom to Die: People, Politics, and the Right-to-Die Movement.* New York: St. Martin's Press.

Jacoby, Kerry N. 1998. *Souls, Bodies, Spirits: The Drive to Abolish Abortion since 1973.* New York: Praeger.

Marwick, Christine M. 1985. *Your Right to Government Information.* New York: Avon Books.

McCorvey, Norma. 1994. *I Am Roe: My Life,* Roe v. Wade, *and Freedom of Choice.* New York: HarperCollins.

McMahan, Jeff. 2002. *The Ethics of Killing: Problems at the Margins of Life.* New York: Oxford University Press.

Murphy, Paul L., ed. 1990. *The Right to Privacy and the Ninth Amendment.* New York: Garland.

Raul, Alan Charles. 2002. *Privacy and the Digital State: Balancing Public Information and Personal Privacy.* Boston: Kluwer.

Strum, Philippa. 1998. *Privacy: The Debate in the United States since 1945.* Fort Worth, Tex.: Harcourt Brace.

Theoharis, Athan G. 1998. *A Culture of Secrecy: The Government versus the People's Right to Know.* Lawrence: University Press of Kansas.

Tribe, Lawrence. 1990. *Abortion: The Clash of Absolutes.* New York: W. W. Norton.

Urofsky, Melvin I. 2000. *Lethal Judgments: Assisted Suicide and American Law.* Lawrence: University Press of Kansas.

Weddington, Sarah. 1992. *A Question of Choice.* New York: Putnam's.

Wenz, Peter S. 1992. *Abortion Rights as Religious Freedom.* Philadelphia: Temple University Press.

Westin, Alan F. 1967. *Privacy and Freedom.* New York: Atheneum.

Racial and Ethnic Minority Rights

Branch, Taylor. 1988. **Parting the Waters: America in the King Years, 1954–1963.** New York: Simon and Schuster.

———. 1998. **Pillar of Fire: America in the King Years, 1963–1965.** New York: Simon and Schuster.

Many excellent books have been written on the civil rights movement and the history of African Americans. Although choosing any one book is quite difficult, Taylor Branch's two-part biography of Martin Luther King clearly stands out from the rest. Both books are exciting narratives that bring to life the tumultuous events surrounding Dr. King's life. As the author makes clear, however, these books are about more than just Dr. King. They cover the "King years," the period from the mid-1950s through the late 1960s when the civil rights movement transformed U.S. society. A veteran journalist, Taylor Branch has unearthed fascinating detail and brings to life both Dr. King and the turbulent events of the civil rights movement.

Carson, Clayborne, David J. Garrow, Bill Kovach, and Carol Polsgrove, eds. 2003. *Reporting Civil Rights.* 2 vols. Library of America. New York: Penguin Putnam.

These two volumes collect original news reports of the civil rights movement. These reports capture the immediate drama of such traumatic events as the integration of the University of Mississippi in 1962, the demonstrations in Birmingham, Alabama, in 1963 and Selma, Alabama, in 1965. Although historical accounts provide perspective, these first-hand reports capture the immediacy of one of the most important chapters in U.S. history.

Carter, Dan T. 1971. *Scottsboro: A Tragedy of the American South.* New York: Oxford University Press.

The Scottsboro case in the 1930s was the first great national civil rights cause and marked the beginnings of the modern civil rights movement. Eight young African American men were convicted of raping two white women in Alabama and sentenced to death. Civil rights activists from around the country rallied to their defense. Eventually two Scottsboro cases reached the U.S. Supreme Court and resulted in two early landmark decisions. Dan T. Carter's thorough history of the case is lively reading, and it vividly brings back the early history of the civil rights movement, when there were no laws or court decisions upholding racial equality.

Friendly, Michael, and David Gallen, eds. 1993. *Martin Luther King: The FBI File.* New York: Carroll and Graf.

One of the most notorious episodes of FBI spying was its campaign to discredit civil rights leader Martin Luther King. In addition to its spying, the bureau passed derogatory information about King to politicians and journalists. This book contains many original FBI documents from their files on King.

Harris, David. 2002. *Profiles in Injustice: Why Racial Profiling Won't Work.* New York: New Press.

Racial profiling emerged as a major civil rights issue in the late 1990s. Racial or ethnic profiling involves police officers making traffic stops based on the color of the driver's skin rather than on bona fide violations of the law. Law professor David Harris played a major role in bringing this issue to public attention through his writings and other activities. This is not a dry law textbook. It is written for a general audience and brings the issue of racial profiling to life through the stories of ordinary people who have been the victims of discrimination. In addition, Harris discusses policies that are designed to control police traffic enforcement activity and reduce racial profiling.

Houston, Jeanne Wakatsuki, and James D. Houston. 1974. *Farewell to Manzanar.* New York: Bantam.

The internment of Japanese Americans during World War II was one of the greatest single violations of civil liberties in U.S. history. More than 110,000 people, most of whom were American citizens, were evacuated from the West Coast and confined in concentration camps. Most lost all of their property and possessions in the process.

Farewell to Manzanar is a moving memoir by Jeanne Wakatsuki Houston, who was seven years old when she and her family were removed from Los Angeles and sent to the relocation center in Manzanar, California. Many other fine books examine the important civil liberties issues involved in the Japanese American internment, but this book brings the story alive as a human tragedy: the shock of losing one's home, the indignities of living in a barracks that cannot keep out the blowing sand, and the devastating psychological effect of internment on the young girl's father. This short first-hand account is an excellent introduction to one of the most important events in the history of civil liberties.

Irons, Peter. 1983. *Justice at War.* New York: Oxford University Press.

Peter Irons is a remarkable scholar-activist. In addition to being a highly respected political scientist and historian, he is a lawyer who played a leading role in reopening the World War II Japanese American evacuation and internment policy cases and winning redress for its victims.

Justice at War is the most thorough history of the evacuation and internment and the resulting court cases. Most notable in this account is that in his research Irons uncovered evidence of misconduct by the federal government in which administration officials covered up evidence that undercut the argument that the Japanese Americans were a threat to national security.

Irons's book *The Courage of Their Convictions* (listed above) includes a chapter with a personal memoir by Gordon Hirabayashi, the plaintiff in the first important Japanese American case to reach the Supreme Court.

Wunder, John R. 1994. *"Retained by the People": A History of American Indians and the Bill of Rights.* New York: Oxford.

Because of the status of Indian tribes as semisovereign nations, the legal status of Native Americans is complex. It is often difficult to determine what laws apply to which people in different situations. As a part of this complexity, the status of civil liberties for Native Americans is often ambiguous. On the one hand, Native Americans are American citizens protected by the Bill of Rights. On the other hand, they are members of Indian tribes that have a certain amount of legal autonomy from the United States. The Indian Bill of Rights, passed by Congress in 1968, attempted to clarify the situation but only partially succeeded.

John R. Wunder offers a brief and admirably clear history of this complex subject. His treatment begins with the culture clash arising from the first settlements by European people in North America and goes on to cover the shifting federal policy toward Native Americans over the years. Of particular value is the chapter devoted to the 1968 Indian Bill of Rights. The book covers the issues of tribal self-determination, hunting and fishing rights, and the increasingly important issue of gaming. This book is definitely the best introduction to this complicated subject.

Acuña, Rodolfo F. 1998. *Sometimes There Is No Other Side: Chicanos and the Myth of Equality.* Notre Dame, Ind.: University of Notre Dame Press.

Altschiller, Donald, ed. 1999. *Hate Crimes: A Reference Handbook.* Santa Barbara, CA: ABC-CLIO.

American Civil Liberties Union. 1999. *Driving While Black.* New York: American Civil Liberties Union.

Amnesty International. 1999. *United States of America: Race, Rights, and Police Brutality.* New York: Amnesty International USA.

Ball, Howard. 1998. *A Defiant Life: Thurgood Marshall and the Persistence of Racism in America.* New York: Crown Publishers.

———. 2000. *The Bakke Case: Race, Education, and Affirmative Action.* Lawrence: University Press of Kansas.

Bradley, David, and Shelley Fisher Fishkin, eds. 1998. *The Encyclopedia of Civil Rights in America.* Armonk, NY: M. E. Sharpe.

Building Blocks for Youth. 2002. *Donde Esta la Justicia?* East Lansing: Michigan State University Press.

Carliner, David, et al. 1990. *The Rights of Aliens and Refugees.* Carbondale: Southern Illinois University Press.

Chávez, Ernesto. 2002. *"Mi Raza Primero!" (My People First!): Nationalism, Identity, and Insurgency in the Chicano Movement in Los Angeles, 1966–1978.* Berkeley: University of California Press.

Chin, Gabriel J. 1998. *Affirmative Action and the Constitution.* 3 vols. New York: Garland.

Cortner, Richard C. 1986. *A "Scottsboro" Case in Mississippi: The Supreme Court and Brown v. Mississippi.* Jackson: University of Mississippi Press.

———. 2001. *Civil Rights and Public Accommodations: The Heart of the Atlanta Motel and McClung Cases.* Lawrence: University Press of Kansas.

D'Emilio, John. 2003. *Lost Prophet: The Life and Times of Bayard Rustin.* New York: Free Press.

Eastland, Terry. 1996. *Ending Affirmative Action: The Case for Colorblind Justice.* New York: Basic Books.

Eisaguirre, Lynne. 1999. *Affirmative Action: A Reference Handbook.* Santa Barbara, CA: ABC-CLIO.

Greenberg, Jack. 1994. *Crusaders in the Courts: How a Dedicated Band of Lawyers Fought for the Civil Rights Revolution.* New York: Basic Books.

Grofman, Bernard, and Chandler Davidson, eds. 1992. *Controversies in Minority Voting: The Voting Rights Act in Perspective.* Washington, DC: Brookings Institution.

Grossman, Mark. 1993. *The ABC-CLIO Companion to the Civil Rights Movement.* Santa Barbara, CA: ABC-CLIO.

———. 1996. *The ABC-CLIO Companion to the Native American Rights Movement.* Santa Barbara, CA: ABC-CLIO.

Hatamiya, Leslie T. 1993. *Righting a Wrong: Japanese Americans and the Passage of the Civil Liberties Act of 1988.* Palo Alto, CA: Stanford University Press.

Higginbotham, F. Michael. 2001. *Race Law: Cases, Commentary, and Questions.* Durham, N.C.: Carolina Academic Press.

Hing, Bill Ong. 1999. *Immigration and the Law: A Dictionary.* Santa Barbara, CA: ABC-CLIO.

Houndsmills, Erica Harth. 2001. *Last Witnesses: Reflections on the Wartime Internment of Japanese Americans.* New York: Palgrave.

Hudson, David Michael. 1998. *Along Racial Lines: Consequences of the 1965 Voting Rights Act.* New York: Peter Lang.

Inada, Lawson Fusao. 2000. *Only What We Could Carry: The Japanese American Internment Experience.* San Francisco: California Historical Society.

Irons, Peter. 2002. *Jim Crow's Children: The Broken Promise of the* Brown *Decision.* New York: Viking.

Irons, Peter, ed. 1989. *Justice Delayed: The Record of the Japanese American Internment Cases.* Middletown, CT: Wesleyan University Press.

Kalven, Harry, Jr. 1965. *The Negro and the First Amendment.* Chicago: University of Chicago Press.

Kanellos, Nicolas, ed. 1993. *The Hispanic-American Almanac: A Reference Work on Hispanics in the United States.* Detroit, Mich.: Gale.

Karson, Jill, ed. 2003. *Civil Rights.* Great Speeches in History Series. San Diego, CA: Greenhaven.

Karst, Kenneth L. 1989. *Belonging to America: Equal Citizenship and the Constitution.* New Haven, CT: Yale University Press.

King, Mary. 1987. *Freedom Song: A Personal Story of the 1960s Civil Rights Movement.* New York: Morrow.

Kluger, Richard. 1975. *Simple Justice: The History of* Brown v. Board of Education *and Black America's Struggle for Equality.* New York: Knopf.

Kymlicka, Will. 1995. *The Rights of Minority Cultures.* New York: Oxford University Press.

Lawrence, Charles R., III, and Mari J. Matsuda. 1997. *We Won't Go Back: Making the Case for Affirmative Action.* Boston: Houghton Mifflin.

League of United Latin American Citizens. 1999. *Civil Rights Manual.* Washington, DC: League of United Latin American Citizens.

Lester, Joan Steinau. 2003. *Eleanor Holmes Norton: Fire in My Soul.* New York: Atria Books.

Levine, Daniel. 2000. *Bayard Rustin and the Civil Rights Movement.* New Brunswick, N.J.: Rutgers University Press.

López, Ian F. Haney. 2003. *Racism on Trial: The Chicano Fight for Justice.* Cambridge, Mass.: Harvard University Press.

Lowery, Charles D., and John F. Marszalek. 1992. *Encyclopedia of African American Civil Rights: From Emancipation to the Present.* Westport, CT: Greenwood.

Maki, Mitchell T., Harry H. L. Kitano, and S. Megan Berthold. 1999. *Achieving the Impossible Dream: How Japanese Americans Obtained Redress.* Urbana: University of Illinois Press.

Marcovitz, Hal. 2003. *Eleanor Holmes Norton.* Philadelphia: Chelsea House.

Márquez, Benjamin. 1993. *LULAC: The Evolution of a Mexican American Political Organization.* Austin: University of Texas Press.

Martin, Waldo E., Jr., ed. 1998. Brown v. Board of Education: *A Brief History with Documents.* Boston: Bedford/St. Martin's.

Martin, Waldo E., Jr., and Patricia Sullivan, eds. 2000. *Civil Rights in the United States.* New York: Macmillan.

Mazón, Mauricio. 1984. *The Zoot-Suit Riots: The Psychology of Symbolic Annihilation.* Austin: University of Texas Press.

McDonald, Laughlin, and John A. Powell. 1993. *The Rights of Racial Minorities.* Carbondale: Southern Illinois University Press.

———. 1998. *The Rights of Racial Minorities: Handbook for Young Americans.* New York: Penguin.

Meier, Matt S., and Margo Gutiérrez. 2000. *Encyclopedia of the Mexican American Civil Rights Movement.* Westport, CT: Greenwood.

Mirande, Alfredo. 1987. *Gringo Justice.* Notre Dame, Ind.: University of Notre Dame Press.

Moses, Robert P., and Charles E. Cobb, Jr. *Radical Equations: Civil Rights from Mississippi to the Algebra Project.* Boston: Beacon Press.

Nieman, Donald G. 1991. *Promises to Keep: African Americans and the Constitutional Order, 1776 to the Present.* New York: Oxford University Press.

Nye, Russell B. 1949. *Fettered Freedom: Civil Liberties and the Slavery Controversy, 1830–1860.* East Lansing: Michigan State University Press.

Olson, James S., ed. 1997. *Encyclopedia of American Indian Civil Rights.* Westport, CT: Greenwood Press.

O'Reilly, Kenneth. 1994. *Black Americans: The FBI Files.* New York: Carroll and Graf.

Patterson, Haywood, and Earl Conrad. *Scottsboro Boy.* Garden City, NY: Doubleday, 1950.

Peacock, Anthony A., ed. 1997. *Affirmative Action and Representation: Shaw v. Reno and the Future of Voting Rights.* Durham, N.C.: Carolina Academic Press.

Pevar, Steven. L. 2002. *The Rights of Indians and Tribes,* 3rd ed. Carbondale: Southern Illinois University Press.

Pfeffer, Paula F. 1990. *A. Philip Randolph: Pioneer of the Civil Rights Movement.* Baton Rouge: Louisiana State University Press.

Pritzker, Barry M. 2002. *Native Americans: An Encyclopedia of History, Culture, and Peoples.* Santa Barbara, CA: ABC-CLIO.

Rosales, F. Arturo. 1996. *Chicano! The History of the Mexican American Civil Rights Movement.* Houston, Tex.: Arte Público Press.

Schultz, Jeffrey D., ed. 2000. *Encyclopedia of Minorities in American Politics.* Phoenix, Ariz.: Oryx.

Shiell, Timothy C. 1998. *Campus Hate Speech on Trial.* Lawrence: University Press of Kansas.

Shimabukuro, Robert Sadamu. 2001. *Born in Seattle: The Campaign for Japanese American Redress.* Seattle: University of Washington Press.

Smith, James Morton. 1956. *Freedom's Fetters: The Alien and Sedition Laws and American Civil Liberties.* Ithaca, NY: Cornell University Press.

Sowell, Thomas. 1990. *Preferential Policies: An International Perspective.* New York: Morrow.

Thernstrom, Abigail M. 1987. *Whose Votes Count? Affirmative Action and Minority Voting Rights.* Cambridge, Mass.: Harvard University Press.

Thomas, Brook. 1997. Plessy v. Ferguson: *A Brief History with Documents.* Boston: Bedford Books.

Urofsky, Melvin I. 1991. *A Conflict of Rights: The Supreme Court and Affirmative Action.* New York: Scribner's.

Vigil, Ernesto B. 1999. *The Crusade for Justice: Chicano Militancy and the Government's War on Dissent.* Madison: University of Wisconsin Press.

Wallenstein, Peter. 2002. *Tell the Court I Love My Wife: Race, Marriage, and Law—An American History.* New York: Palgrave.

Wunder, John R. 1994. *"Retained by the People": A History of American Indians and the Bill of Rights.* New York: Oxford University Press.

Wunder, John R., ed. 1996. *The Indian Bill of Rights, 1968.* New York: Garland.

Religious Liberty

Frankel, Marvin E. 1994. *Faith and Freedom: Religious Liberty in America.* New York: Hill and Wang.

This short book does an outstanding job of taking the complex church-state issues and presenting them in a clear fashion that illuminates the underlying core values. Most important, Frankel avoids technical, legalistic analysis and discusses the place of religion in a diverse and free society. For readers who are looking for a good introduction to an enormously complicated and often emotional subject, this book is absolutely the place to start.

Long, Carolyn N. 2000. *Religious Freedom and Indian Rights: The Case of* **Oregon v. Smith**. Lawrence: University Press of Kansas.

The status of Native Americans in the United States represents a complex clash of cultural and legal traditions. One particularly controversial aspect of this clash involves the use of peyote, a hallucinogenic drug, in some Native American religious practices. When this issue reached the U.S. Supreme Court in 1990, the Court ruled that the state of Oregon could fire two employees who had used peyote as part of a religious ceremony. Congress responded by passing the Religious Freedom Restoration Act (RFRA) to protect the free exercise of religion, for all groups and not just Native Americans. The Supreme Court then ruled this law unconstitutional.

Long's book is an absorbing account of this ongoing controversy. To set the context for the Court's decision in *Oregon v. Smith,* she examines the role of peyote in Native American religion as well as the Supreme Court's position on the free exercise of religion generally. Then she covers the tangled history of the *Smith* case and its aftermath. Focusing on this one case, this book is an excellent introduction to Native American rights.

Peters, Shawn Francis. 2000. *Judging Jehovah's Witnesses: Religious Persecution and the Dawn of the Rights Revolution.* Lawrence: University Press of Kansas.

The national controversy over the Jehovah's Witnesses that embroiled the nation for about fifteen years and brought more than two dozen cases to the U.S. Supreme Court is nearly forgotten today. But from the late 1930s until the early 1950s, members of this faith were hounded all across the country. Local communities passed laws specifically designed to limit their proselytizing activities—including bans on door-to-door canvassing—and vigilante groups assaulted them and chased them out of town. The title of Chapter 4 of this excellent book accurately characterizes the whole affair as "A Shocking Episode of Intolerance in American Life." Most important in terms of civil liberties, the cases that reached the Supreme Court resulted in a series of landmark decisions that greatly expanded First Amendment protection of speech and religion.

This well-written book recounts this forgotten national crisis in U.S. religious liberty. The author describes the nature of the Witnesses' faith and activities and chronicles the wave of persecution that erupted against them. The author also describes the major court cases that resulted, including two involving the Witnesses' refusal to salute the American flag and the first important "fighting words" decision. This book is highly recommended as an important chapter in the history of religious intolerance in U.S. history and an analysis of how the First Amendment emerged as a protector of unpopular groups and ideas.

Eller, Cynthia. 1991. *Conscientious Objectors and the Second World War: Moral and Religious Arguments in Support of Pacifism.* New York: Praeger.

Epps, Garrett. 2001. *To An Unknown God: Religious Freedom on Trial.* New York: St. Martin's Press.

Evans, Carolyn. 2001. *Freedom of Religion under the European Convention on Human Rights.* New York: Oxford University Press.

Finkelman, Paul, ed. 2002. *Religion and American Law: An Encyclopedia.* New York: Garland.

Lynn, Barry, Marc D. Stern, and Oliver S. Thomas. 1995. *The Right to Religious Liberty,* 2nd ed. Carbondale: Southern Illinois University Press.

Moskos, Charles C., and John Whiteclay Chambers II, eds. 1993. *The New Conscientious Objection: From Sacred to Secular Resistance.* New York: Oxford University Press.

Murphy, Paul L., ed. *Religious Freedom: Separation and Free Exercise.* Vols. 6 and 7 of *The Bill of Rights and American Legal History.* New York: Garland.

Urofsky, Melvin I. 2002. *Religious Freedom: Rights and Liberties under the Law.* Santa Barbara, CA: ABC-CLIO.

Separation of Church and State

Ginger, Ray. 1974. *Six Days or Forever? Tennessee v. John Thomas Scopes.* New York: Oxford.

The *Scopes* "Monkey" Trial is one of the most famous events in twentieth-century U.S. history. John T. Scopes, a biology teacher, was prosecuted for teaching Darwin's theory of evolution in violation of a Tennessee law prohibiting such teaching. Although Ray Ginger's book, first published in 1958, is almost fifty years old, it is still a brisk, very readable, and factually accurate account of the *Scopes* case. There are several more recent scholarly books on the case that have considerably more detail (see below), but none challenge the facts as presented by Ginger. His book is an excellent introduction to this famous civil liberties case.

Larson, Edward J. 1985. *Trial and Error: The American Controversy over Creation and Evolution.* New York: Oxford University Press.

————. 1997. *Summer for the Gods: The Scopes Trial and America's Continuing Debate Over Science and Religion.* New York: Basic Books.

Edward Larson's two books are the most recent and thorough scholarly accounts of the *Scopes* case. *Summer for the Gods* won the Pulitzer Prize for History in 1998. One of the fascinating aspects of Larson's account of the *Scopes* trial is his examination of the image of the case in U.S. memory and the extent to which it has achieved almost mythic status. *Trial and Error* places the Scopes case in the larger context of the struggle over the teaching of evolution in public schools. Particularly interesting is the author's analysis of the long-term aftermath of the case and its impact on the teaching of biology and the issue of evolution in the United States. He brings the story down to the present and the current controversies of "balanced treatment" of evolution and the idea of "creation science."

Conkin, Paul K. 1998. *When All the Gods Trembled: Darwinism, Scopes, and American Intellectuals.* Lanham, Md.: Rowman and Littlefield.

Curry, Thomas J. 1986. *The First Freedoms: Church and State in America to the Passage of the First Amendment.* New York: Oxford University Press.

Doerr, Edd, Albert J. Menendez, and John M. Swomley. 1996. *The Case against School Vouchers.* Amherst, NY: Prometheus Books, 1996.

Drakeman, Donald L. 1991. *Church-State Constitutional Issues: Making Sense of the Establishment Clause.* New York: Greenwood Press.

Fenwick, Lynda Beck. 1989. *Should the Children Pray? A Historical, Judicial, and Political Examination of Public School Prayer.* Waco, Tex.: Baylor University Press.

Hall, Timothy L. 1998. *Separating Church and State: Roger Williams and Religious Liberty.* Urbana: University of Illinois Press.

Haynes, Charles C., and Oliver Thomas. 2001. *Finding Common Ground: A Guide to Religious Liberty in Public Schools.* Arlington, Va.: First Amendment Center.

Hester, Joseph P. 2003. *The Ten Commandments: A Handbook of Religious, Legal, and Social Issues.* Jefferson, N.C.: McFarland.

Jurinski, James John. 1998. *Religion in the Schools: A Reference Handbook.* Santa Barbara, CA: ABC-CLIO.

Lawrence, Jerome, and Robert E. Lee. 1955. *Inherit the Wind.* New York: Random House.

Levy, Leonard. 1994. *The Establishment Clause: Religion and the First Amendment.* Chapel Hill: University of North Carolina Press.

Menendez, Albert J. 1985. *School Prayer and Other Religious Issues in American Public Education: A Bibliography.* New York: Garland.

Moore, Randy. 2002. *Evolution in the Courtroom: A Reference Guide.* Santa Barbara, CA: ABC-CLIO.

Moran, Jeffrey P. 2002. *The Scopes Trial: A Brief History with Documents.* Boston: Bedford/St. Martin's.

Morgan, Edmund S. 1967. *Roger Williams: The Church and the State.* New York: Harcourt, Brace.

National Academy of Sciences. 1999. *Science and Creationism: A View from the National Academy of Sciences.* Washington, DC: National Academy Press.

Ravitch, Frank S. 1999. *School Prayer and Discrimination: The Civil Rights of Religious Minorities and Dissenters.* Boston: Northeastern University Press.

Scopes, John T. *Center of the Storm.* 1967. New York: Holt, Rinehart, and Winston.

Smout, Kary Doyle. 1998. *The Creation/Evolution Controversy: A Battle for Cultural Power.* New York: Praeger.

Souraf, Frank J. 1976. *The Wall of Separation: The Constitutional Politics of Church and State.* Princeton, N.J.: Princeton University Press.

Viteritti, Joseph P. 2001. *Choosing Equality: School Choice, the Constitution, and Civil Society.* Washington, DC: Brookings Institution.

Weil, Danny. 2002. *School Vouchers and Privatization: A Reference Handbook.* Santa Barbara, CA: ABC-CLIO.

Withman, Larry A. 2002. *Where Darwin Meets the Bible: Creationists and Evolutionists in America.* New York: Oxford University Press.

Students', Seniors', People with Disabilities', and Poor People's Rights

Bernstein, Nina. 2001. *The Lost Children of Wilder: The Epic Struggle to Change Foster Care.* New York: Pantheon Books.

This prize-winning book tells a terribly sad and moving story and provides an important account of the role of the courts in bringing about social change. In the early 1970s, the ACLU challenged the foster care system in New York City on the grounds that it discriminated against Protestant African American children. At the outset of the case, the facts of the discriminatory practices by the major religious charities that ran the foster care system seemed obvious. But as this detailed story makes clear, changing a large bureaucratic system is not easily done. The special value of this book is that takes a large and complicated legal and political struggle and presents it in human terms through the lives of people who were the victims of an unjust system.

Annas, George J. 2004. *The Rights of Patients,* 3rd ed. Carbondale: Southern Illinois University Press.

Brown, Robert N. 1989. *The Rights of Older Persons.* Carbondale: Southern Illinois University Press.

Bryan, William A., and Richard H. Mullendore, eds. 1992. *Rights, Freedoms, and Responsibilities of Students.* San Francisco: Jossey-Bass.

Cary, Eve, and Alan H. Levine, and Janet Price. 1997. *The Rights of Students.* New York: Puffin Books.

Davis, Martha F. 1993. *Brutal Need: Lawyers and the Welfare Rights Movement, 1960–1973.* New Haven, CT: Yale University Press.

Hershkoff, Helen, and Stephen Loffredo. 1997. *The Rights of the Poor.* Carbondale: Southern Illinois University Press.

Hinchey, Patricia H. 2001. *Student Rights: A Reference Handbook.* Santa Barbara, CA: ABC-CLIO.

Hushbeck, Judith C. 1989. *Old and Obsolete: Age Discrimination and the American Worker, 1860–1920.* New York: Garland.

Levy, Robert M., and Leonard S. Rubenstein. 1996. *The Rights of People with Mental Disabilities.* Carbondale: Southern Illinois University Press.

O'Neil, Robert M. 1981. *Classrooms in the Crossfire: The Rights and Interests of Students, Parents, Teachers, Administrators, Librarians, and the Community.* Bloomington: Indiana University Press.

Pelka, Fred. 1997. *The ABC-CLIO Companion to the Disability Rights Movement.* Santa Barbara, CA: ABC-CLIO.

Robertson, John A. 1983. *The Rights of the Critically Ill.* Cambridge, Mass.: Ballinger.

Rothman, David J., and Sheila M. Rothman. 1984. *The Willowbrook Wars.* New York: Harper and Row.

Rubenstein, William B., Ruth Eisenberg, and Lawrence O. Gostin. 1996. *The Rights of People Who Are HIV Positive.* Carbondale: Southern Illinois University Press.

Smith, Christopher E. 1991. *Courts and the Poor.* Chicago: Nelson-Hall.

Stefan, Susan. 2001. *Unequal Rights: Discrimination against People with Mental Disabilities and the Americans with Disabilities Act.* Washington, DC: American Psychological Association.

West, Guida. 1981. *The National Welfare Rights Movement: The Social Protest of Poor Women.* New York: Praeger.

Willis, Clyde E. 2002. *Student's Guide to Landmark Congressional Laws on the First Amendment.* Westport, CT: Greenwood.

Women's Rights

Brownmiller, Susan. 1999. ***In Our Time: Memoir of a Revolution.*** New York: Dial Press.

Susan Brownmiller, a noted writer and activist, opens her book by asserting that she was not present at the creation of the women's movement. This disclaimer is laudably modest, but Brownmiller has been deeply involved in many of the most important struggles of the modern women's rights movement. This is a vivid and compelling narrative, part history, part memoir, of such important events as the founding of the National Organization for Women, the early hears of the abortion rights movement, and the feminist antipornography effort, of which Brownmiller was a leader.

Rosen, Ruth. 2000. *The World Split Open: How the Modern Women's Movement Changed America.* New York: Viking.

Whereas Susan Brownmiller's *In Our Time* covers particular chapters in the history of modern feminism in a vivid and highly personal fashion, Ruth Rosen's *The World Split Open* provides a solid and well-written history of the women's movement, beginning in the 1950s. The special value of this book is indicated in its subtitle. It is not just about the women's rights movement itself but about the profound change this movement had on American society.

Brodie, Laura Fairchild. 2000. *Breaking Out: VMI and the Coming of Women.* New York: Pantheon Books.

Dooling, Richard. 1996. *Blue Streak: Swearing, Free Speech, and Sexual Harassment.* New York: Random House.

Eisaguirre, Lynne. 1997. *Sexual Harassment: A Reference Handbook.* Santa Barbara, CA: ABC-CLIO.

Evans, Sara. 1979. *Personal Politics: The Roots of Women's Liberation in the Civil Rights Movement and the New Left.* New York: Knopf.

Feinberg, Renee. 1986. *The Equal Rights Amendment: An Annotated Bibliography of the Issues, 1976–1985.* Westport, CT: Greenwood.

Freedman, Estelle B. 2002. *No Turning Back: The History of Feminism and the Future of Women.* New York: Ballantine.

Friedan, Betty. 2001 (originally published in 1963). *The Feminine Mystique.* New York: W. W. Norton.

Greenburg, Hazel, ed. 1976. *The Equal Rights Amendment: A Bibliographic Study.* Westport, CT: Greenwood.

Hardy, Gale J. 1993. *American Women Civil Rights Activists: Biobibliographies of 68 Leaders, 1825–1992.* Jefferson, N.C.: McFarland.

Howard, Angela M., and Frances M. Kavenik, eds. 2000. *Handbook of American Women's History.* Thousand Oaks, CA: Sage.

Hurley, Jennifer, ed. 2002. *Women's Rights.* Great Speeches in History Series. San Diego, CA: Greenhaven.

Janda, Lance. 2002. *Stronger Than Custom: West Point and the Admission of Women.* New York: Praeger.

MacKinnon, Catharine A. 1978. *Sexual Harassment of Working Women: A Case of Sex Discrimination.* New Haven, CT: Yale University Press.

Moss, Kary. 1998. *The Rights of Women and Girls.* New York: Puffin Books.

Ross, Susan Deller, Isabelle Katz Pinzler, Deborah A. Ellis, and Kary L. Moss. 1993. *The Rights of Women.* Carbondale: Southern Illinois University Press.

Stein, Laura W. 1999. *Sexual Harassment in America: A Documentary History.* Westport, CT: Greenwood Press.

Strum, Philippa. 2002. *Women in the Barracks: The VMI Case and Equal Rights.* Lawrence: University Press of Kansas.

U.S. Secretary of Education. 2003. *Open to All: Title IX.* Washington, DC: U.S. Department of Education.

Court Transcripts

Goldman. Jerry. 1999. **The Supreme Court's Greatest Hits.** Oyez Project. Available at www.oyez.org.

Audio excerpts from oral arguments before the Supreme Court.

Irons, Peter. 1997. **May It Please the Court: The First Amendment—Transcripts of the Oral Arguments Made before the Supreme Court in Sixteen Key First Amendment Cases.** New York: New Press.

Irons, Peter, and Stephanie Guitton. 1993. **May It Please the Court: The Most Significant Oral Arguments Made before the Supreme Court since 1955.** New York: New Press.

Audio excerpts from oral arguments before the Supreme Court.

Supreme Court Historical Society. Available at www.landmark-cases.org.

Excerpts of oral arguments from many important Supreme Court cases.

Various Artists. 1997. **Voices of the Civil Rights Movement.** 2 CDs. Washington, DC: Smithsonian/Folkways.

Videos

A. Philip Randolph: For Jobs and Freedom
Type: VHS
Length: 86 minutes
Date: 1996
Cost: $49.95 for high school and public libraries; $195.00 for
          college and university libraries
Source: California Newsreel Order Dept.
          P.O. Box 2284
          South Burlington, VT 05407
          http://www.newsreel.org

A biography of one of the most important civil rights leaders of the period from the 1940s to the 1960s. Randolph proposed a civil rights march on Washington in 1941, which was eventually canceled, and he was the official leader of the famous 1963 March on Washington.

Access Denied
Type: VHS
Length: 28 minutes
Date: 1991
Cost: $175.00
Source: Women Make Movies
          462 Broadway, Suite 500WS
          New York, NY 10013
          http://www.wmm.com

Documentary on antiabortion protests around abortion clinics that addresses the conflict between the First Amendment rights of speech and assembly and the constitutionally protected right to abortion services.

The ACLU: A History
Type: VHS
Length: 57 minutes
Date: 1998
Cost: $22.00
Source: ACLU Publications
          P.O. Box 4713
          Trenton, NJ 08650-4713
          http://www.aclu.org/store

This is a documentary on the history of the American Civil Liberties Union, which has been the principal defender of civil liberties in the United States since its founding in 1920. It was produced in conjunction with Diane Garvey's book, *Defending Everybody* (1998) and provides a good introduction to the mission of the ACLU and some of its major achievements.

After Stonewall
Type: VHS
Length: 88 minutes
Date: 1999
Cost: $29.95
Source: First Run Features
         153 Waverly Place
         New York, NY 10014
         http://www.firstrunfeatures.com

Sequel to *Before Stonewall* (see below). A documentary on gay and lesbian Americans after the 1969 riot at the Stonewall bar in New York City (see Chapter 4). The film examines how the Stonewall incident gave birth to the modern lesbian and gay rights movement and how this changed peoples' lives.

All Different, All Equal
Type: VHS
Length: 25 minutes
Date: 2000
Cost: $195.00
Source: Bullfrog Films
         P.O. Box 149
         Oley, Pennsylvania 19547
         http://www.bullfrogfilms.com

Documentary on progress in women's rights around the world. Places women's rights in the United States in an international perspective.

Battle over School Choice
Type: VHS
Length: 60 minutes
Date: 2000
Cost: $19.98
Source: Shop PBS

1320 Braddock Place
Alexandria, VA 22314
http://www.shoppbs.org

PBS documentary on proposals to improve public schools, including the idea of government-funded vouchers to help parents send their children to private schools. Examines separation of church and state issues surrounding government support for religious schools.

Before Stonewall
Type: VHS
Length: 87 minutes
Date: 1986
Cost: $24.95
Source: First Run Features
          153 Waverly Place
          New York, NY 10014
          http://www.firstrunfeatures.com

This is a documentary on the history of gay and lesbians in the United States prior to the 1969 riot at the Stonewall bar in New York City. The sequel, *After Stonewall,* examines the lives of gay and lesbian Americans after the Stonewall incident (see above).

Berkeley in the Sixties
Type: VHS and DVD
Length: 117 minutes
Date: 1990
Cost: $29.95
Source: First Run Features
          153 Waverly Place
          New York, NY 10014
          http://www.firstrunfeatures.com

Documentary on political protests and the counterculture in Berkeley, California, in the 1960s. Includes coverage of the free speech movement at the University of California in the fall of 1964, which was the first important student protest movement.

Casting the First Stone
Type: VHS
Length: 58 minutes

Date: 1991
Cost: $245.00
Source: First Run/Icarus Films
         32 Court Street, 21st Floor
         Brooklyn, NY 11201
         http://www.frif.com

Documentary focusing on six women in the town of Paoli, Pennsylvania—three who oppose abortion and three who support the right to abortion.

Censorship: The Unseen Cinema
Type: VHS
Length: 50 minutes
Date: 1991
Cost: $18.99
Source: Movies Unlimited
         3015 Darnell Road
         Philadelphia, PA 19154
         http://www.moviesunlimited.com

This video is a documentary on the history of censorship of Hollywood films. It is an excellent supplement to the books on censorship listed in the previous section, as it contains many original scenes deleted from the commercially released versions of films.

Children of the Camps
Type: VHS
Length: 57 minutes
Date: 1999
Cost: $150 for school and public libraries; $225 for college
         and university libraries
Source: National Asian American Telecommunications
         Association
         346 Ninth Street, 2nd Floor
         San Francisco, CA 94103
         http://www.naatanet.org

Children of the Camps, produced by Satsuki Ina, is a PBS documentary on Japanese American children who were interned during World War II. It provides an excellent supplement to the many books on this subject.

Conscience and the Constitution
Type: VHS
Length: 50 minutes
Date: 2000
Cost: $165 for high schools and public libraries; $280 for
           college and university libraries
Source: Resisters
           3811 South Horton Street
           Seattle, WA 98144
           http://www.resisters.com

Documentary directed by Frank Abe on young Japanese American men who refused to be drafted from the internment camps into the U.S. armed services during World War II (see Chapter 4).

Crisis: Behind a Presidential Commitment
Type: DVD
Length: 53 minutes
Date: 1963
Cost: $24.98
Source: Barnes and Noble
           76 Ninth Avenue, 9th Floor
           New York, NY 10011
           http://video.barnesandnoble.com

Documentary produced by Gregory Shuker on the 1963 desegregation crisis at the University of Mississippi when James Meredith attempted to enroll in the previously all-white university. Riots erupted and federal troops were mobilized to protect Meredith.

The Crucible
Type: VHS
Length: 123 minutes
Date: 1996
Cost: $9.98
Source: Barnes and Noble
           76 Ninth Avenue, 9th Floor
           New York, NY 10011
           http://video.barnesandnoble.com

The film version of Arthur Miller's *The Crucible,* starring Wynona Ryder, vividly portrays the hysteria and presumption of guilt that surrounds crusades against alleged "evil." The film's interpretation of the Salem events emphasizes the sexuality of the young women who were accused of being witches.

Do Not Enter: The Visa War against Ideas
Type: VHS
Length: 58 minutes
Date: 1987
Cost: $59.00 for high school and public libraries; $99.00 for college and university libraries
Source: New Day Films
         190 Route 17M
         P.O. Box 1084
         Harriman, NY 10926
         http://www.newday.com

Documentary on government denial of visas to writers and filmmakers because of their political beliefs and associations.

Equal Rights Amendment: Unfinished Business for the Constitution
Type: VHS
Length: 17 minutes
Date: 1998
Cost: $24.95
Source: Alice Paul Institute
         P.O. Box 1376
         Mt. Laurel, NJ 08054
         http://www.equalrightsamendment.org

Documentary on the history of the proposed Equal Rights Amendment to the U.S. Constitution, which would guarantee equal rights for women.

Founding Fathers
Type: DVD, VHS (four parts)
Length: 200 minutes
Date: 1998
Cost: $31.95 VHS; $39.95 DVD
Source: A & E Home Video
         687 Marshall Avenue
         Williston,VT 05495
         http://store.aetv.com

Four-part documentary series on the American Revolution, the Constitution, and the Bill of Rights.

Four Little Girls
Type: VHS
Length: 102 minutes
Date: 1998
Cost: $95.00
Source: Direct Cinema LTD.
          P.O. Box 10003
          Santa Monica, CA 90410
          http://www.directcinema.com

Documentary directed by Spike Lee on the bombing of an African American church in Birmingham, Alabama, in 1963 that killed four young African American girls.

Freedom on My Mind
Type: VHS
Length: 110 minutes
Date: 1994
Cost: $69.95 for high schools and public libraries; $195 for
          college and university libraries
Source: California Newsreel
          P.O. Box 2284
          South Burlington, VT 05407
          http://www.newsreel.org

Documentary produced by Connie Field and Marilyn Mulford on Bob Moses, an important civil rights figure in the 1960s who was a leader of the Student Non-violent Coordinating Committee (SNCC), led the civil rights movement in Mississippi, and later developed a pioneering program to teach mathematics to African American children.

The Front
Type: DVD
Length: 94 minutes
Date: 1976
Cost: $19.98
Source: Barnes and Noble
          76 Ninth Avenue, 9th Floor

New York, NY 10011
http://video.barnesandnoble.com

The Front is a Hollywood film starring (but not directed by) Woody Allen on movie and television writers who were blacklisted because of their political views. It vividly illustrates how some victims of the Cold War managed to survive. Interestingly, the screenwriter and some of the actors in the film had been blacklisted during the 1950s.

George Mason and the Bill of Rights
Type: VHS
Length: 28 minutes
Date: 1991
Cost: $18.95
Source: Gunston Hall Plantation
           Mason Neck, VA 22079
           http://www.gunstonhall.org

Biography of one of the intellectual leaders of the American Revolution and the principal author of the Virginia Declaration of Rights (see Chapter 4), which was a model for the Bill of Rights.

Ghosts of Attica
Type: VHS
Length: 90 minutes
Date: 2001
Cost: $440.00
Source: First Run/Icarus Films
           32 Court Street, 21st Floor
           Brooklyn, NY 11201
           http://www.frif.com

This video is a documentary on the 1971 prisoner rebellion at the New York State penitentiary at Attica and the retaking of the prison by New York State troopers that left more than forty people dead. It is a valuable supplement to Wicker's book, *A Time to Die*, because it was produced thirty years later and consequently adds some valuable historical perspective.

God in the Classroom
Type: VHS
Length: 50 minutes

Date: 1996
Cost: $24.95
Source: A & E Home Video
          687 Marshall Avenue
          Williston, VT 05495
          http://store.aetv.com

Documentary on the issue of separation of church and state, and religion in public schools in particular. Traces the history of church-state controversies in U.S. society, including the major Supreme Court cases.

The Good War and Those Who Refused to Fight It
Type: VHS
Length: 57 minutes
Date: 2002
Cost: $250.00
Source: Bullfrog Films
          P.O. Box 149
          Oley, PA 19547
          http://www.bullfrogfilms.com

Documentary on young men who became conscientious objectors during World War II, many of whom went to prison for their beliefs.

Guilty by Suspicion
Type: DVD
Length: 100 minutes
Date: 1991
Cost: $14.98
Source: Barnes and Noble
          76 Ninth Avenue, 9th Floor
          New York, NY 10011
          http://video.barnesandnoble.com

Hollywood drama directed by Irwin Winkler about the experience of a film director who is blacklisted during the Cold War because of his political beliefs.

Hollywood on Trial
Type: VHS
Length: 100 minutes

Date: 1976
Cost: $19.98
Source: Barnes and Noble
         76 Ninth Avenue, 9th Floor
         New York, NY 10011
         http://video.barnesandnoble.com

Documentary directed by David Helperen on the anti-Communist crusade in the motion picture industry and the blacklisting of actors, directors, and writers accused of being Communists. Includes interviews with many of the victims of the blacklist and members of their families.

Inherit the Wind
Type: VHS
Length: 127 minutes
Date: 1960
Cost: $14.98
Source: Barnes and Noble
         76 Ninth Avenue, 9th Floor
         New York, NY 10011
         http://video.barnesandnoble.com

Inherit the Wind, directed by Stanley Kramer, is a dramatization of the *Scopes* trial. The main figures in the original controversy have been recreated as fictionalized characters, and some additional events have been invented, but much of the testimony in the court room scenes is taken directly from the trial transcripts. The clash between the fictionalized Darrow and Bryan figures is still dramatic more than seventy-five years after the original event. Spencer Tracy gives a magnificent performance in the Clarence Darrow role, and Gene Kelly is very good in the role based on the journalist H. L. Mencken, who offers cynical and amusing commentary on the trial.

Although entertaining, *Inherit the Wind* is not good history. The authors show their liberal biases by turning the Darrow character into a virtual saint and portraying the William Jennings Bryan character as a complete simpleton. The facts of the case, as the books by Ginger and Larson make clear, were a lot more ambiguous. The video is well worth watching, but reading one of the books is needed to get the facts straight.

J. Edgar Hoover
Type: VHS
Length: 50 minutes
Date: 1998
Cost: $29.95
Source: A & E Home Video
             687 Marshall Avenue
             Williston, VT 05495
             http://store.aetv.com

This video is an A&E Network biography of former FBI director J. Edgar Hoover. It covers his entire career, including issues related to FBI spying and other violations of civil liberties.

Joseph McCarthy
Type: VHS
Length: 50 minutes
Date: 2000
Cost: $19.95
Source: A & E Home Video
             687 Marshall Avenue
             Williston, VT 05495
             http://store.aetv.com

Biography of Senator Joseph McCarthy, of Wisconsin, the most prominent leader of the anti-Communist crusade during the Cold War.

Just the Facts: The U.S. Constitution and Bill of Rights
Type: VHS
Length: 100 minutes
Date: 1999
Cost: $49.95
Source: Goldhil Home Media
             137 East Thousand Oaks Boulevard, 2nd Floor
             Thousand Oaks, CA 91360
             http://www.goldhil.com

Documentary on the Constitution and the Bill of Rights. Available in English and in Spanish.

Lone Star Hate
Type: VHS

Length: 76 minutes
Date: 1997
Cost: $75 for high school and public libraries; $300 for
            college and university libraries
Source: Frameline Distribution
          145 Ninth Street, Suite 300
          San Francisco, CA 94103
          http://www.catalog.frameline.com

Documentary directed by Paul Yule on a fatal gay bashing incident in Texas in which a young gay man was murdered because of his sexual orientation.

Martin Luther King
Type: VHS
Length: 50 minutes
Date: 1997
Cost: $19.95
Source: A & E Home Video
          687 Marshall Avenue
          Williston,VT 05495
          http://store.aetv.com

Biography of civil rights leader Martin Luther King, covering the major events of his career.

Mississippi Burning
Type: DVD, VHS
Length: 128 minutes
Date: 1988
Cost: $14.98
Source: Barnes and Noble
          76 Ninth Avenue, 9th Floor
          New York, NY 10011
          http://video.barnesandnoble.com

A Hollywood dramatization directed by Alan Parker of the murder of three civil rights workers in Mississippi in the summer of 1964. The film has been heavily criticized by civil rights leaders and historians for presenting a distorted picture of the events. In particular, it presented an overly favorable view of the role of the FBI in civil rights cases.

Monkey Trial
Type: VHS
Length: 90 minutes
Date: 2002
Cost: $19.98
Source: Shop PBS
          1320 Braddock Place
          Alexandria, VA 22314
          http://www.shoppbs.org

Documentary on the 1925 *Scopes* "Monkey" Trial, in which a biology teacher was prosecuted for violating a Tennessee state law that banned the teaching of evolution.

Out of the Past: The Struggle for Gay and Lesbian Rights in America
Type: VHS
Length: 65 minutes
Date: 1998
Cost: $14.98
Source: Barnes and Noble
          76 Ninth Avenue, 9th Floor
          New York, NY 10011
          http://video.barnesandnoble.com

Documentary directed by Jeff Dupre on the history of the gay and lesbian rights movement. The story of a seventeen-year-old high school student who attempted to organize a gay-straight club at her school.

Point of Order
Type: VHS
Length: 93 minutes
Date: 1964
Cost: $29.98
Source: Barnes and Noble
          76 Ninth Avenue, 9th Floor
          New York, NY 10011
          http://video.barnesandnoble.com

Documentary on the famous U.S. Senate hearings conducted by Senator Joseph McCarthy that have become known as the Army-McCarthy Hearings. The original footage in this video clearly illustrates Senator McCarthy's style and helps explain what the phrase "McCarthyism" has come to mean. This video also includes the famous rebuke of Senator McCarthy by attorney Joseph Nye, which helped to start the Senator's downfall.

Procedure 769: Witness to an Execution
Type: VHS
Length: 80 minutes
Date: 1995
Cost: $440.00
Source: First Run/Icarus Films
          32 Court Street, 21st Floor
          Brooklyn, NY 11201
          http://www.frif.com

Documentary directed by Jaap van Howijk on the procedure for executions that focuses on the execution of Robert Alton Harris in the San Quentin gas chamber in 1992.

The Rodney King Incident: Race and Justice in America
Type: VHS
Length: 57 minutes
Date: 1998
Cost: $89.95
Source: Films for the Humanities and Sciences
          P.O. Box 2053
          Princeton, NJ 08543
          http://www.films.com

This video is a documentary on the beating of Rodney King, an African American, by Los Angeles police officers in 1991. It includes the famous home video of the incident, which was broadcast around the world and had a huge impact on public opinion. The bulk of the video involves the criminal trial of the officers involved.

Seeing Red
Type: VHS
Length: 100 minutes
Date: 1993
Cost: $29.95
Source: Facets Multimedia
          1517 West Fullerton Avenue

Chicago, IL 60614
http://www.facets.org

Documentary on the anti-Communist hysteria in Hollywood. It includes interviews with victims of the anti-Communist blacklist of actors, writers, and directors.

Scottsboro: An American Tragedy

Type: VHS
Length: 90 minutes
Date: 2001
Cost: $19.98
Source: Shop PBS
          1320 Braddock Place
          Alexandria, VA 22314
          http://www.shoppbs.org

Documentary on the famous Scottsboro case, in which eight young African American men were accused of raping a white woman. The case led to two landmark Supreme Court decisions regarding the right to a fair trial.

Skokie

Type: DVD
Length: 125 minutes
Date: 2003 (orig. 1990)
Cost: $9.99
Source: CD Universe
          101 N. Plains Industrial Road
          Wallingford, CT 06492
          http://www.cduniverse.com

This video is an ABC Television docudrama on the 1977–1978 Skokie free speech case in which an American Nazi group attempted to hold a demonstration in the predominantly Jewish community of Skokie, Illinois. By focusing on one (fictionalized) individual the film succeeds in presenting the hate speech controversy in personal terms.

Skokie: Rights or Wrong

Type: VHS
Length: 28 minutes
Date: 1987

Cost: $99.00
Source: New Day Films
   190 Route 17M
   P.O. Box 1084
   Harriman, NY 10926
   http://www.newday.com

Documentary on the 1977–1978 free speech case in Skokie, Illinois, in which an American Nazi group attempted to hold a demonstration in the predominantly Jewish community of Skokie, Illinois (see Chapter 4).

Smothered: The Censorship Struggles of the Smothers Brothers Comedy Hour
Type: VHS, DVD
Length: 93 minutes
Date: 2002
Cost: $19.98 VHS; $24.98 DVD
Source: Barnes and Noble
   76 Ninth Avenue, 9th Floor
   New York, NY 10011
   http://video.barnesandnoble.com

Documentary on the tribulations of the Smothers Brothers television show in the 1960s when a number of scenes were censored because of their political content.

Stop the World, We Want to Get On
Type: VHS
Length: 26 minutes
Date: 1992
Cost:
Source: Bullfrog Films
   P.O. Box 149
   Oley, Pennsylvania 19547
   http://www.bullfrogfilms.com

Documentary on the rights of disabled persons.

Super Chief: The Life and Legacy of Earl Warren
Type: VHS
Length: 88 minutes
Date: 1989

Cost: $34.95
Source: Direct Cinema Ltd.
          P.O. Box 10003
          Santa Monica, CA 90410
          http://www.directcinema.com

A biography of Chief Justice Earl Warren, who played a major role in landmark civil liberties and civil rights cases during his tenure as chief justice.

Thurgood Marshall: Justice for All

Type: DVD, VHS
Length: 50 minute
Date: 1992
Cost:
Source: A & E Home Video
          687 Marshall Avenue
          Williston,VT 05495
          http://store.aetv.com

Biography of Thurgood Marshall, who was the lead attorney for the NAACP in some of the most important civil rights cases and later became a U.S. Supreme Court Justice.

When Abortion Was Illegal: Untold Stories

Type: VHS
Length: 28 minutes
Date: 1993
Cost: $95.00
Source: Bullfrog Films
          P.O. Box 149
          Oley, Pennsylvania 19547
          http://www.bullfrogfilms.com

Documentary by Dorothy Fadiman featuring personal stories of women who had illegal abortions before the 1973 *Roe v. Wade* decision that made abortion legal.

Whitewash

Type: VHS
Length: 25 minutes
Date: 1995
Cost: $8.97

Source: Source: First Run Features
          153 Waverly Place
          New York, NY 10014
          http://www.firstrunfeatures.com

Film directed by Michael Sporn about an African American girl
who is the victim of a hate crime.

Zoot Suit Riots
Type: DVD, VHS
Length: 60 minutes
Date: 2002
Cost: $19.98
Source: Shop PBS
          1320 Braddock Place
          Alexandria, VA 22314
          http://www.shoppbs.org

Documentary directed by Joseph Tovares on the Los Angeles
riots in 1943. Examines the prejudice and discrimination against
Latinos that surrounded the event.

Table of Cases

Index

About the Author

Samuel Walker is Isaacson Professor of Criminal Justice at the University of Nebraska at Omaha. He is the author of twelve books on various aspects of policing, criminal justice policy, and civil liberties. He is the author of *In Defense of American Liberties: A History of the ACLU* (2nd ed., 1999) and *Hate Speech: The History of an American Controversy* (1994).

The author would like to thank several people for their assistance in writing this book. Teresa Gleason and Amy Miller reviewed an early draft of the manuscript and provided a number of suggestions that greatly improved the book. Jim Shaw of the UNO Library provided invaluable help at the last minute with the bibliography. Many thanks to all three.